lasting
happiness

In search of deeper meaning and fulfilment

Dr Andrew Parnham

DARTON·LONGMAN + TODD

First published in 2018 by
Darton, Longman and Todd Ltd
1 Spencer Court
140 – 142 Wandsworth High Street
London SW18 3HB

ISBN: 978-0-232-53359-0

A catalogue record for this book is available from the British Library

Designed by Judy Linard

Printed and bound in Great Britain by Bell & Bain, Glasgow

CONTENTS

ACKNOWLEDGEMENTS

Like any good journey, life goes so much better when you have companions to share the adventures, joys and sorrows along the way. I am very grateful to have had plenty of company on my travels. From the start my mum was my closest companion and at 93 years old she's still journeying!

Jill and I celebrated our thirty-fourth wedding anniversary last year and I can safely say that her support, admonitions, wisdom and insight have kept me on track throughout that time. The context and ethos of this book flow from many years of dreams, disappointments, faith and hope, as well as large doses of study, reflection and (attempted) practice. There are many people with whom I have shared these experiences, but some in particular spring to mind, for example John and Lynne Quanrud, Simon and Paula Thomas, Phil and Julie Stokes and Simon and Shunu Pellew. Andy and Jo Thomas were key players in the development of the Healthy Brockley community initiative, with Phil and Jo Ratcliff as companions along the way. And of course Sherry Clark, who introduced me to Positive Psychology and inspired me to take The Happiness Course further. Thanks so much all of you for your companionship and comradeship!

In preparing the material for the book itself I am especially grateful to my nephew Philip, with whom I have engaged in many stimulating and challenging discussions over the past twenty years – setting the world to rights and planning ways to make it happier! Specifically, Phil came up with the framework for the foundational diagrams in the book, which have helped to bind it all together (I hope you agree!). My daughter Anna has brought her understanding of infant development and her psychotherapeutic experience to bear, especially in the preparation of chapters five and six. Phil and Anna also spent time reviewing the whole text of the book – a labour of love, if ever there was one! My son-in-law Andrew, with his customary

5

artistic flair, drew the Tree of Life, and my younger daughter Kate has lent her wisdom too across nearly thirty years!

There are many other people who have contributed to my life and experience. More recently, colleagues at Livability (in particular Adam Bonner and Corin Pilling) have enriched my thought and practice. Thanks too to Denis and Lorna Wade, who have been a great support in recent years.

I hope you'll get a taste of my own life journey and passions as you read – and find some lasting happiness along the way!

FOREWORD

I first met Andy some nine years ago, when he visited me at the University of Kent to present his Happiness Course to my colleagues and me. I was immediately struck by its agreement with contemporary psychological thinking. I subsequently visited the community in which he worked and saw some of the principles outlined in his course acted out in practice on the ground.

Andy possesses a special awareness of the human condition, stemming from his medical training and a wide range of experiences working with people in his community, some of whom have severe physical and psychological issues. All readers of his book, whatever their background, will benefit from his enthusiasm to help people achieve a sense of meaning and fulfilment in their lives.

Lasting Happiness provides a unique insight into wellbeing and happiness. The eight chapters are presented in the form of a journey, starting with a discussion of happiness as perceived from a UK and global perspective. The paradox of other nations' positive perception of the UK versus domestic commentaries that focus on negative aspects of life, highlights the complexity of trying to understand and help people develop a sense of happiness and wellbeing. Moving through concepts of happiness and wellbeing, as understood from biological, psychological and social approaches, in chapters 1-4, the author takes us on a journey of discovery into existential perspectives of relationships, meaning and belonging.

From Chapter 5 onwards, after the earlier neuroscience and psychologically informed insights into brain function, deeper revelations emerge to help us understand the fundamental human need for relationships, and an 'integrated life'. The author's personal journey provides a useful backdrop and well-referenced approach to help people find and maintain happiness. Lasting happiness, in contrast to transient pleasure seeking states, is interdependent on other people and on healthy relationships.

This book provides a countercultural perspective on wellbeing and the recognition that happiness is unlikely to be achieved through 'an impoverished worldview that is itself materialistic'. It provides a well-needed and balanced contribution to a narrow traditional perspective often pursued by people seeking the relief of psychological distress and searching for meaning and belonging. It is useful as an informed text to support The Happiness Course (Appendix 1), which has also been developed by the author. But although helpful prompts/questions are presented at various points in the book, this is much more than a course primer; it provides a concept of happiness accessible to all. I warmly commend the book and am sure that each reader will find it of value in their own pursuit of lasting happiness.

Professor Adrian Bonner
Honorary Professor in the School of
Applied Social Sciences, University of Stirling
December 2017

INTRODUCTION

I Googled 'Happiness' today.[1] There were 581 million results. A search for 'How to be happy' turned up 626 million results (by comparison 'Donald Trump' brought up 237 million, and 'Brexit news' just 90 million). It appears that many of us want to know about happiness and how to achieve it. But why is it such a popular issue, and why is its pursuit so significant – and elusive – for so many of us?

The simplest answer perhaps is that 'everyone wants to be happy', or 'what's not to like about happiness?' Who doesn't want a happy life, with a reasonable standard of living, healthy relationships and a clear sense of direction? However, being happy can mean different things to different people. I'm 'happy' when I'm eating an ice cream or tucking into my favourite dish. But when a long-lost relative turns up decades after I thought they'd perished, or I'm grateful that my marriage has lasted for forty years, should I describe my happiness in the same terms? What do all these states of happiness have in common? And is happiness just a matter of feeling good? If so, what happens when I'm *not* feeling good? Does my state of happiness depend on other people, my circumstances, what I've just eaten, or what the government does for me? Can I take steps to make myself happier and is that all there is to be said about the subject? These are important questions, and I hope to address them in this book.

The origin, or etymology, of the word happy is a little surprising. It started off centuries ago meaning 'lucky' or 'favoured by fortune' – that is, how you end up when events turn out well. Only later did it come to mean 'greatly pleased.' We still retain words that have the original sense: 'happen', a chance occurrence; 'perhaps', maybe, possibly; 'haphazard', mere chance, aimless; 'hapless', unlucky; and 'heap', a group of things thrown together.

> *So on this basis happiness is pretty random, more a matter of chance or luck than a settled state that we produce ourselves. We can't control or predict it – it just 'happens' to us.*

That may seem rather scary – even fatalistic – but it does emphasise our ambivalence towards happiness. On the one hand, we want to be happy and therefore go to great lengths to achieve it, with mixed success. On the other hand, we realise that many things in life are beyond our control and there's only so much we can do to influence them, although we 'hope for the best.' This possibly explains why we are often rather cynical about achieving happiness and some of us in any case might agree with Thomas Hardy's comment (never known for his optimistic view of humanity), 'Happiness was but the occasional episode in a general drama of pain.'[2] We are left with a familiar dilemma – we all want to find happiness but are not convinced we can or will! Nor do we know *how* to achieve this fabled state.

Not that this ambivalence and cynicism stops us pursuing happiness. On the contrary, contemporary society seems almost obsessed with it, as my Google search implies. Every culture has what might be called a 'dominant narrative' about how life should best be lived.[3] The Western world is no exception and at the risk of over-simplification its narrative might be summarised with three words: *health, wealth and happiness.* If we have these in abundance (or at least enough to keep us going, although no one can agree on what constitutes 'enough') then we will continue to enjoy ever-growing prosperity – The Good Life. Or so the story goes. But for several generations now, more and more people have been questioning whether this apparently assured narrative is strong, deep or durable enough. We're not nearly as certain about it as we once were, although we're not sure what the alternative is. So we plough on with what we know.

Let's take a journey

Following a narrative or storyline is a powerful metaphor that helps us understand what our lives are about (and we will return to it in Chapters 7 and 8). But there are others we could use. One is journey. I'd like to take us on a journey, one whose goal is lasting happiness (although we will find that the expression 'happiness' is not quite up to the task to portray the destination and we will discover other, more consequential descriptions as we travel). Although the three priority-words I've used above are a helpful starting point in the journey, they won't take us to the finishing line, because in themselves they come up short and need something more.

> *I propose that three other words, relationships, meaning and fulfilment are needed to fill out and complete those first three words.*

That is not to say that health, wealth and happiness are made redundant – we need them all. But they are not enough to satisfy the longings of the human heart. They do have the advantage that they are concrete, immediate and fairly easily grasped and measured. The other three take a lot more effort to achieve, but they are ultimately more significant – and more *lasting*. To help us navigate the journey I will use a simple diagram of a circle. It comes in two halves, with our first three words on one side and the other three opposite them. With each chapter, the picture will develop and the journey will unfold, as increasingly the two sides come to stand in mutual contrast. It *is* possible to seek to live primarily out of the left-hand-side values and priorities, but over-dependence on them risks damage to the right-hand-side principles – and the cost can be severe. In our journey, the left-hand-side characteristics are helpful resources (or fuel, if you like) to keep us going along the way. But they are simply not enough to take us the whole distance.

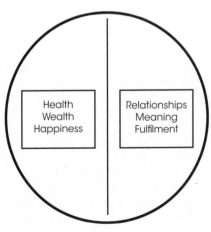

Chapter 1 begins our journey by exploring our Western interpretation of The Good Life, with its emphasis on finding happiness (perhaps better described as 'pleasure') and cutting down the risks as much as possible. The dominant narrative is spelt out through politics, economics, medicine, commerce, advertising and the media. But there is also a downside too, as the scales have tipped too heavily onto the left side of our diagram. The less material parts of our lives are aching and crying out to be heard.

Chapter 2 examines what we mean when we use those overused words, happiness and wellbeing. Of course, the title of this book includes the word happiness (would you have started reading it if it was called 'Lasting wholistic fulfilment'?), which again shows how much leverage it has in our culture. But as we will see, it's not necessarily the most helpful word to take us further. So we will try to unpack the notions of happiness and wellbeing and enquire about the state of relationships and meaning in our culture. Can we redress our diagram's imbalance?

In Chapter 3 we go further along our route – or rather, a little deeper, beyond the science, asking more of the heart than the brain. Why do we have a deep need to connect and what is this universal yearning about? Will that take us further towards lasting happiness and how does it link in with the right hand side of our diagram – relationships, meaning and fulfilment? Is the way we live today enabling or crushing that longing?

Chapter 4 takes us on to the brain and discovers how neuroscience has opened the way to an amazing understanding of how we experience the world around us, other people and ourselves (don't worry, it's not particularly technical). This contrasts the two sides of our diagram in a startling way, building on the discoveries we have already made. Our journey towards life satisfaction has already taken several turns.

Chapter 5 focuses again on connection, but this time it is with people – starting from our first breath and continuing on into our adult lives. Our ability to relate to other people is hard-wired into our system in the most remarkable way, but our early upbringing is equally significant in determining whether we will flourish relationally or not in later life. Again, the distinction between our diagram's two sides is fundamental to comprehending how we can live successfully.

Having described the foundations for healthy relationships, in Chapter 6 we discover how those relationships can develop and how our minds' well-worn patterns affect our thoughts and feelings about ourselves and other people. That begs the question, if we have not experienced positive beginnings, is it possible to change? Can we develop healthier ways to relate to others and move beyond the restrictions of our past? I believe the answer is a resounding 'yes', but the way forward may be demanding in time and effort if we are to find lasting happiness in our relationships.

Chapter 7 takes our journey further, as we dig deeper into our individual and societal mindsets. What is foundational in the way we think, hope, dream and act? This is the domain of worldviews. We all have one, but we spend almost no time thinking about or examining it. By definition a worldview is a set of assumptions that by and large we don't scrutinise or challenge. They are just 'there' and everything we think, say or do is based on them. There are several different worldviews in our society; parts of them overlap, but the deeper you dig, the more dissimilar they are. That matters, because the way in which we view the world and beyond has a huge impact on our attitudes, values and behaviour – and therefore on our happiness and wellbeing. We will explore our culture's dominant worldview, reflect on some of its outworkings and consider how that relates to all that we've investigated in earlier chapters.

Chapter 8 takes us on to the final stage of our journey, as we try to bring all the strands together. If a worldview is so significant, determining so much of our thoughts, dreams and behaviour, then the one we follow needs to be broad, deep and robust enough to both provide a vision for a thriving and flourishing life for ourselves and everyone else on planet earth *and* help us cope with the challenges and difficulties we face! I want to give you an insight into my own worldview, and how I believe it provides a strong framework that leads to lasting happiness.[4]

The Appendices are an added extra. The first is an outline of The Happiness Course, which I developed over recent years as a way to aid people in their reflections on and choices for their lives. The second provides some practical ways forward to help you develop your happiness in life!

If that all sounds a little complex, let's take a short break for a simple but enlightening exercise. It's one that I've run scores of times, coming at the very beginning of The Happiness Course. It has become a favourite of mine and consists of just one question: What makes you happy?

What makes you happy?

On a piece of paper, simply write out a list of things, people and activities that make you happy, from the simplest to the most profound.

Better still, do it with others and see how your results compare.

Although I've led this activity many times, the responses are almost always the same. They include friends, family, walks in the countryside, a good dinner, pets, volunteering, achieving something and the deeper matters of life, philosophy or faith (what did you write down?). The most interesting thing about this list is that it contains very little that costs much money or comprises goods or possessions. For example, in all the times I've run the exercise, rarely if ever have people put down 'computer', 'car' or 'designer clothes'.

The pursuits that make us happy are largely uncomplicated, unsophisticated and inexpensive and tend to focus on people and meaningful activities.

On that basis, most people can find some satisfaction in most situations, with relatively little financial investment. But here's the irony: in our culture *it appears to be the very things that bring us most happiness (especially relationships and meaning) that are being squeezed out by other things* (literally – things) that bring *less* satisfaction. How did we get to such a point?

Happiness – the destination?

My own responses to the question, 'What makes you happy?' emerge very quickly. They include spending time with my wife, family and friends, walking in the park behind my home, enjoying a good film with friendly company, eating my favourite dish, playing or watching sport, reading an absorbing book, having a deep conversation with someone I trust not to dismiss my thoughts and feelings ... you probably know the sort of thing. But the fundamental question of this book is, how *lasting* is all that? I'd like to think that they are based on durable foundations, but is that right?

As we've already seen, 'happiness' is a tricky word. It can refer to so many different phenomena, from the trivial to the profound. Life throws challenges at us at many levels: superficial, deep, good, bad, intimate, cosmic…the list is very long, and the questions raised aren't really answered by simply having more pleasant experiences. Wellbeing certainly isn't summed up with just the one word, 'happiness' and the route to life satisfaction is not necessarily easy and smooth.

One man whose view of life's experiences might carry more weight than most is Viktor Frankl. He was an Austrian neurologist and psychiatrist who practiced in Vienna before the Second World War. Frankl spent three years in concentration camps. His bestselling book, *Man's Search for Meaning* is an account both of his experiences and his approach to life. After the war he pioneered a new type of therapy called Logotherapy, based on the premise that pursuing meaning in life is the most significant motivating force in human beings. A quote from his book gives us some idea of his principles and priorities:

> Don't aim at success. The more you aim at it and make it a target, the more you are going to miss it. For success, like *happiness, cannot be pursued; it must ensue, and it only does so as the unintended side effect* of one's personal dedication to a cause greater than oneself or as the by-product of one's surrender to a person other than oneself. Happiness must happen, and the same holds for success: *you have to let it happen by not caring about it. In the long-run success will follow you precisely because you had forgotten to think about it* [my italics].[5]

This evaluation is so counter-cultural today that it is worth repeating: happiness and success are very slippery goals and they regularly turn out to be a disappointment if and when we finally achieve them. Making them our primary goals in life will almost certainly doom us, like adventurers looking for treasure at the end of the rainbow, to frustration and disappointment.

But Frankl wasn't alone in his convictions. Rudyard Kipling's famous poem, 'If' is really about the same issue:

> If you can meet with Triumph and Disaster
> And treat those two impostors just the same....
> You'll be a Man, my son!

The apostle Paul took a similar view when he wrote, 'I have learned in whatever situation I am to be content. I know how to be brought low, and I know how to abound. In any and every circumstance, I have learned the secret of facing plenty and hunger, abundance and need.'[6] That sounds a lot like lasting happiness, but it's worth pointing out that Paul's route there involved many experiences that most of us would consider anything but 'happy'. But it does raise the question, how do you learn such a secret? Does it come quickly and easily? Intuitively we know it doesn't. It turns out that how we *respond* to both ease and adversity is one of the keys. Our choices in life are crucial, both for good or ill.

Just in case we harboured any further doubts, here is one of the leading experts in the field of happiness and wellbeing research today, psychology professor Sonja Lyubomirsky. Speaking of our universal tendency to get used to happy and positive experiences (called in the trade 'hedonic adaptation'), she says:

> What's particularly fascinating about this phenomenon is that it's most pronounced with respect to your happiest experiences due to the creeping normalcy and the constant ramping up of expectations that causes you to seek out more, more and more. While the rate at which we adapt to happiness seems to vary between people and situations, there can be no doubt that our brains thrive on novelty *which is why happiness and wellbeing should never be the destination but the journey* [my italics].[7]

So, according to Lyubomirsky, happiness helps us along the way, but it isn't the purpose of our journey. But, given that this book is called 'Lasting *Happiness*', isn't that all rather confusing? Is happiness a good thing or not? Should we be pursuing it or not? Well, the answer, it seems, is that it all depends on what we mean by happiness. We'll unpack that in Chapter 2 and try to get beyond the trivial ('just think positive and keep that smiley face going') and technical ('if you learn enough psychology and philosophy you'll get the idea eventually') to explore the deeper yearnings of the human heart (in Chapter 3). Remember, the other word in this book's title is *'lasting.'* And satisfaction that keeps going to the end is really what life is about. But there's the rub – how do we keep the contentment and serenity going till we get to the finishing line?

Symptoms – and cure

I said at the beginning that we feel a certain ambivalence towards happiness. We want it, but it's difficult to hold on to when we find it. And the relentless pursuit of it seems to lead to a fair amount of *un*happiness. We focus on the most obvious routes towards happiness, but discover that the result is less satisfying than we thought when we started our journey. It's as if there's something not quite right, but we can't quite work out what that 'something' is (more of that in the next chapter).

There are two steps forward. The first is to discern what is wrong, and as I've hinted, that is a task in itself. For a doctor, diagnosis is crucial (don't try to treat something if you're uncertain of the cause!)[8] and a lot depends on getting it right. But that's only half the story. There is a second step: unless the physician finds some kind of remedy, the patient won't be sending back any thank you cards! The solution, the cure, the therapy, is just as crucial as the analysis.

What then is the therapy for Western society's maladies? That is the motivation behind and focus of this book. But whatever the healing balm might be, it will not simply be found on the surface. When someone visits their doctor, their presenting symptom is only the external indicator of, or a signpost towards an underlying condition, and the physician needs to delve deeper to find the source of the problem. That longstanding headache or sudden loss of vision point to something serious within. So too, in our case, any remedy must address the root causes of unhappiness or un-wellness.

I referred to 'Western society', but the predicament is not limited to that part of the world. Nations with very different cultural origins, who have recently adopted Western lifestyles, are encountering very similar issues. Two examples will suffice. Qatar is the richest country in the world, by some distance, if Growth Domestic Product (GDP – the main measure of a nation's overall wealth) per head of population is anything to go by.[9] Its experiment with material wealth and consumerism is a case study of how a nation can be transformed in a few years. It will host the football World Cup in 2022, at a cost of $200 billion. Towering skyscrapers dominate the horizon of the capital Doha and the streets are clogged with traffic. 'We have become urban,' says sociology professor Kaltham Al Ghanim. But that's not the whole story. Qatar has not only imported the material trappings of a Western lifestyle, it is now also experiencing the social consequences. 'Our social and economic life has changed – families have become separated, consumption culture has taken over', says Al Ghanim. Although there is high employment and free education and healthcare, the social cost is mounting: stress, obesity (two thirds of the population), divorce (40% of marriages) and family break up are all on the increase. One insider's verdict? 'Qataris have lost almost everything that matters.' Does this sound familiar? It seems that the social consequences follow on from the material changes, as surely as night follows day.

The second example is Japan. Although it had become an industrialised nation by the beginning of the twentieth century, the Second World War devastated the country. Its economic recovery was spectacular and by the 1970s its Gross Domestic Product was the world's third largest. But once again, the social cost has been devastating. The condition known as *karoshi* (literally, 'overwork death') first appeared in 1969 and is referred to as an 'epidemic'. Workers may spend twelve or more hours, six to seven days a week at work, with overtime going unpaid.[10] Japan's suicide rate is the highest in the developed world, with more than 25,000 people taking their own lives in 2014.[11] As men prioritise their jobs, becoming less involved in family life, the family suffers and rates of depression soar. I probably don't need to add any more.

We will spend more time reflecting on the challenges of twenty-first-century Western life in Chapter 1, but most of the book is more upbeat, seeking to find fruitful and lasting ways forward. As I've hinted already, that almost always involves making choices. This *capacity to choose* is one of the greatest human characteristics. We almost always have a choice (even if it seems very limited and initially impacts our inner life more than externals). Making that choice matters, because what and how we choose will often determine our pathway thereafter, taking us either closer to or further away from our destination – lasting happiness.

Change is possible - choices make the difference

You don't have to be an expert in psychology to realise that change really is possible in our thoughts, feelings, behaviour – and in our relationships. Of course, the older we get the more challenging it is to change, but with strengthened motivation and good support from other people, we can do it. Research has shown that there are three main determinants of our happiness or subjective wellbeing: our genetic make-up, our present circumstances and our own voluntary choices.[12]

So here's a question. What relative proportions do you think these three factors contribute to our individual happiness? Most people guess that genetics is quite small and that our choices count for a lot.[13] They are therefore surprised (and sometimes upset) to find that *genetics* is responsible for 50% of our sense of happiness – our dispositions count for a lot.

It's as if we all have a 'set point', like a thermostat, that brings us back towards the same level of wellbeing whatever joy or sorrow we have experienced. The second finding is that our *circumstances* (where we live, our social standing, housing, etc.) account for just 10% – quite a revelation, given the emphasis placed on this by advertisers, the media and popular culture.

This of course leaves the *40% determined by our choices – our own volition.* That may not seem very significant, but think for a moment. The 50% genetically determined part is by definition beyond our ability to change, but the remaining 50% lies at least to some degree within our power to influence. Consider this segment to be 'the 100% that is within our capacity to change'. We can influence our circumstances to a varying degree, although that still only accounts for 20% of this '100%'.

> *But our own choices lie completely within our own capability and they contribute 80% of what is amenable to change.*

No one else is responsible for them – and they are wholly within my power to change. Even if I simply don't bother to act into my situation, that is still a decision, a choice, albeit by default. I may not consider myself advantaged; I may feel life has dealt me a poor hand; but I still have choice and with support from others, I can choose to make changes. So seizing the moment may turn out to be more life changing than we imagine.

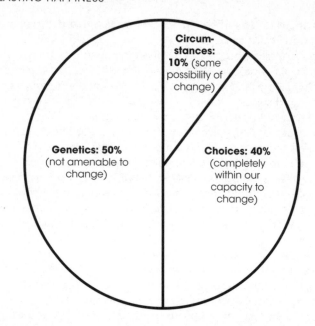

Circum-
stances:
10% (some
possibility of
change)

Genetics: 50%
(not amenable to
change)

Choices: 40%
(completely
within our
capacity to
change)

Carpe diem

The Roman poet Horace wrote these words over two thousand years ago. Usually translated as 'seize the day', a more literal translation would be, 'pluck the day, as it is ripe'. In nature, there are different times and seasons and one 'time' is not the same as another. What happens in autumn, when the fruit is ripe, is very different from spring, and requires different actions and choices. Plucking the day, like a fruit, should be done when it is 'ripe' and not at any other time. But, how do we know when the day is ripe?

There are two ancient Greek words for time. One is *chronos*, which is how we usually understand time – each moment, minute, hour or year follows another in regular, predictable succession (think chronology or chronometer). But another word for time, *kairos*, refers to 'a special, particular moment' in history (or my-story), which will perhaps come only once – and it may turn out to be vitally important that we make a good decision at that point. *Chronos* has to do with quantity, *kairos* with quality. One is mundane; the other is profound. Discerning one from the other could make the difference between, on the one hand, bemused frustration and (on the other hand) discovering the reason why we are on planet earth. We are all on a journey through life and at key moments we are called upon to make crucial decisions (although they may not appear to be so decisive at the time).

There have been *kairos* moments in my life, as I'm sure there have in yours. Some have declared themselves as such very clearly, for example, when I got married or had children. Others have come a little more subtly and at the time they didn't seem so profound. For example, I once found myself at loggerheads with my boss and the decision I took to react to his (as I saw it) intransigence resulted in a series of events that changed the course of my career and the rest of my life! Another *kairos* moment turned out to be my decision to rent a bed-sitter in Lewisham borough (south London), which, amongst other factors, resulted in my living in that area for the following thirty-seven years. (I'm still there to this day!) We can't always predict which decisions will turn out to be *kairos* moments and which others will simply be more *chronos* occasions, but being aware that both will happen may help us to prepare for the big ones.[14] Either way, it's well worth reflecting on our lives, past and present, because that may help us to recognise the patterns and themes that in turn enable us to identify the *kairos* moments when they come. Such an approach can give us clues about how to spend our *chronos* days – and even more importantly, what we should do with the *kairos* events. When it comes to lasting happiness, our decisions really do matter, as we will see in Chapter 5.

As you read through this book, you may be prompted to consider stages in your life that, as you think about them, reveal themselves to be *kairos* moments – amidst all those other *chronos* periods. Or you might be at a point in which *kairos* events are about to happen, so it might well be worth spending some time considering how you might act into your situation.

Carpe diem
- What have been the seasons of your life?
- Can you think of times when you 'seized the day' – and others when, looking back on it, you wish you had?

- What is your current season and what choices are significant for you at this kairos moment?
- Is there anything you could do to help you move forward?

Inspiring people

Role models are very important for us, since they offer us a hope that things can be different – and what kind of people it takes to make that difference. Who has been a role model to you? Life has plenty of uncertainty and ambiguity, but having some guides along the way can help us to negotiate those difficulties (even if we take the guides for granted much of the time and only recognise what they have given to us after they have left us!). We all need at least one person to inspire us. Without that, our lives become tedious and diminished. Famous people like Nelson Mandela, Mother Teresa or Martin Luther King may come to mind, and it's certainly worth reflecting on the characteristics that we admire in them. However, generally we don't know such people personally, and so there is a large gap between what we know of them and our own lives. They may also seem to have existed on a plane way above and beyond what we can expect, living lives that we could never attain to! People nearer home can therefore be more powerful, even if they seem less dazzling.

Inspiring people
- Who do you know who inspires you?
- What precisely is it about them that stirs and elevates you?
- How might you take on some of that strength and character – and what would you need to do to make that happen?

Summary

I am very grateful that human life includes moments of sheer exuberance and delight. Such times often come when we connect with other people, the world around us and the activities that give us pleasure. But pleasurable experiences are interspersed with less happy times and in the journey of life we need to navigate both the satisfying and the painful. In any case, for many of us today, the pursuit of enjoyment through health, wealth and happiness seems often to be accompanied by unhappiness and stress. Finding a balance in life involves pursuing other goals also, especially strong and durable relationships and lasting satisfaction and significance. Without these, we are more likely to encounter enduring frustration than lifelong fulfilment.

Our quest for lasting happiness has begun.

ONE

THE GOOD LIFE

How it works today[1]
- Hello! Gordon's Pizza?
- No sir, it is Google Pizza.
- So, I have the wrong number?
- No, Sir, Google bought Gordon's Pizza.
- Okay. Take my order please.
- Well, Sir, you want the usual?
- The usual? How do you know me?
- According to your caller ID, the last 12 times, you ordered pizza with cheese, sausage, thick crust ...
- Okay! Okay! That's it.
- Sir, may I suggest to you this time ricotta cheese, arugula with sun-dried tomatoes?
- No, I hate vegetables.
- But your cholesterol is high!
- How do you know?
- Through the Lab Subscriber's Guide. We have the results of your blood tests for the last 7 years.
- Okay, but I want my regular pizza, I already take medicine.
- But sir, you have not taken your medicine regularly. Four months ago, you only purchased a box with 30 tablet at Drug sale Network.
- I bought more from another chemist.
- It is not showing on your credit card.
- I paid in cash.
- But you did not withdraw that much cash according to your bank statement.
- I have other sources of cash.
- This is not showing on your last Income Tax return, unless you got it from an undeclared source.
- WHAT THE HECK?! Enough! I'm sick of Google, Facebook, Twitter, WhatsApp. I'm going to an island without Wi-Fi or internet. Where there are no cell phones or satellites to spy on me!
- I understand, Sir, but you'll need to renew your passport, as it expired 5 weeks ago!

What is your definition of The Good Life

- What ingredients would go into it? No doubt there would be enough health and wealth to keep you more than alive and flourishing.
- Would there be people there – who would they be?
- What would you and they be doing?
- What would there be more of than there is now – and what would there be less of?

When you've finished, take a look again at the exercise in the Introduction, 'What makes you happy?' How does the list of things that you wrote then compare with what you've just written? Are they different? If so, why? What can you conclude from that?

Despite everything we hear in the news, the UK is statistically among the more happy nations of the world. The World Happiness Report tells us that although it is not *the* happiest nation on earth (that accolade consistently goes to Denmark or Norway), we are certainly in the top few divisions. It was ranked nineteenth in the world by the Report's Update in 2017.[2] Australia came ninth, the United States fourteenth, Ireland fifteenth and Germany sixteenth. Reasons for happiness included the nation's wealth, levels of health, freedom to make life choices, perceptions of corruption and positive affect (i.e. feeling good). A report by the Organisation for Economic Cooperation and Development (OECD) concluded that the UK was one of the best places to live and work, citing such reasons as high environmental quality, personal security and civic engagement.[3] Britain is one of the most generous foreign aid donors in the world (third according to gross amount, at $19.9 billion and seventh by percentage of Gross Domestic Product (GDP) at 0.71%).[4] Ireland spent €648 million ($726 million), representing 0.36% of GDP.[5]

There is much then to appreciate in our nation, with its heritage of democracy, tolerance and generosity. Other states certainly seem to think so. A poll for the British Council revealed that many other nations hold the UK in high esteem, especially after the high profile events of recent years (including the London Olympics and the Queen's Diamond Jubilee). Britain is seen positively by others as a place to visit, study and do business. This is in stark contrast with the poor view British people have of themselves: only 24% think the UK a good place to invest, compared with 42% of foreigners![6] Ireland too is generally regarded positively, with 72% of foreigners living in the country expressing general satisfaction (though not with the weather!), especially with regard to friendly locals and an easily accessible culture.[7]

So, how would you best sum up our society's view of life? What do most people aim for and what might be a good slogan to sum it all up? Based on much of what we see and hear around us one appropriate maxim might be, *'the pursuit of pleasure and the avoidance of pain'*. This comes in two parts. First, we appear to think that the search for material gratification and happiness is the greatest pursuit in life; and secondly, we seek to free our lives from hurt and suffering as much as possible – as someone once put it, 'Stay safe till you die.'

Life in your country
- What's your view of your nation's society as a whole?
- Is it a happy place to live?
- Is your answer based on your personal experience and the views of your friends – or from somewhere else (like the media)?
- How would you get a wider view?
- Do you think what you find there might surprise you?

The pursuit of pleasure ...

There's nothing new about all this. Some of the ancient Greeks certainly thought the same way. The Cyrenaics and Epicureans of the fourth and fifth centuries BC saw more pleasure and less pain as the highest good in life. And ever since, people have urged that nations and individuals should make human happiness their main aim. Jeremy Bentham, the eighteenth-century philosopher and reformer, promoted his philosophy of utilitarianism, with its clarion call, 'It is the greatest happiness of the greatest number that is the measure of right and wrong.' [8]

In the modern era, over the past couple of centuries, at

least in the West, this has been understood to apply primarily to economic, political, scientific and now, technological dimensions of life. As long as our standard of living (i.e. material wellbeing) is high and growing, all will be well. Indeed, in the past century and a half, there have been amazing leaps forward, including the combatting of infectious diseases (culminating in the eradication of smallpox worldwide in 1979), the growth in living standards and the mushrooming of easily available technology, to name just a few. With rising standards of education, society, we are told, will become more and more equipped to meet the challenges it faces, bringing inevitable progress to all areas of our world. This is modernism, with its optimistic and progressive philosophy, anticipating the final victory over all ills and ushering in a form of utopia. You might call it The Western Dream. Of course, this vision, most fully promoted in the nineteenth and early twentieth centuries, now sounds a little hollow and the rise of postmodernism has sounded a timely warning against such over-optimistic rhetoric.

The need for novelty

Nevertheless, wellbeing or even happiness in our day are often primarily expressed in physical or material terms of health and wealth. If we were to ask someone in the West, 'Are you well off?' or 'do you enjoy The Good Life?' we would probably expect to hear the answer expressed in financial, material or medical terms – health and wealth. Even if we twenty-first century Westerners are more cynical about the possibilities and achievements of capitalism and science, the Western Dream still seems very much alive and well. We might say that 'the pursuit of pleasure' has come to mean something like 'accumulating wealth to the extent that I'm able to enjoy all the material benefits that our culture can provide'. Our advertising industry is built upon this conviction. According to writers like Jeremy Rifkin and Kenneth Galbraith, corporations from the 1920s began to create the desire for the very products that the companies were manufacturing.[9] Or to put it another way, 'In recent years marketers have discovered a very effective way to persuade us to increase our appetites for MORE. They have sought to convince us that in addition to the basic human needs of air, water, food and shelter from the elements we all have a fifth human need – the need for novelty ... By far the majority of us ... seem to have bought this propaganda.' [10]

Here's a fun but serious activity to do with a group of friends. Buy some magazines, preferably of the glossy kind, though others will probably do the job. Leaf through the pages until you find an article, advertisement or other item that includes a picture or two. Then ask yourselves the question: in order to enjoy The Good Life, what does this picture or article tell us we need to (a) have; (b) be? Take special note of what is present materially and what kind of person is being highlighted.

Or consider the lyrics of the 1933 song, 'Keep young and beautiful': 'Keep young and beautiful ... *if you want to be loved.*' We smile at the sentiment, but it's still a powerful message eighty years on. One organisation estimates that the worldwide cosmetics industry amounts to $170 billion dollars annually,[11] so someone, somewhere, must be agreeing with those lyrics.

The Western Dream
- What do you think of this talk of The Western Dream?
- Is it a fair summary of our aims and hopes?
- What impact does it have on your daily life (family, job, leisure, etc.)?
- What about your hopes, dreams and aspirations?

... and the avoidance of pain

But if that is one way of looking at the first part of our motto, 'the pursuit of pleasure', what about the second part, 'the avoidance of pain'? There can't be many people in our world who actually enjoy pain, and given the choice most of us would want to avoid it. But this phrase is saying something more than that. We are not only pain-averse, we are also often risk-averse, and anxious to limit exposure to pain of any kind, physical or otherwise. We love our comfort zones, and having achieved a fairly high degree of comfort we do all we can to hold on to them.

Materially, we have done well; witness the amelioration of severe poverty, huge advances in science and technology and (despite our constant moans and groans about the National Health Service) generally high quality medical provision.[12] In less material domains the picture is not so rosy, as we shall see shortly. But our 'medical model' is primarily a material, physical one, which views illness and dis-ease as a malfunction of the material and physical dimensions of the human being. So not only are diabetes and kidney dysfunction of biological origin, but mental illness, emotional problems and less tangible matters of despair and meaninglessness (*anomie* is the technical term) are ultimately biological too. The metaphor for this model views the human being as a machine, which is helpful if we want to understand physical mechanisms. But as the psychiatrist Iain McGilchrist puts it, 'if we…take the machine as our model, we will uncover the view that – surprise, surprise – the body, and the brain with it, is a machine.' He goes on to say that a model is 'a comparison with something else…(but for) the human body – there isn't anything that *that* can be compared with.'[13] Another psychiatrist, Martin Seager, puts it this way: 'we don't hypothesise that the suffering we call 'mental' has a physical basis; we simply assume it. But what if the whole medical paradigm were completely and demonstrably false?'[14]

If the problems are physical and biological, so are the treatments. We intervene surgically in some disorders, but mostly we give drug treatment. The pharmaceutical industry occupies a significant place in the British economy (in 2014 it contributed £32.4 billion to the UK's GDP).[15] Ireland is the largest net exporter of pharmaceuticals in the EU – they account for over 50% of all its exports.[16] After all, if chemical imbalance is at the root of dysfunction, then chemicals will no doubt alleviate it. The average family doctor spends just a few minutes with each patient, and because of time pressure the result is usually a prescription, even though (s)he knows the patient really wants to simply talk about the problem. (Actually, patients themselves also drive the prescription machine – many people won't be happy as they walk out the door unless they have a prescription in their hands.)

A common finding among patients visiting their doctor is a condition called 'Medically Unexplained Symptoms' (MUS). The patient complains of pain or other symptom, but the doctor can find nothing objectively wrong. Is there pain? Yes there is. Does it trouble the person? Yes it does. But the medical model cannot find a demonstrable cause. This is surprisingly common. One study found that 52% of patients experienced MUS, rising to 66% in the gynaecology clinic.[17] The existence of MUS illustrates an important issue: the less physical or material the context, the trickier it is to nail down either the problem or the solution.

Physical conditions are largely explicable and remediable in our culture, but emotional, social and existential matters are more difficult – much more difficult. The less tangibly material the issue, the more difficult we seem to find it.

The darker side of modern life: epidemics

We don't live in Utopia, but we are so much richer and healthier than previous generations. In 1900 a British baby could expect to reach 50 years of age.[18] By 1960 this had increased to 71 years, but in 2014 figure stood at 81 years – a whole decade's increase in just over 50 years! Ireland's life expectancy has improved in a similar way.[19] The UK's GDP has risen ten-fold over the past century, from £184 billion in 1900 to £1,869 billion in 2015, and nearly all that increase has happened since the end of the Second World War.[20] On a material level, we have achieved so much – as a nation we're enjoying increased health and wealth.

There is however another dimension of our national life that isn't flourishing quite so well. Health professionals speak of social 'epidemics' in society. One of these is stress, which affects one in five of the working population and is the single largest cause of sickness absence (40 per cent of all work-related illnesses). One hundred and five million days are lost to stress each year, costing employers £1.24 billion.[21] Only 17 per cent of employees are engaged with their work, with 63 per cent not engaged and 20 per cent disengaged.[22]

Another epidemic is depression and anxiety. Nearly one third of sick notes are issued by Britain's GPs for mental health issues.[23] One in four people experience a mental health problem each year, with one in six suffering anxiety and depression.[24] Worryingly, a quarter of girls in the UK show signs of depression at the age of 14 (for boys it is a tenth).[25] Depression is set to become the second most burdensome disorder in the world by 2020, and the first by 2030.[26] A recent report by the UK's Mental Health Foundation revealed some even more disturbing statistics:

- 65% say they have experienced a mental health problem at some point in their life
- 42% have experienced depression
- 70% of women have experienced a mental health problem
- Only 13% of Britons are living with high levels of positive mental health.[27]

31

Ironically, NHS workers, charged with responsibility for the care of people with illness, experience some of the highest sickness absence rates in the country, with an annual cost of £2.4 billion.[28]

Many today speak of another social epidemic – loneliness. Studies show that loneliness is as damaging to health as obesity or smoking thirty cigarettes a day. It increases amounts of both the powerful stress hormone cortisol and depressive symptoms, producing a vicious cycle of isolation and poor health.[29] One recent UK study found that 13 per cent of people don't have a single close friend. Alarmingly, loneliness seems to be growing especially amongst young people. 65 per cent of 16-24 year olds say they feel lonely at least some of the time, and 32% report feeling lonely often or all the time (just 32% per cent and 11 per cent, respectively, of over-65s report these problems).[30] Ireland too has its loneliness problems.[31] Humans are intensely social beings and one of the most robust findings in wellbeing research is that strong relationships are by far and away the most significant factor in promoting life satisfaction.[32]

So if our relationships are not healthy, our wellbeing will be damaged.

(Relationships are such an important determinant of lasting happiness that I've devoted two chapters of this book to them.) Loneliness is a clear indication that something is wrong. With nearly eight million people living alone in Britain, this is an epidemic that shows no signs of going away.[33]

Epidemics – really?
- What do you make of all this talk of epidemics?
- Is it a little overblown?
- What is your experience?

A deeper malaise

One of the reasons for the dramatic improvement in life expectancy during the twentieth century was the containment, and in some cases, eradication of infectious diseases – bubonic plague, smallpox, measles and the like. We take it all for granted now, but through most of history these diseases have been the scourge of humanity. Yet their effects have largely been reversed through improvements in sanitation, the revolution of antibiotics and breakthroughs in immunisation.

Today, we are much more likely to die from a very different type of disorder, and the primary cause is closer to home – us. We now suffer from 'lifestyle diseases'. The top five causes of *premature death* in this country are cancer, heart disease, stroke, respiratory disease and liver disease. All of these are strongly influenced by our lifestyles – what *we* eat and drink, *our* sedentary lifestyles, *our* smoking habits, stress responses, etc. According to NHS England Chief Executive, Simon Stevens, 'obesity is the new smoking', with two thirds of adults and a quarter of children between two and ten years of age being overweight or obese.[34]

These conditions, as well as being causes of pain and suffering in their own right, are also *symptoms of a deeper malaise.* Unhealthy habits like excessive alcohol intake and overeating point to psychological, emotional and experiential issues of discontent and dissatisfaction. It is these underlying issues that we will seek to understand and explore.

All of this comes at a time when state care provision is under great strain. Cuts in services are exerting a major impact on individuals and communities. But there is an underlying, longer-term societal phenomenon, which transcends shorter-term political changes. The post-war welfare state was designed to deliver physical, material support, and assumed that social 'shock absorbers' like family, neighbours, churches and community groups would provide the relational foundation that all of us need. However, these have atrophied in subsequent decades, leaving many to struggle with loneliness and depression.[35] *Once again, we have shown ourselves adept at rising to the challenge of material problems, but curiously inept at doing the same for relational and existential difficulties.* I believe there are deep-seated reasons for this, which we will examine as we continue our journey into lasting happiness.

Here is Mother Teresa's take on it:

> The greatest disease in the West today is not TB or leprosy; it is being unwanted, unloved, and uncared for. We can cure physical diseases with medicine, but the only cure for loneliness, despair, and hopelessness is love. There are many in the world who are dying for a piece of bread but there are many more dying for a

little love. The poverty in the West is a different kind of poverty – it is not only a poverty of loneliness but also of spirituality. There's a hunger for love.[36]

Arguably today then, our social, communal and existential needs are greater than our physical and material deficiencies.

One further twist to this perplexing tale comes through research that has shown that the very pursuit of happiness can lead to unlooked-for negative consequences. People who set happiness as a major goal in life are more likely to feel disappointed about their feelings, be lonely and experience depressive symptoms.[37] In part, this is probably because, on the one hand, Western conceptions of happiness are very individualistic and on the other hand, social connection is one of the most significant factors in a person's happiness. Our individualised, materialism-orientated focus has ironically led to us being less satisfied and more lonely.

Life in Western nations, then, is a paradoxical affair, with material affluence mingled with relational and existential poverty. The challenges are not likely to disappear in the near future. Of course this begs lots of questions, not the least of which are, who is influencing our attitudes and behaviour and what is our role and responsibility in it all?

Who's writing your script?

I watched the TV news today and made a note of the various topics mentioned. Here they are, in order:[38]

1. Concern for the future of workers' jobs, after a British car company was sold to a foreign corporation.
2. The American President orders a travel ban on people from some Muslim countries to the USA for security reasons.
3. Thirteen terror attacks in the UK were averted over the past four years, amidst fears of more to come.
4. Supermarket chain fined £300,000 for food safety breaches.
5. Zoo ordered to close after 500 animals in its care had died in less than four years.
6. The World Health Organisation reports that air pollution is one of the greatest dangers to health around the globe.
7. Talks have started to persuade parties to form a new power-

sharing government in Northern Ireland. If they fail, the British government will have to impose direct rule.

8. The 30-year anniversary of a ferry crossing disaster was commemorated. 193 passengers died.

9. Three British-based scientists have won a prestigious prize for work on the brain.

Watching the news
- What strikes you about that list?
- What is your emotional response to the kinds of issues raised?
- Do we get inured to shock and pain?
- How does the one piece of good news at the end of the bulletin affect you?

So what, you might say. Does it really make any difference to the way we live or think? In fact, research into the impact of news reporting on our emotional and psychological state is not encouraging. One study showed that just a few minutes of negative news had a significant effect on mood. People who watched just three minutes of negative news in the morning were 27% more likely to report their day as unhappy six to eight hours later. The impact was not just on mood – their work performance was also affected.[39] Another survey found that watching negative news resulted in people becoming more anxious and sad, not just about the news items, but also about their own personal worries, concluding that negative news can 'exacerbate a range of personal concerns not specifically relevant to the content of the program itself'.[40]

We are deeply impacted by what goes on around us, especially via the media and advertising industries. It is claimed that in one 45-minute journey, the average London commuter is exposed to more than 130 adverts, rising to 3,500 in a whole day.[41] Although half of them do not make an impact, clearly many do. Like the proverbial frog being slowly boiled in water we are so saturated with marketing messages that we are unaware of their powerful effect.[42] Successful advertising rests on two key foundations: create dissatisfaction with the present and then portray a better future – accessible only of course if you purchase the product. Advertising is very effective, but it promotes a lifestyle of autonomy and self-focus that some have called narcissistic – and has severely affected long-lasting, mutually dependent, healthy relationships.[43]

Socially connected – or moving apart?

Increasingly 'everyone is connected' through social media, but there is mounting evidence that their use can be detrimental to relationships and wellbeing.[44] Face-to-face interactions have faded over the past several years, raising the question: Does substituting technology for direct human contact lead to unforeseen negative consequences?

Social media are now such a fundamental part of life, particularly among young people, that it's difficult to remember what life was like before their invention. But evidence is increasing that constant, continuous use of social media brings trouble as well as blessing. Technology use late at night reduces children's sleep, and the consequences are alarming. If children are sleep deprived by just one hour a day their cognitive academic performance can be reduced by up to two years – the equivalent of them being two whole years behind.[45] One study into the use of multiple social media platforms among 19-32 year olds found that those who used the most platforms were 3.3 times more likely to experience high levels of anxiety symptoms than peers who used the fewest platforms.[46] 'Technology has fundamentally changed our world and this generation in particular', says professor of psychology Jean Twenge. 'This generation is more confident, assertive, entitled – and more miserable. We are malnourished from eating a junk-food diet of instant messages, Facebook posts, email and phone calls'.[47]

What is to blame? The finger has been pointed at a number of culprits: the pressure to look good on Instagram; ensuring we have many followers (not necessarily the same thing as real friends); distraction from other activities (like school work); and of course the dreaded 'fear of missing out' ('FOMO') – the anxiety that someone somewhere is having a better time than me.

But it may be the *lack of face-to-face contact* that is the most important reason. The biologist Aric Sigman says that a lack of face-to-face networking can alter the way genes work, upset immune responses and hormone levels and influence mental performance. He considers that electronic media undermine people's social skills and their ability to read body language.[48] Professor of Social Studies, Sherry Turkle, writes that *conversational skills, connection and intimacy are fast disappearing*, mostly because of technology. We don't like to be bored and doing nothing, so our phones offer us an escape from unwelcome feelings. But as a result we don't learn the empathy so crucial for nurturing healthy relationships: 'Every time you check your phone in company, what you gain is a hit of stimulation, a neurochemical shot, and what you lose is what a friend, teacher, parent, lover, or co-worker just said, meant, felt.' The result of all this is that we are losing contact and perspective.[49]

In one section of Turkle's book, entitled 'I'd rather text than talk', she writes, referring to a recent study amongst students, 'In-person conversation led to the most emotional connection and online messaging led to the least. The students tried to 'warm up' their digital messages by using emoticons … and using the forced urgency of TYPING IN ALL CAPS. But these techniques had not done the job. *It is when we see each other's faces and hear each other's voices that we become most human to each other*[50] [my italics].[51] I stopped making jokes and humorous comments very early on in my emailing career. There was just too much scope for miscommunication.

This issue of communication is central to our understanding and developing of relationships. Only a small amount of our interpersonal connections is in fact conveyed by the words we use. The rest is down to intonation and crucially, non-verbal gestures and body language. There is some disagreement on the precise relative proportions (the figures I have most often encountered are 7 per cent verbal, 38 per cent intonation and 55 per cent non-verbal body language) but that non-verbal exchange is much more significant than words alone is not in dispute.[52] It is therefore clear that using words-only in a text or email can never adequately convey what we mean to express.

All of which brings us back to our question, who's writing our script? It's very likely that the media, advertisers and other people are having a big say, composing a life narrative that we unconsciously follow from cradle to grave. We generally don't it give it a moment's thought, but how often have you stopped and asked yourself that question, 'Whose script am I following?'

Who's writing your script?
- Thinking of your life as a story – who is writing your script?
- What are the main elements of the drama of your life?
- What are the priorities, and who decides?

Happiness and money

'Money makes the world go round.'   John Kander, Fred Ebb

'When I was young I thought that money was the most important thing in life; now that I am old I know that it is.'
Oscar Wilde

'Money cannot buy peace of mind. It cannot heal ruptured relationships, or build meaning into a life that has none.'
Richard M. DeVos

Happiness has a strange relationship with money.[53] As the diagram below shows, if we have very little money, it's not surprising to find that we're not very content. As our income increases, we do become more satisfied (the part of the line marked 'A' in the diagram), but that then begins to plateau (point 'X') until no matter how much more money we get, our happiness hardly increases at all (the part of the line marked 'B').[54] Experts are disagreed about the precise level of income at which the graph begins to plateau but it is clear that although money does bring satisfaction, it does so only up to a point. [55]

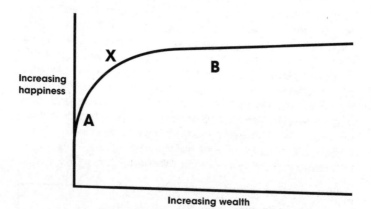

Increasing happiness

X   **B**

A

Increasing wealth

In the decades that followed the end of the Second World War, income in Western nations soared, but life satisfaction did not follow suit. Instead, a striking paradox emerged, in which the proportion of people who consider themselves very happy did not change at all (see diagram on next page).

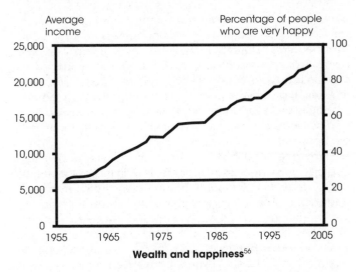

Average income

Percentage of people who are very happy

Wealth and happiness[56]

But there is more. It isn't simply how much we earn that matters, but rather *how we spend it* that impacts our wellbeing. People who spend their money on material things (and therefore primarily on themselves) are less satisfied than those who spend it on experiences – and especially those with other people.[57] When we share our possessions (and ourselves) it makes us happier!

Money and me
- What is your relationship with money and possessions like?
- Who's in control of whom?
- To what extent can money buy you happiness?

Professor Tim Kasser's research on the impact of materialism is very revealing. He and others have shown that:

Materialism is associated with lower levels of wellbeing, less pro-social (the opposite of anti-social) behaviour, worse academic outcomes and more spending problems and debt.

More materialistic people tend to be less empathetic, more

competitive, manipulative and selfish. Following a review of the literature on materialism and happiness he concluded, 'The negative relationship between materialism and well-being was consistent across all kinds of measures of materialism, types of people and cultures.' Kasser also takes the view that adverts promote more materialistic attitudes, probably because they 'send messages suggesting that happy, successful people are wealthy, have nice things, and are beautiful and popular.'[58]

Why does wealth only promote happiness to a limited degree – and why does it tail off? To explain this, psychologists talk of *hedonic adaptation.* Human beings are remarkably adaptable, able to live (nearly) at the North Pole and at the Equator, and all places in between. We adapt not only physically, but emotionally too. If we are bereaved, we feel loss and pain, but most people are eventually able to recover their wellbeing, even if it takes several years. This is emotional adaptation. But here's the rub – *we adapt, not only to negatives, but also to positives in our lives, and especially materially.* Very quickly we become accustomed to a pay rise, a better car or more expensive clothes. This is hedonic adaptation – adjusting to things that bring material pleasure. The effect is much less marked with relationships and activities that bring meaning.

Materially rich, but relationally poor

In the Introduction, I outlined the simple exercise that I start off with in The Happiness Course: 'What makes you happy?' The responses are almost always along the lines of simple but meaningful things that often involve other people and bring some kind of meaning to our lives. They do *not* usually include much in the way of material possessions. You'll remember my conclusion: in our culture it appears to be the very things that bring us most happiness (especially relationships and meaning) that are being squeezed out by other things that bring less satisfaction.

It gets worse. It is precisely in the arena of relationships and community where the trends are most troubling. One survey found that levels of trust and belonging among British under-50s are the lowest in Europe.[59] Another study ranked the UK twenty-sixth out of 28 European countries by the proportion of people who say they have someone on whom they could rely if they have a serious problem, giving Britain the dubious label of 'the loneliness capital of Europe'.[60]

A study by the relationship charity Relate found that one person in five feels unloved and one in 10 people said they did not have a close friend.[61]

The huge significance of relationships (both personal and communal) will emerge throughout this book, simply because they are indisputably the most significant factor for wellness among human beings.

If you want to be happy, you need to have at least one person to whom you can be close and with whom you can share your life. The eminent sociologist Robert Putnam makes the claim that if you belong to no groups but decide to join one, 'you cut your risk of dying over the next year in half.'[62] A more recent study in the UK showed that the more a person identified with a particular group, such as family, local community or via a hobby, the happier they were with their life.[63]

Finding the balance

This seems a good point to refer back to the diagram that I launched in the Introduction, contrasting the popular dimensions of The Good Life with other less tangible but more profound elements. I wrote there that over-prioritising the values on the left hand side risks jeopardising those on the right hand side, which are eclipsed by the pursuit of pleasure and avoidance of pain. I think the evidence of this chapter emphasises that risk even more and shows that as a culture we have tipped alarmingly far over to the left. It is not yet too late to redress the balance, but currently we appear to be surging headlong in the direction of health and wealth and away from relationships and meaning. That raises the inevitable question – how do we bring these components together to live a more joined-up life?

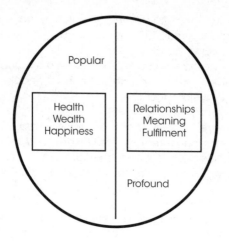

The search for more

Given our culture's inconsistencies regarding what actually makes us happy, it is perhaps not surprising that over the past generation or two there has been a strong and sustained reaction against the dominant narrative of our age, i.e. 'the pursuit of pleasure (primarily through acquiring material possessions) and the avoidance of pain (primarily through physical health via the medical model).' Materialism shows no signs of fizzling out any time soon, but there is nonetheless widespread dissatisfaction with its social and existential consequences in Western nations. So, what alternatives are there to our culture's downsides and 'symptoms of a deeper malaise'?

One way of looking at it is to take a step back and consider the spectrum of contemporary global worldviews and cultures stretching from the West's individualistic, materialistic emphasis right over to the East's traditional stress on the corporate and immaterial. Here is my take on it. The first diagram is my attempt to encompass the many dimensions of an *individual person's life* in our Western context, spanning physical, psychological and emotional spheres right over to relational, communal and spiritual arenas.

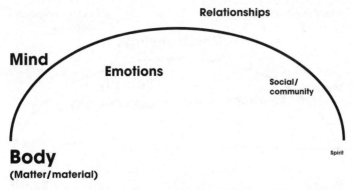

Western view: materialistic, deterministic

The underlying worldview in the West is material. Just as the universe is material, so is humanity. Both our understanding and advancement of human experience are based on this material foundation. In the diagram, 'body' represents not only the human body, but also material wellbeing. Since material flourishing and wellbeing are dominant, so the font of the word 'body' is large. The mind is also conceived of as a machine, made up of material components, so the word 'mind' is in large font too, though not quite so big as 'body'. Emotions are perhaps a little trickier, since they aren't so easily formulated and compartmentalised. In fact the further to the right of the diagram one goes, the less clearly are the entities characterised, the less they flourish in our society and therefore the smaller is the font. Relationships and community thrive less now than they once did, and the spiritual domain has increasingly become a matter of private, rather than public, concern.

The last fifty years, however, have seen a reaction to the dominant Western narrative. In their frustration with a purely materialistic perspective, many people have sought alternative worldviews and perceptions in order to discover a more holistic, less compartmentalised explanation for their existence, and practical ways of living that transcend the material and physical. You might call this 'the flight to the East', - seeking out self-consciously spiritual mindsets and practices. Interestingly though, this flight is not complete. It has tended to restrict itself to the private sphere, leaving the public domain still largely occupied by the materialistic narrative – exemplified by Alastair Campbell's famous comment, 'We don't do God' (he was referring to politics, but it could as easily have been expressed in the economic, commercial or cultural spheres).

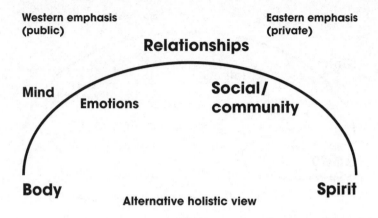

This flight is illustrated by the rise of Complementary and Alternative Medicine.[64] Up to a third of people with cancer use CAM at some point in their illness.[65] Types of CAM include herbal medicine, homeopathy, aromatherapy, massage and reflexology. Some of these have been present in the UK for many centuries, but others are much more recent imports, including yoga and acupuncture. Although opinion is divided on why CAM has become more popular, one reason seems to be people's dissatisfaction with a purely medical model of disease and its treatment.[66] The embracing of mindfulness and meditation practices also indicates a desire for more than sheer rationalistic and cognitive perspectives.

World view wars
- Which of these two worldviews due you relate to most: Modern or Alternative?
- Or to put it another way, do you mostly 'stick with the West' or join the 'flight to the East'?
- What are the practical consequences of living in a culture that contains both worldviews?
- Is anything still missing?

In the early stages of the twenty-first century then (at least in the West), we find ourselves standing in a rather odd place – with one foot based on a firmly materialistic yet un-joined-up foundation, and the other seeking out a more holistic, joined-up base. It leaves many people confused, even though they don't really know why. Let's take a closer look.

Pursuing wholeness

For many of us, life today is compartmentalised, fragmented and incoherent. Compartmentalised, because we box the various parts of our lives into different sealed-off categories: work, personal, business, leisure, etc. Fragmented, because the different aspects of life are disconnected from each other – there is not much joined-up living. And incoherent, because when everything is put together, it doesn't necessarily add up – there's not much integration and consistency. Why? Because ...

> *We lack an underlying framework to help us to make sense of, interpret and give meaning to all the disconnected and occasionally conflicting experiences of our lives.*

Our existence becomes anecdotal and we continue our mad dash through life, not really understanding what we are about. The actor Robert Morley put it bluntly, 'We are raucous and boorish, and we are alive because we don't know what else to be.' That might be an overstatement for some of us, but it makes the point quite well!

But there often seems to be a reticence to take things further than that. When I first began to put The Happiness Course together, I remember my collaborator (who worked in the NHS, running wellbeing programmes) relating to me a conversation she had recently had with one of her work colleagues. She had referred to some matters the two of us had been discussing, especially about meaning and purpose in life. Bearing in mind that their job was to help people find more health and wellbeing, the response she received surprised and even shocked her: 'Oh that's a bit deep isn't it – can't we talk about something else?' For me, that exchange illustrated well the unease many of us feel about exploring the deeper places of our lives, and spending time reflecting on the key issues, to try and make sense of it all. Perhaps underneath there is an unspoken question in many of our minds that highlights our ambivalence: I'd like to know what my life adds up to, but do I really want to explore it to find out? Or to put it another way, everyone wants to find satisfaction – but is it just too scary or painful? As the Rolling Stones put it, 'I can't get no satisfaction, though I try and I try and I try' ....

Signposts for the journey

Two words may act like signposts to help us find our way. The first is *connection*. It means to link, unite or bind together two or more previously separate things. The psychiatrist Edward Hallowell wrote a whole book entitled *Connect*. Here is part of his introduction:

> For most people, the two most powerful experiences in life are achieving and connecting. Almost everything that counts is directed toward one of these goals. While we are doing well at achieving, we're not doing well at connecting. There are many kinds of connections people make. You can connect with your family, your friends, neighborhood, job, garden, nature, your past, and with whatever is beyond knowledge – with the transcendent, with whatever you call God.[67]

That covers a lot of things! But his words point to two key features of contemporary life. First, as Hallowell says, we moderns are very keen on achieving, but don't seem to be so successful with our connecting. Whole cultures, communities, cities, neighbourhoods, families and even our individual lives are profoundly *dis*-connected. We will explore some of the reasons for this in the chapters that follow. Secondly,

> *The kinds of things with which we fail to adequately connect are the very ones that matter for our wellbeing and fulfilment: relationships, community and meaning and purpose.*

My connections
- With what and whom do you feel connected?
- What does that connection look like?
- In what ways do you feel disconnected?
- What prevents you from connecting with matters beyond the immediate world of 'me and mine'?

The second word is *integration*. It's one thing to make a connection with something. It's quite another thing to then unite and merge disparate elements together to gain one whole, united entity. The word integrate means, 'to bring together or incorporate parts into a whole; to *combine to produce a whole* or larger unit' [my italics].[68] In an age characterised by fragmentation and extreme individualism, we could do with large doses of integration. It is lacking in many of our lives. We busy ourselves with everyday activities, of which many are pressing and some are lastingly significant. But we struggle to 'incorporate (these) parts into a whole' and find a way to join them together 'to produce a whole' life.

A related word of course is *integrity*, which means, 'an unimpaired condition, the quality of being *complete or undivided* [my italics again].[69] If something loses integrity it becomes unstable and can easily come apart. For example, we might say, 'The nation was losing its integrity – the place was falling to bits!' The principle of being 'undivided' correlates well with a wholistic[70] approach to life – something that holds together.

But there is more to this word. It can also mean, 'the quality of being *honest and having strong moral principles* that you refuse to change' [my italics].[71] When we speak of inanimate things having integrity, we mean simply that they hold together. But when we apply it to people ('he was a man of great integrity') we mean much more. More than simply bringing parts together, more even than living healthy lives, it has to do with morality and ethics – things that many of us prefer not to dwell on. Integrity is an important character attribute and there is surely a vital link between character and wholistic wellbeing.

So, being connected and having integrity involves:

> *Bringing together important strands, themes and elements that so often get separated, to generate something whole and meaningful from them.*

Most non-Western cultures and societies are more connected and integrated than ours. There is an organic connection with nature, with an acknowledgment that humans are very much part of the natural world. And because most recognise an unseen, spiritual realm, there is generally much less separation between the visible and the invisible. The West suffers from a dualism (separating the visible material from the less 'tangible' realm) that inevitably brings disconnection and dis-integration – not just to the big picture but also to our everyday lives (we will explore this in later chapters).

A life of integrity

- Who do you know to whom the description, 'a person of integrity' might apply?
- What is it precisely about them that leads you to label them in that way (e.g. conscientiousness, reliability, generosity, etc.)?
- What would you need to change in your life to take you towards:

   1. Greater integration: i.e. where all the disparate parts of your life come together to make some kind of whole?

   2. Greater integrity: i.e. developing your character to the extent that others would look at your life and say, 'There's someone of integrity'?

Summary

In this chapter we have explored our society's priorities, which I have characterised as the pursuit of pleasure and avoidance of pain. We've seen that these carry some unwanted side effects with them (all those epidemics) that uncover the malaise many of us experience. We live fragmented, disconnected lives and aren't sure how to bring everything together. Technology and materialism often seem to complicate, rather than simplify our lives and we are left wondering whether there is an alternative – hence the pursuit of alternative therapies and lifestyles. Perhaps if we could discover ways to connect and integrate the disjointed parts of our lives, we might begin to find our way towards lasting happiness and fulfilment.

TWO

HAPPINESS AND WELLNESS

What this chapter is about

We've started our journey towards lasting happiness by examining the way in which our society prioritises the material dimensions of life, summarised by the words *health, wealth and happiness* (where happiness could easily be substituted by pleasure). We've seen that this leads to a lop-sided picture in which the deeper dimensions of relationships, meaning and fulfilment shrink and fade; and that the blights of stress, anxiety and depression are inexorably on the rise. There seems to be a malaise, which our consumer society is unable to control.

So in this chapter we will unpack these pressing issues further and endeavour to set our feet on more solid ground. We will ask what happiness and wellbeing really mean and whether we are discovering how to live them out. We will also explore two of our 'right-hand-side' characteristics, relationships and meaning and see why they are so important. But, to lead us in gently, try this exercise.

What was the happiest period of your life?

I don't mean a time when there was nothing wrong and you had no problems (although if that was true for you at some point, that's definitely what you need to write about). Rather, a time (weeks, months, even years) when basically life went well.

- What was going on at that stage of your life?
- Why was it such a good time?
- Who contributed to making it a positive period?
- What was your contribution?
- What might be helpful to apply to your current situation?

Starting with the basics – rather like eating your greens

There are plenty of articles these days promising us almost unlimited happiness if we just follow the list of six ... eight ... ten activities they then go on to outline.[1] Reading it through often makes me want to respond, 'So, is that it then? You just do these things and a life of unalloyed pleasure will follow?' It tends to make a lot of us a little cynical about 'How to ...' lists.

And yet there are some things in life that do have a lasting impact on our mood and health. It's a little like cleaning your teeth or eating your greens. Although most of these activities aren't at all glamorous or exciting, they build strong foundations and robust health. They don't hit the headlines, nor do they make lots of money for corporations – which is a good thing for most of us, because although they can be expensive in time and effort they don't empty your wallet. So, what are they?[2]

Well, they turn out to include everyday things like getting enough sleep, taking adequate exercise, eating healthy foods, getting outside more and generally looking after your body. ('What?' I hear you say, 'Is that it?' Well, yes, actually.) Whenever some newfangled food or other product appears on the news, claiming to revolutionise our lives, often, at the end of the report, a nutritionist appears briefly to tell us that of course it's a healthy balanced diet and regular moderate exercise that is *really* necessary for our health, whatever else has just been claimed.

But it's not just our bodies that need care. The same goes for our inner lives and relationships. Living an appreciative life, maintaining inner stability in our minds and emotions, balancing (better still, integrating) the various dimensions of work, home and leisure, staying connected with other people and living for more than the latest fad or fashion all contribute hugely to a life lived well, or if you like, The Good Life. There is more to add to this list, but the key point is that if we don't have these elements in place, it won't matter much what else we do, because we're unlikely to find that elusive and mysterious factor to make us 'happy'. I like watching rugby and there's nothing more irritating than seeing your favourite team make basic errors like dropping the ball or giving away a 'soft' penalty. It's the same in life: get the basics right and the rest will (most likely) follow. Or, if you prefer it the other way round, get the basics wrong and it won't matter what else you do.

Here's another illustration. A successful life is like a building –

if constructed properly it rests securely on solid, healthy, reliable foundations. With those in place, you're on your way to success. Start off wrong, and whatever else you build on top won't stand much of a chance. It is just as true for our lives. Foundations are crucial for a life that thrives. (That begs lots of questions of course, not least, what our background was like and how we live our lives in the present. We will investigate the first of these later, in our chapters on relationships.) So, here is some helpful advice – not rocket science, but simple, practical steps we can all take.

The psychologist Stephen Ilardi has developed what he calls the Therapeutic Lifestyle Change programme.[3] It has six elements. He claims that anyone who institutes these changes will see a positive difference in their life. The elements are:

1. Omega-3 fatty acid supplements: these substances have been shown to have antidepressant and anti-inflammatory properties. We do not produce them naturally, so we need foods (oily fish like salmon or mackerel, or walnuts) or supplements to provide them.
2. Exercise: some people call this the 'miracle cure', because encouraging people to undertake moderate exercise for 30 minutes several times a week improves their health measurably – sometimes dramatically.
3. Sleep hygiene: lack of sleep is associated with increased risk of diabetes, high blood pressure, heart disease and mood disorders. British people are apparently amongst the world's worst sleepers. One survey found that 37% (more than one in three) of people said they did not get the right amount of sleep.[4] Advice for better sleep includes establishing a routine, eating dinner earlier and avoiding screens of various types before bed.
4. Light exposure: we should get out more – it's good for our bodies, minds and relationships.
5. Anti-rumination strategies: rumination consists of dwelling on negative thoughts and feelings, rather like cows chewing the cud. Finding someone to talk to, going for a walk or discovering something pleasant to do can all help to break the cycle of rumination.
6. Social support: as we've seen already, this is probably one of the most helpful things we can do to bring us health and happiness.

> **Your foundations**
> - How would you describe the foundations of your life: solid, reliable and healthy … or shaky and vulnerable?
> - How are you doing with the 'basics' of life?
> - What could you do to improve them?

What is happiness?

Traditionally, amongst scholars, there have been two ways of understanding happiness. The first, the *hedonic tradition*, focuses on how we feel and our satisfaction in life. Hedonism views pleasure as the highest good and encourages us to experience as much of it as possible. Down through the centuries many people have lived according to this principle – getting the most pleasure out of life, and minimising pain as much as possible. The Epicureans (Greeks of classical times who held to a particular philosophy and practice) saw pleasure as the highest good. More recently, the authors of the United States Constitution included in their preamble the statement, 'We hold these truths to be self-evident, that all men are created equal, that they are endowed by their Creator with certain unalienable Rights, that among these are *Life, Liberty and the pursuit of Happiness*' [my italics]. As we have seen, the principle is still alive and well in the twenty-first century, focusing on 'the pursuit of pleasure and the avoidance of pain'.

The second, the *eudaimonic tradition*, can be traced all the way back to the Greek philosopher Aristotle. The word *eudaimonia* is often translated as 'happiness' but is better rendered 'flourishing', since it emphasises not just feeling well, but living well, or virtuously. Aristotle saw *eudaimonia* as the highest human good, in which how you lived (excellently or virtuously) counted for at least as much as simply enjoying life. Unlike his rivals the Stoics, he accepted that external things such as health and wealth were also important – which the Stoics rejected. But for him, happiness could not be divorced from virtuous living, involving thoughtful moral and ethical behaviour.

The psychologist Paul Wong has referred to a third type of happiness, which he calls *chaironic*.[5] The word is derived from the Greek word for joy, and so Wong describes this type of happiness as a gift of joy, often happening in unlikely places (he gives Mother Teresa as a classic example).[6] It is neither simply consumed, like hedonism, nor is it attained or earned, as in eudaimonic living, but is received as a gift. After all, many of the things we enjoy in life have come to us, not through our own efforts, but freely as a gift. That is true for the world as we find it, nature and its life, much that is good in humanity (relationships, laughter, kindness, etc.) and meaning that transcends individual desires and attainments. Such happiness includes a sense of awe about our existence and the cosmos and the fruit of reflecting on one's life. On this basis pleasure and satisfaction come as a consequence or side effect of pursuing something beyond 'me and mine'. I wonder if Viktor Frankl would have agreed.

Some things are clear then. The pursuit of happiness is very long-standing and the topic is not likely to fade away any time soon. The principles have been worked out over the centuries and we moderns are not inventing anything new when we talk about it. All three of the traditions described above have a part to play and recent research simply confirms that, as the next section describes.

Happiness in the twenty-first century

In recent years, there has been a huge amount of interest and research into happiness and wellbeing. This century, a new branch of psychology has emerged, known as Positive Psychology. Psychology professor Martin Seligman, who for many years had researched ways to develop human flourishing, first coined the term, but other researchers such as Mihaly Csikszentmihalyi,[7] Ed Deiner, Sonja Lyubomirsky and Barbara Fredrickson have also played a significant part in this burgeoning arena. Seligman is careful about the limitations of the answers science can give to questions like 'What is the meaning of life?' but adds, 'science can illuminate components[8] of happiness and investigate empirically what builds those components.' For me, one of his most helpful contributions has been his categorisation of the different types or dimensions of happiness. He has proposed three: pleasure, engagement and meaning.[9]

The Pleasant Life is the hedonic dimension of happiness, including positive emotions and our usual understanding of 'pleasure'. It focuses especially on material wellbeing – anything from enjoying a good drink or lying in the sun by a swimming pool to more developed experiences of pleasure like a meal with friends or a night on the town. But this type of happiness will only take us so far, whatever the advertising industry tells us. It is usually quite transient too – that glass of wine, slice of chocolate cake or bowl of ice cream only lasts for minutes, and any effort to maintain the pleasure leads to diminishing returns. This is hedonic adaptation, in which repeated doses of pleasure paradoxically bring less and less pleasure – the law of diminishing returns. It is also the bane of many of our lives – the more we pursue pleasure, the less we attain. A warning should probably be written over every shopping mall and supermarket in the country: 'Beware of hedonic adaptation'!

But there is another dimension. Pleasurable pursuits don't just rapidly fade, they also habituate – that is, you have to take just a little more of them each time to get the same buzz. The first bite of chocolate tastes best, but if you eat too much you'll get ill. Addiction is the price we pay for indulgence. We conventionally think of drugs and alcohol as addictive, but think – what is retail therapy? I remember talking to one of my friends some years ago. She always looked forward to Fridays because that was when after work she would reward herself with a new top or other item of clothing. The trouble was that her wardrobe was full of unopened clothes – the delight she got just by buying them only lasted as long as the journey home! For many of us today material wealth and physical health have become the 'highest good' in life – the main script or narrative of our society. As long as we have plenty of material things and are physically healthy, our lives will flourish. But as we have seen already, this is not all there is to be said.

The Engaged Life (or Good life) goes beyond the Pleasant life, since it demands more of us.[10] It has a lot in common with the eudaimonic life we encountered in the previous section. With pleasure we are simply consumers – that's what makes it pleasurable. We receive whatever is being served up and have to do very little to obtain it. But in the second, eudaimonic realm of happiness, we are initiators and participants in the process. Examples include training for a sport, working in an allotment or spending time with our family. Unlike pleasures, investments build for the future. They may not give the same quick burst of pleasure, but the satisfaction they bring is deeper and much longer lasting (if fleeting pleasures last for minutes or hours, engagements are more enduring, perhaps for years or even a lifetime), and this often involves development of character.

Seligman puts this lucidly when he writes (he uses the term 'gratifications' to refer to those activities that enable the Engaged life):

> Mounting over the last forty years in every wealthy country on the globe, there has been a startling increase in depression. This is a paradox, since every objective indicator of wellbeing has been going north, while every indicator of subjective wellbeing has been going south. How is this epidemic to be explained?
>
> There is[a] factor that looms as a cause of the epidemic: the over-reliance on shortcuts to happiness ... television, drugs, shopping, loveless sex, spectator sports and chocolate to name just a few. One of the major symptoms of depression is self-absorption. In contrast, the defining criterion of gratification is the absence of feeling, loss of self-consciousness, and total engagement. Here, then is a powerful antidote to the epidemic of depression: strive for more gratifications, while toning down the pursuit of pleasure. The pleasures come easily ... the gratifications are hard-won. Playing three sets of tennis, or participating in a clever conversation ... takes work. The pleasures do not.
>
> People ask, 'How can I be happy?' This is the wrong question, because without the distinction between pleasure and gratification it leads all too easily to a total reliance on shortcuts, to a life of snatching up as many easy pleasures as possible. I am not against the pleasures. When an entire lifetime is taken up in the pursuit of the positive emotions, however, authenticity and meaning are nowhere to be found. The right question is 'What is the good life?' My answer is tied up in the identification and the use of your signature strengths.[11]

One aspect of this approach has been given the name 'flow' by psychologists. Have you ever been so wrapped up in what you're doing (i.e. 'engaged' with it) that you lose track of time completely? Hours can pass without you realising it. This is called a state of flow and is what Seligman means in the quote above when he speaks of 'the absence of feeling, loss of self-consciousness, and total engagement.' He advocates prioritising these kinds of activities, with the aim of discovering and using your 'signature strengths.' You can test yourself and discover your own strengths by visiting the University of Pennsylvania's 'Authentic Happiness' website.[12]

Getting into flow

What do you do that takes you into a state of 'flow'? (To give you an idea, I've heard people referring to activities such as gardening, playing a sport, reading a book, cooking, etc.)

How could you develop this more?

But there is still one more dimension to discover. **The Meaningful Life** takes us deeper still, into meaning and purpose. Seligman sums it all up when he says, 'Just as the good life (another expression for the Engaged life) is something beyond the pleasant life, the meaningful life is beyond the good life.'[13] The major difference here is the importance of *being part of, belonging to and contributing towards something larger and more lasting than 'me and mine'*. This can include social groups or organisations, the natural world, belief systems and the transcendent. The satisfaction that comes from this is of a different order to the other two arenas. That is why Wong's description of the chaironic life is appealing, since it takes life satisfaction further even than *eudaimonia*. A meaningful or chaironic life is the most enduring, for its legacy persists even beyond a person's lifetime (think of the lasting impact of key figures in history).

More recently, Seligman has developed his classification, giving it the acronym 'PERMA.'[14] This stands for 'Positive emotions' (equating to pleasure), 'Engagement', 'Relationships', 'Meaning' and 'Accomplishments'. The last three are expansions of the 'Meaningful Life' from his earlier formulation. This brings more nuance but for me at least it doesn't negate the simpler three-fold framework.

Positive Psychology research has ventured into many and varied avenues, including emotions, gratitude, mindfulness, optimism, self-compassion, resilience, goal setting, relationships, marriage, work, education, volunteering, spirituality – the list goes on and on. Buckingham University became Europe's first 'positive' university in 2017, using Positive Psychology to develop a more engaging culture. Of course, the movement is not without its critics, who see it all as 'happiology' and an effort to get everyone smiling whatever the circumstances. Some of this disparagement is unfair, since it tends to caricature the discipline, deliberately setting up a straw man, which then gets enthusiastically knocked down. However, there is a real danger that Positive Psychology's focus on strengths, positive emotions and optimism can eclipse the deep significance of 'negative' emotions like fear, sadness and anger, all of which are vital for healthy human functioning. Life is not simply a bed of roses and reflection on the inevitable pains and losses we all encounter leads to a deeper – if not always jollier – life.

One other researcher worth mentioning is Carol Ryff, who has been working in the field of wellbeing (especially in older people) for many years. She has constructed a six-fold model of wellbeing comprising self-acceptance, personal autonomy, personal growth, environmental mastery, positive interpersonal relationships and purpose in life, which has stood the test of time.[15] What is particularly helpful is her recognition that wellbeing is multi-dimensional and cannot be forced into one simple model. I think her framework resonates well with Seligman's perspective. But as we will see below, wellbeing needs to include material and non-material dimensions; personal and corporate spheres; and theoretical principles as well as lived reality.

What are you grateful for?

One of the most significant and robust findings of Positive Psychology is that people who live lives of appreciation and gratitude are healthier, happier and more fulfilled. The top expert on gratitude research, Robert Emmons, says, 'I am not neutral about gratitude. I believe it to be the best approach to life.'[16] So how about trying this exercise?

Write down as many things as you can think of that you are grateful for in your life.

They can be small, inconsequential things, as well as hugely important aspects.

Take it further by writing down three things you're grateful for every day. Try it for three months and see what difference it makes to your attitudes.

Health, wellbeing and happiness

This chapter is entitled 'Happiness and wellness' so I should attempt to explain the link, if there is one. I've added another word, health, because all three words are used very commonly today and are often seen as the sum of all that is good in life. How do they connect?

The World Health Organisation defined health seventy years ago with a short, pithy statement: 'health is a state of complete physical, mental, and social wellbeing and not merely the absence of disease or infirmity.'[17] This definition has stood the test of time and it is noticeable that health is not viewed as a state you arrive at once you've thrown off the negatives of disease. Rather it is something tangible in its own right. We don't enjoy health because we have *no* disease but because we possess *something real and positive* – health. It is concrete, vital and vibrant and we will return to this vitally important theme in our last chapter.

But how does health relate to wellbeing? Are they the same thing? Today they are often used synonymously (think 'Health and Wellbeing Boards' in the NHS), but actually they refer to different things. Health is another way of talking about 'fitness'. If my body is healthy, it means that it is fit, suitable, ready, competent and able to carry out the activities a body exists for. Similarly, psychological or emotional health is necessary for me to live successfully and relate to other people. But what is it, exactly, that we need to be physically or emotionally fit and healthy *for*? That's where wellbeing comes in. We have healthy bodies and minds in order that we can live well. Living well (i.e. wellbeing) is much broader and deeper than simply being fit – it is of course the reason for which we need to be fit in the first place (if you'll excuse my circular reasoning). 'Health is too dependent on fate, fortune or luck ... health and wealth are mere instrumental goods.'[18]

In passing, it's interesting to note that frequently fitness or health are seen as ends in themselves, rather than a means to a further end. Health promotion is commonplace in the NHS (note, it's called the National *Health* Service, not the National *Wellbeing* Service, because in helping us to be healthy, it enables us to go on to *live* our lives – but that's down to us, not the government or the NHS),[19] and the aim is commendable – to help everyone to be healthy in body and mind. But when we become physically healthy, what then? Is there no more to living that that? I go to the gym fairly often and I'm constantly impressed by the effort that some people put into getting that best body or peak fitness. It sometimes crosses my mind to wonder whether the rest of their lives match their impressive outer forms. I have no idea about that – you can't tell from external appearances – but it does highlight again the prominence our culture gives to the physical and material.

So if health is something that enables wellbeing, how should we understand wellbeing itself? In fact there is no agreed definition of wellbeing. The health expert Allan McNaught sums up the situation by saying, 'the search for a generally accepted definition (of wellbeing) is fruitless, frustrating and ultimately impossible.'[20] Why? Because 'wellbeing' encompasses all aspects of life, from physical to spiritual, from individual to global, reaching into every sphere of human existence. It has to do with so much more than how healthy my body or mind is, since it goes far beyond me and mine. McNaught bravely attempts a framework for defining wellbeing by overlapping spheres of the individual, family, community and society and then subdividing each of these. For example, the 'Individual' category includes the physical, psychological, social and spiritual; whilst 'Society' incorporates amongst other things identity, economic security, political and geographical integrity of the state and fairness, equity and social justice.[21] Try summing all that up in one pithy sentence!

So that brings us to happiness. It may have become clear by now that human life is immensely complex and no one simple phrase can sum it all up. Wellbeing (which we all want) incorporates many different elements, and they all need to be largely healthy to bring about the desired overall result. It's perhaps not surprising then that happiness is a little tricky to obtain, especially if we see it primarily as manufactured by material wealth and physical health. And yet – some people seem to be remarkably happy, without having degrees in health science, marketing or philosophy.

Perhaps being happy has more to do with our attitudes than our bank balances; with our mindsets than our socio-economic status.

We'll pursue that further in the next sections.

Drawing it together

We've seen how happiness can be understood in a number of different ways, and throughout history people have sought to describe what those ways might look like. The distinction between hedonic, eudaimonic and chaironic perspectives attempts that, as does Seligman's threefold lives – Pleasant, Engaged and Meaningful. They all shed more light on our guiding diagram. The hedonic and Pleasant perspectives are over on the left, with eudaimonic and Engaged in the middle and chaironic and Meaningful on the right. Our society's emphasis on the material and physical aspects of health and wealth has skewed things to the left, but wellbeing research clearly shows that there is much more to life satisfaction than that and more attention is needed to correct the imbalance.

If we wanted to sum it all up in just four words, spanning from left to right, I would suggest the following. First, 'What' defines the concrete, explicit nature of the material world ('What *is* this thing exactly?'). Beyond that lies the 'How' of life ('So how does that work – how do we apply all those 'what' things?'), which edges us towards the centre. The third word, 'Who' takes us well into the right hand side ('Who am I, who are we – and how do we find out?') and 'Why' moves us further to the right ('Why am I (we) here anyway?'). We will pick this up again in later chapters.

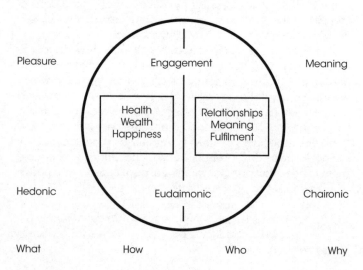

So let's turn to the key features of a 'right-hand-sided' life – relationships and meaning.

The first essential: Relationships

If we want to be happy, there is one dimension of life that we cannot afford to ignore: social connections, other people, community – in a word, relationships. So much research bears this out. For example, neuroscience has shown that our brains function best when our relationships are healthy. The opposite is also true – social isolation activates the same nerve pathways as physical pain.[22]

But one study stands out strongly for me and I find it compelling. The Study of Adult Development is a (nearly) eighty-year survey of men in the USA. It actually consists of two studies: the Grant Study looked at college graduates and the Glueck Study at less advantaged people. Data on health, career, retirement and relationships has been gathered over many years. You can hear the current director of the study, Robert Waldinger, talking about it in an absorbing TED Talk.[24]

He points to the three key conclusions that connect with relationships:

1. Men in both studies who say they are *closer to their family*, friends or community tend to be happier, healthier and longer-living than the others
2. The *quality of their relationships* has an impact on their wellbeing
3. Men whose marriages had *remained intact* until age fifty actually performed better on memory tests later in life than others.

His conclusion? *Strong relationships are critical to our health.* To quote Waldinger: 'Over and over, over these 75 years, our study has shown that the people who fared the best were the people who leaned in to relationships, with family, with friends, with community.' A previous director, George Vaillant agrees: 'Warmth of relationships throughout life have the greatest positive impact on "life satisfaction".'[24]

Looking outwards towards other people and their concerns turns out to be a two-way street. There is much evidence to show that focusing on others' interests and acting for their good is health-giving both for the giver and receiver. It benefits our physical, mental and emotional health by reducing stress, getting rid of negative feelings, giving us a sense of belonging, keeping things in perspective and even helping us to live longer! Paradoxically, socially isolated older adults gain the most from volunteering.[25] This focus on others is yet another example of the significance of that word that we encountered in Chapter 1 – connection.

John Ortberg sums it all up well:

> The yearning to attach and connect, to love and be loved, is the fiercest longing of the soul. Our need for community with people ... is to the human spirit what food and air and water are to the human body ... We need face-to-face interactions; we need to be seen and known and served and do these same things for others. We need to bind ourselves to each other with promises of love and loyalty made and kept ... Community is essential to human life. Rene Spitz showed that infants who are not held and hugged and touched, even if they have parents who give them food and clothes, suffer from retarded neurological development.[26]

But as with so many aspects of our culture, we tend to view relationships primarily from the individual's perspective: 'I'll grow my relationships because it's good for my happiness and health.' This of course is true, but it turns the matter on its head – and destroys its fragile nature in the process. The reason relationships are good for me is that I choose to situate myself where others can truly know me, depend on me and draw out the best in me (and vice versa of course). It's the very opposite of autonomous independence.[27] It gives the group at least as important a role as the individual and that person him/herself grows happier and healthier as (s)he fits in with the group. This is the norm in so many non-Western cultures, where behaving in this way literally 'goes without saying', but in the West it is hugely counter-cultural.[28] We lived in the Middle East for some years and I remember clearly one occasion when we had lost our way in Cairo and asked a passer-by for directions. Without hesitation he took us by the arm and walked us to our destination (fortunately not far away) – something I have never encountered in London! We were astounded at his willingness to redirect his priorities, but for him it was completely normal.

Our culture's preoccupation with mechanisms, control and individualism has momentous though unintended consequences for our everyday relationships. The bureaucratic and impersonal outworkings of an efficiency-focussed society lead inevitably to regarding people as 'productive' and 'functional' – or not. The expression 'human resources' used in organisations always screams that attitude out to me. If they are too old, disabled (physically, mentally or emotionally) or otherwise dysfunctional, we shut them away, either physically or in our minds. We feel awkward and unable to 'fix' the problem, so we move away from the dilemma, back towards the places where we feel at home. [29]

In 1964, Jean Vanier founded a community in France for people with intellectual disabilities. He called it 'l'Arche', meaning 'the Ark' and it has now become a global federation of communities, spread over 35 countries. Vanier has received many honours for his work.[30]

A film has recently been made about the work of l'Arche, called *Summer in the Forest*.[31] In it Vanier sums up his perspective:

> What is it to be a human being? Is it the power? If it's power, then we would kill each other! You see, the wise and powerful lead us to ideologies, whereas the weak are in the dirt. *They're not seeking power, they're seeking friendship.* It's a message for all of us. It's about all of us.

The second essential: Meaning

Clearly then, relationships really are essential for lasting happiness. But what about meaning and purpose? Is this also 'essential' to get us to our final destination? We will delve into this much more towards the end of the book, but let me begin by asking another question: what do we *mean* by 'meaning'? What is the meaning of meaning? Tricky? Well, here's my working definition:

> *Meaning is the implicit intention or representation lying behind the explicit entity – be that a word, gesture, action or something more profound.*[32]

The key phrase is 'the implicit lying behind the explicit' (or the invisible behind the visible). Something unseen and implied lies beneath the outward appearance *that requires more exploration and explanation* – in fact we sometimes talk of a 'hidden' meaning. Meaning is less obvious than surface, material, visible things and it takes more time to discover and fathom. In our culture, that doesn't come very naturally, but it is well worth the effort, especially if we are considering the whole of our lives.

That may all sound a bit abstract so let me give a few practical examples. During the time that we as a family lived in the Middle East, I travelled a fair amount and therefore had lots of cross-cultural encounters. I soon discovered that words and actions that meant one thing in my own culture came across very differently in another person's context. One of my best friends was Lebanese and early on in our relationship I asked him a simple question, something like, 'Are you going to catch the bus?' To my shocked surprise, he just tutted, tilting his head back as he did so. I thought, 'What did I say to make him react like that?' (In the UK you only tut when you're irritated or disapproving.) It was only later that I discovered that he simply meant, 'No'. On other occasions, we hosted groups of young people from Western Europe for a few weeks at a time. They had great fun and would often joke about in mixed gender groups, with plenty of banter and friendly hugging, poking and general touching (appropriately!). But some of my Middle Eastern friends were appalled by the seeming *in*appropriate physical contact between the sexes – something just not done in their circles.

A final illustration. For someone who grew up with a loving father the word 'father' conveys feelings of warmth and security; but for another person who never knew their father or experienced abuse at his hands, their immediate response is likely to be one of anger or pain. The word itself is simply six letters strung together, but its perceived meaning could not be more different. The point in all these examples is that the visible outer word or act is the same for both parties, but the meaning perceived by different people is drastically different.

All of this shows that 'meaning' is an even trickier word than 'happiness'. But it also demonstrates that if we are to discover meaning, we will have to do more than stay in our comfort zones of obvious and surface affairs. Everything in life conveys meaning of some kind, but often that meaning is far from evident at first sight. (How much misunderstanding and conflict might be avoided if we took more time to discover *precisely* what someone meant by their words or action?) We will have to dig deeper. This is especially important with relationships and more intangible matters such as 'the meaning of life'. In Chapter 7 we will pursue this theme more fully.

But here's the rub. Just as with relationships, a sense of meaning and purpose is lacking in so many of our lives. Over a century ago, the sociologist Emile Durkheim coined the expression *anomie*, signifying 'a condition of instability resulting from a breakdown of standards and values or from a lack of purpose or ideals'.[33] At the same time, another sociologist, Max Weber wrote about the rigid and rationalistic bureaucracies that had come to dominate society.[34]

Peter Berger (another sociologist!) spoke later of the loss of the 'sacred canopy' of meanings that traditionally had explained life, death and the world around us.[35]

The title of one of his books, *The Homeless Mind* communicates well the loss of purpose and direction that modern people have experienced.[36]

The pace quickened as the twenty-first century arrived, with increased mobility, speed of change and social fragmentation. It has left many people walking the treadmill but feeling homeless and wondering what life is all about.

Happiness versus meaning

One of the most absorbing and revealing studies into meaning (and happiness) that I have come across was conducted by Roy Baumeister and colleagues in 2013.[37] They investigated the similarities and differences between the Happy Life (akin to Seligman's The Pleasant Life) and the Meaningful Life (elements of The Engaged Life and The Meaningful Life). They surveyed people across the nation (the USA) and their findings and conclusions were fascinating. From the results of the study, they came to understand happiness as 'natural', with its narrow focus on pursuing and enjoying needs and desires, like any other sentient animal. If life is easy, health is good and both feelings and finances are satisfactory, then we are happy. In other words, *happiness is about the present moment and comes from getting what we want.*

Meaning on the other hand is 'cultural'[38] and a specifically human characteristic. It is more complex and less immediate, requiring us to both reflect on the past and imagine the future. This in turn helps us to link and integrate our experiences and events across the past, present and future. Though social connections increase both happiness and meaning (loneliness is detrimental to both), helping others actually *diminishes* happiness, benefitting meaningfulness only. Parenting is the classic example. Many people want to become parents, but find the reality anything but pleasurable. However, it is profoundly meaningful, with the deepened meaning offsetting losses in happiness.

Meaning then is associated with doing things for others, whereas happiness equates with doing things for oneself. Sacrifice builds meaning, but bears little relation to happiness. Paradoxically, meaning is associated with anxiety, stress and arguing because it connects with important activities beyond the self – even though this is clearly not a state of happiness!

> *Meaning is characterised by giving and focuses on the longer, deeper picture.*

Let's make that a little more real by painting some personal portraits. Consider Harry, who is keen to live a happy life and pursues it enthusiastically. He doesn't hold back on enjoying food, drink, holidays and other pleasures. He relishes living in the present moment and doesn't spend too much time planning for the future – nor does he reflect much on his past. He revels in being with people but isn't great at keeping in touch with people when he doesn't see them often. He tries to keep his distance from situations that might lead to demanding entanglements.

Mary, on the other hand, engages quite seriously in more difficult undertakings. This brings her more worry, stress, anxiety and arguments, none of which result in lashings of happiness. She too is interested in people, but her focus isn't just on the present moment – she reflects a lot on her past experiences and future hopes. This can sometimes make her relatively unhappy, but it enables her to self-regulate well. She is known as a giver more than a taker.

These are of course stark caricatures (and there are aspects of them that aren't mutually exclusive), but they reflect the patterns that Baumeister describes. In fact he paints a picture of a *'highly meaningful but unhappy life'* – essentially that of Mary above – which contrasts glaringly with Harry's 'happy but meaningless life'. The researchers conclude that the essence of happiness is satisfying needs and wants. A happy person is similar to an animal (with a little more complexity of course), whereas meaningfulness is human and is all about expressing the self and thinking integratively about the past and future.

> *Like animals, we strive for happiness (what we get) but like humans, we also quest for meaning (what we give).*[39]

This all brings us to the horns of our modern dilemma: we want happiness (by which we often mean pleasure) and are encouraged to do so by the media, advertisers, commerce and government. But we have been discovering for a long time now that such a focus only takes us so far and if we push it to its conclusion it ends up making us *un*happy and *un*well! 'There has to be more to life', we cry – and of course there is. But pursuing that 'more to life' takes us into less comfortable territory – places we don't often search out because more is required of us than simply being 'consumers' who spend a lot of their time – well, consuming.

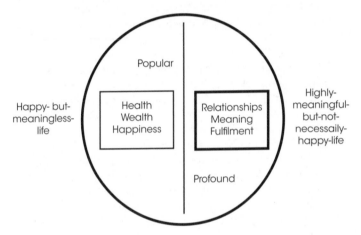

Summary

In this chapter we have explored what we mean by happiness and found that it can mean many different things, from sheer material pleasure to deep sacrificial living. We have also examined wellbeing and seen that it spans the whole range of human life and experience. It certainly conveys more than what we usually think of when we hear the word 'happiness'. We've sought to travel more from the left side of our diagram towards the right, investigating the key areas of relationships and meaning, and again finding that all that is worthwhile is not necessarily on the surface – we have to dig deeper. And that is precisely what we will do in the next chapter.

LONGING FOR MORE

We are torn between nostalgia for the familiar and an urge for the foreign and strange. As often as not, we are homesick most for the places we have never known.[1]

Carson McCullers

It seems to me we can never give up longing and wishing while we are still alive. There are certain things we feel to be beautiful and good, and we must hunger for them.

George Eliot

Standing at the front of a small lecture hall, Ed Diener, University of Illinois psychologist and world-renowned happiness teacher, held up a real brain in a jar with a blue liquid, which he called 'joy juice,' trickling into it from a small plastic pouch held above. He asked the audience to pretend that their brains could be treated with a hormone (i.e. joy juice) that would make them ecstatically happy, and that they could be happy *all the time*. Then he asked the crucial question, 'How many people in this room would want to do this?' Of the 60 audience members, only 2 raised their hands to signify their desires for perpetual happiness.[2]

Joy juice

Suppose you had been in Diener's audience that day:

- How would you have voted?
- Why?
- What's the issue with non-stop happiness on tap?

Longing – the ache that won't go away

Have you ever gazed towards a stunning sunrise or sunset, or over a beautiful natural scene, say, of mountains, coastland, forests or lakes, and found yourself carried into a place that lies far beyond what you can physically see? Or experienced an intimacy with another person that transported you way beyond your present circumstance? (Why do people say 'Oh God!' when they experience something climactic?) Or listened to a particularly poignant piece of music, only to discover that you've been reduced to tears, when you weren't previously in the least bit sad or upset? (I remember doing the ironing one evening in my front room – how prosaic is that? – listening to an especially expressive and emotional piece of music, and suddenly realising that I was now sobbing my heart out. I'm not usually given to tears, but music can sometimes have a very powerful effect on me. I remember at the time part of me thinking, 'What on earth are you weeping about? It's only a piece of music!').

If so, you are certainly not the first person to experience such things. There is a strange poignancy to them, to such an extent that it is almost impossible to find a label or description for them – again, words prove very inadequate indeed. But one word that may fit the bill better than most is *longing*, i.e. a reaching out towards or yearning for something that you can't describe but which draws you very powerfully with a mixture of joy and sadness – even melancholy. Augustine was a great thinker of the fourth century. He reflected and wrote much about the human condition, which was essentially the same in his day as it is in ours. He wrote that all people have hopes and longings for something 'more' (even though we often don't recognise or understand what it is we are longing for). But because the things we pursue can never adequately fulfil our deepest desire, we remain dissatisfied and frustrated. One of Augustine's well-known sayings was 'longing makes the heart deep'.

Many centuries later, the British writer C. S. Lewis wrote about this universal human longing. He suggested that each person possesses a deep and intense yearning, which no object or experience can fully satisfy. He called this longing 'joy', and described it as 'an unsatisfied desire which is itself more desirable than any other satisfaction ... anyone who has experienced it will want it again'. Here is what he goes on to say about our age-old quest for beauty:

The books or the music in which we thought the beauty was located will betray us if we trust to them; it was not in them, it only came *through* them, and what came through them was longing. These things—the beauty, the memory of our own past—are good images of what we really desire; but if they are mistaken for the thing itself they turn into dumb idols, breaking the hearts of their worshippers. *For they are not the thing itself; they are only the scent of a flower we have not found, the echo of a tune we have not heard, news from a country we have never yet visited.*

Almost our whole education has been directed to silencing this shy, persistent, inner voice; and yet it is a remarkable thing that (they) bear reluctant witness to the truth that our real goal is elsewhere. Do what they will, then, we remain conscious of a desire which no natural happiness will satisfy. Here, then, is the desire, still wandering and uncertain of its object and still largely unable to see that object in the direction where it really lies [my italics].[3]

No matter how we seek to reduce life to solid, tangible and predictable activities and laws, some things seem to creep up on us and pull the rug from underneath our neat and certain lives. And these things generally are emotional, reducing us to tears or producing within us a state of joy and sorrow all at the same time. Such phenomena are at the heart of music, art, poetry and expressions of faith. They cannot easily be nailed down and contained – they just don't work that way. That makes them perplexing and difficult, and therefore often consigned to the margins of 'mainstream' life. It's as though we say, 'art, music and faith are all very well, but we can probably manage without them, although life would be a bit mundane that way'.[4]

But they are still there and tend to intrude at the most inconvenient moments. We will see as we go on that underrating and undervaluing them comes at a heavy cost.

The verb, 'to long' derives from Anglo-Saxon '*longen*', meaning, 'to yearn after, grieve for'. Literally it means, 'to grow long, lengthen', which gives us a sense of that feeling of stretching out towards something or someone. It is related to the German 'verlangen', 'to desire'.[5] But as the literary scholar Iain McGilchrist (of whom more later) points out,

> This form suggests something about longing that differentiates it from wanting or desiring a thing. *Wanting* is clear, purposive, urgent, driven by the will, always with its goal clearly in view. *Longing*, by contrast, is something that 'happens' between us and another thing. It is not directed by will...with the ultimate goal of acquisition; but instead is a desire for union – or rather it is experienced as a desire for re-union. (It) remains in the realms of the implicit or intuitive, and is often spiritual in nature. Longing suggests a distance, but a never interrupted connection or union over that distance... It is somehow experienced as an elastic tension ... the pull, tautness as in a bow string [my italics].[6]

This takes us into very different territory from the life in which we seek to be in control and exert our wills in the world.

> *With longing, the focus is not really on ourselves, but rather on something or someone that occupies our view but lies beyond our grasp or control. We are drawn after something but we can't quite reach it.*

That's an uncomfortable place, but it is as happy as it is sad (actually neither of these words adequately describes the feeling, which is perhaps better rendered joyful and melancholic). McGilchrist's comment on 're-union' is significant in that we yearn to be *re*-united with something or someone that is not completely new to us – a part of our lives from which somehow we have been separated. Incidentally, his contrast between wanting and longing is reminiscent of the distinction between The Pleasant Life and The Engaged and (especially) Meaningful Life. Pleasure, especially material pleasure, is explicit, concrete, tangible, easily described and understood. But the further one goes towards meaning the more implicit things become and therefore more difficult to describe, capture and encapsulate. Wanting goes with *taking* (pleasurable things), longing goes with *receiving* (meaningful living).[7]

What does longing look like?

This may all sound a bit abstract, so let me try and ground it in reality with a few examples. Think of some popular songs you know. What are they about? Most seem to concentrate on relationships, especially romantic ones, in which love is sought, gained and lost; or on the hopes, dreams, joys and sorrows of people who want to experience more in their lives. And they always involve emotion – lots of emotion! Here are the four main categories as they appear to me:

1. We sing about *persons* (i.e. individuals) to whom we look to bring an end to our *loneliness*: love me, be with me, hold me, take me home, don't leave me, don't reject me.[8]

2. We also sing about *place(s)*: we are *lost* and homesick for home and we want to go back there – not simply alone, but with those we care about.

3. We sing about *people*, by which I mean, a group of people with whom we want (need) to be – we ache for a family to *belong* to.

4. And sometimes we simply have a strong *desire*: our song is a deep heart-cry for *something more* than we experience right now.

You could probably think of lots of songs to fit these different groupings, but here is my selection:

Longing for a person

'Yesterday'[9] was a best-selling song by Paul McCartney, mourning the loss of a lover. You probably know the words by heart, but for me, his yearning could be summed up with, 'Oh, if only I could have yesterday again.' If that's not a song of longing, I don't know what is! It was voted the twentieth century's best song in a poll in 1999 – an indication, if we needed one, of its power and resonance.[10]

'I Will Wait for You'[11] was written for a French musical in 1964. The singer promises to wait for her lover forever, for a thousand summers.

More recently, Martin Garrix and Dua Lipa wrote 'Scared to be Lonely' (2017).[12] The relationship (of the couple in the song) has started so well. Now, despite all the fights and flaws, they are still together. But why? Is it simply because they are too afraid to be left alone and lonely? The question is asked over and over, but there's no answer.

Longing for a place

'Jerusalem',[13] popularised by Edward Elgar in 1922, is sung every year at the London Promenade concerts. It begins with the words, 'And did those feet in ancient time walk upon England's mountains green?' and ends with, 'Nor shall my sword sleep in my hand, till we have built Jerusalem in England's green and pleasant land'. For some people at least it arouses visions of past might, patriotic fervour and the longing for a greater nation.

The final film of the 'Lord of the Rings' series ends with the haunting song 'Into the West'.[14] It encourages the listener to lay down their head, because night is falling and the journey has ended at last. Those who have gone before call from a distant shore and sleep is finally coming. The whole poem is a powerful song of longing for a place that can only be reached by travelling far across the ocean.

And of course there is 'Somewhere Over the Rainbow'[15] with its aching for that place beyond the rainbow, far away beyond our reach. It's a paradise where the skies are always blue and dreams really do come true. But the pang comes when the singer realises that although birds seem to find their way there past the rainbow, she can never reach it. All of which goes to show that longing is often tinged with the sadness of dreams that haven't yet come true.

Longing for a people

You may find your nation's national anthem moving. Just watch athletes standing on the Olympic medal podium and notice how many are moved to tears as they listen to their anthem. Or sports people, deeply moved as they stand to attention for the national hymn before the match starts. Why is that?

'Jerusalem of Gold'[16] is an evocation of the significance of Jerusalem to the Jews and therefore perhaps belongs equally in the 'place' category. But it is also a fervent craving to belong to a people. The song was written by Naomi Shemer just three weeks before the Six Day War broke out, which resulted in the taking of the Old City of Jerusalem – back in Jewish hands for the first time in nearly 2000 years. You can sense the longing and nostalgia in the words, 'Jerusalem of gold, and of bronze, and of light, Behold I am a violin for all your songs.'[17]

Just desiring

The musical *Cats* gave us the poignant song, 'Memory',[18] sung by the character Grizabella, who is mourning her lost youth and hankering for a new life above. But she dares to hope that a new future is possible if she can but find up there the meaning of happiness. It's a song of longing.

John Mayer released his album *Heavier Things* in 2003. One of the songs was called 'Something's Missing'.[19] Once again, the singer searches for joy, but somehow he just can't satiate that inner hunger and thirst. He checks off all the things he's got (friends, money, 'opposite sex'), but over and over he cries out for that missing something, which he doesn't know how to fix. You can feel the pain and yearning in his words.

The list goes on and on. Of course the power isn't just in the words, although poetry has its own intensity.

So before you read any further, why not listen to the songs yourself and see what impact they have on you (both words and music).

You probably know and love songs that hold powerful meaning for you, because of memories of people, places or experiences ('Hey, they're playing our song!'). Often the melodies are haunting, evoking feelings that itch and resonate in unexpected ways.

The same could be said for the *best stories*. Like songs of longing, they prompt in us a yearning for adventure, love, connection, kinship and meaning. They put us in touch with memories, experiences, dreams and longings that transcend the words on the page. Different stories often share a similar plot, which goes something like this: In the beginning there is home, family, relationship. But most of the narrative consists of epic struggles and adventures as evil seeks to overthrow good. This leads inexorably to the climax or denouement, entailing an epic battle with the final overthrow of evil. The concluding scene consists of a world put to rights and a final homecoming celebration. Think Greek epics, *The Pilgrim's Progress*, *The Lord of the Rings*, the *Harry Potter* series, the *Narnia* books, most fantasy books and many Hollywood blockbusters![20] Again, you probably have a favourite of your own, but it may well have similar elements in it. We identify with the hero(es) and yearn wistfully for a 'happy-ever-after' outcome, since it reverberates with the longings of our own hearts.

Longing for home

Why is all this so? Surely it's because we sing songs or tell stories about things that really matter (i.e. they're *meaningful* to us). How many ballads and moving songs do you know that focus on cars, fridges, the office or the local supermarket? I can't think of any. They are nearly all about love, connection, meaning, hope and a vision for a better future. As Alexander Pope wrote,

> Hope springs eternal in the human breast;
> Man never is, but always to be blessed:
> The soul, uneasy and confined from home,
> Rests and expatiates[21] in a life to come.

That word *home* crops up often in songs, poems and stories. Part of our universal longing is bound up with a yearning for home – as if we have wandered away and are looking for a homecoming. We want to be with people we care about, but we also desire to be in a place we can call 'home'. The group Keane released the song, 'Sunshine' in 2004. Their key question focuses on home over and over again: Can anyone discover their home? We're lost in the sun, but come on, can we find our home?[22]

The writer Richard Rohr comments on 'home and homesickness':

> The archetypal idea of 'home' points in two directions at once. It points backward toward an original hint and taste for union, starting in the body of our mother ...[23] And it points forward, urging us toward the realization that this hint and taste of union might actually be true. It guides us like an inner compass or a 'homing' device ...
>
> To understand better, let's look at the telling word *homesick*. This usually connotes something sad or nostalgic, an emptiness that looks either backward or forward for satisfaction ... We are both driven and called forward by a kind of deep homesickness, it seems. I think also of Hermann Hesse's *Steppenwolf*, in which he says, 'We have no one to guide us. Our only guide is our homesickness'...We are homesick, although today most would probably just call it loneliness, isolation, longing, sadness, restlessness, or even a kind of depression.[24]

Rohr refers to *nostalgia*, which expresses well what we have been reflecting on. It means 'pain or grief' (*algos*) connected with 'homecoming' (*nostos*) – i.e. the pain of homesickness. Why the pain? We're not here being transported into the realm of pleasure or hedonic-happiness-as-we-usually-understand-it. Rather, there is a sense of loss – we once had something good but now it's lost, at least in part, and we yearn to reconnect with it. But pain isn't the only characteristic. There's hope and anticipation there too. Either way, both homesickness and nostalgia convey very powerful emotions of loss and disappointment combined with hope and desire – in fact, longing!

Homesick or nostalgic
- When have you felt homesick?
- For what, or whom, were you yearning?
- If you tried to put the feeling into words, what words would you use?
- How does that feeling about a specific experience you had relate to the deeper, wider longings we all feel in life?

The human condition

Henri Nouwen was a Roman Catholic priest who, in later life, lived in a community that cared for people with major disabilities. As he dwelt among and contributed into the community he became more and more convinced of the need for a deeper life. He refers to a 'second loneliness':[25]

It is important to learn to move from a 'first loneliness' to a 'second loneliness.' The first loneliness is sort of the emotional loneliness: you need friends, you need family, you need home. *But when you satisfy all those needs, you have to suddenly learn that there is another loneliness ... [a] deep, personal intimacy, and it is an intimacy that is very demanding.* It requires letting go of many things that are emotionally, intellectually and affectively very satisfying. You must grow to realise and to trust that this deeper loneliness is not to be overcome, but lived. You must live it with trust, standing tall. You must try to say, 'Yes, I am lonely, but *this particular loneliness sets me on the road to intimacy...it brings me closer to the source of love in the depths of my being* [my italics].'

The sentiments that Nouwen expresses here are not easy to grasp. (I remember once reading the above quote out to a group. One person responded, 'Wow, that's so powerful and meaningful'; another just looked confused and said, 'I have no idea what that is talking about!') But they nonetheless provide the context to all that we will investigate in the later chapters of this book, especially with reference to 'the source of love in the depths of our beings'.

It turns out that the expression of longing is not limited to one culture. The idea is articulated more deeply in languages other than English – German has *sehnsucht*, Welsh *hiraeth*,[26] Portugese *saudade* and Romanian *dor*. *Sehnsucht* derives from two words meaning 'ardent longing' and 'addiction' or 'insatiable craving' (notice the parallel with homesickness) and represents something very profound. Apparently the word enjoys great popularity amongst German speakers, having come third in a public competition for 'the most beautiful German word' (after *lieben*, 'to love', and *gemutlichkeit*, 'coziness'. This latter word can apparently include qualities of 'peace of mind' or 'belonging'. I wonder whether all three sentiments could be summed up with the phrase, 'We long for love and belonging'?) One researcher says that it has several components: our longings are rich and symbolic; we long for an ideal world, a utopia; but since we also realise that this is unattainable we end up with bittersweet or ambivalent emotions; the panorama stretches across a lifetime, looking back, forward, and to the present;[29] and longing leads to deep reflection on our lives.[30]

It is as if we all have within us a very strong (though mostly unconscious and incompletely understood) awareness. We have a reasonably clear idea of what life and the world is *supposed* to be like and hold a deep conviction that things *ought* to be good, as the songs and stories we compose reveal. But in practice, all is *not* as it should be – we look around (and within) and realise that reality doesn't measure up to our longings. The result is an ambivalent and conflicted perspective, part hopeful and part despondent. In fact, if we didn't have the hope and desire for life-as-it-should-be inside us, the pain of disappointment wouldn't be so great. This, in my view, summarises the Human Condition.

We know intuitively what life should be like, yet somehow we can never quite reach or grasp it – and often we feel we don't come within light years of it! We try to fill the gap with all kinds of 'things' but they never quite do the job, and we are still left with that ache that won't go away.

This chimes with our guiding diagram, in which the words on the left hand side equate with the world of explicit, concrete 'reality', whereas the right hand side entities are trickier to get hold of. We *grasp* the left hand side elements, but *long for* the ones on the right hand side.

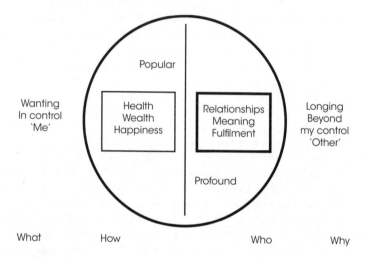

Wanting
In control
'Me'

Popular

Health
Wealth
Happiness

Relationships
Meaning
Fulfilment

Longing
Beyond
my control
'Other'

Profound

What   How   Who   Why

C. S. Lewis – a case study in longing

No one exemplifies the desire and ambivalence of longing more than the writer C. S. Lewis, perhaps because he is better known to us from his writings than many other people, but also because from his childhood his main passion in life was to pursue longing. He called it 'Joy'. Alister McGrath has written a very accessible and revealing biography about him,[31] and many of that book's pages refer to Lewis' longings. Speaking for example of Lewis's childhood home in Northern Ireland, McGrath writes,

From Little Lea, the young Lewis could see the distant Castlereagh Hills, which seemed to speak to him of something of heartrending significance, lying tantalisingly beyond his reach. They became a symbol of liminality, of standing on the threshold of a new, deeper, and more satisfying way of thinking and living. An unutterable sense of intense longing arose within him as he contemplated them. He could not say exactly what it was that he longed for, merely that there was a sense of emptiness within him, which the mysterious hills seemed to heighten without satisfying. [32]

At around the age of seven or eight years, Lewis experienced three powerful imaginative encounters, which broke in on an otherwise 'astonishingly prosaic' life.[33] The first came on a summer's day when the fragrance of a nearby bush triggered a memory that evoked 'enormous bliss...a sensation of desire', though he could not place what the desire was for. Almost immediately the desire was gone, but he was left with 'a longing for the longing that had just ceased.' The second glimpse came as he was reading Beatrix Potter's *The Tale of Squirrel Nutkin*. The 'shock' he experienced as he read it could only be described as the 'Idea of Autumn'; again came that 'intense desire', which seemed to him to be of 'incalculable importance'. Thirdly, while reading Longfellow's 'Saga of King Olaf', he read the lines:

> I heard a voice that cried,
> Balder the beautiful
> Is dead, is dead –

He was 'uplifted into huge regions of northern sky' and 'desired with almost sickening intensity, something never to be described'.[34] A measure of the importance Lewis attached to this dimension of life is found in his decision to call his autobiography, 'Surprised by Joy'. In the paragraph that follows his recounting of the three experiences in that book, Lewis writes about Joy:

> The reader who finds these three episodes of no interest need read this book no further, for in a sense the central story of my life is about nothing else. For those who are still disposed to proceed I will only underline the quality common to the three experiences: *it is that of an unsatisfied desire which is itself more desirable than any other satisfaction. I call it Joy*, which is here a technical term and must be sharply distinguished both from Happiness and from Pleasure. Joy (in my sense) has indeed one characteristic, and one only, in common

with them: the fact that anyone who has experienced it will want it again. Apart from that ... it might almost equally well be called a particular kind of unhappiness or grief [my italics].[35]

As the child Lewis grew into adulthood, particularly following his experiences in the First World War, he learnt to disregard such phenomena. Although he still retained 'his deep longing for the safety and security of the past ... a wistfulness over the irretrievability of a loved past',[36] he came to mistrust the imaginative realm. Nonetheless he could not shake off the constant internal conflict between rationality and imagination, summing it up in this way:

> The two hemispheres of my mind were in the sharpest contrast. On the one side a many-islanded sea of poetry and myth; on the other a glib and shallow 'rationalism'. *Nearly all that I loved I believed to be imaginary;[37] nearly all I believed to be real I thought grim and meaningless* [italics mine].[38]

He was of course an Oxford English Literature don, and lived much of his adult life there. One of his closest friends was J. R. R. Tolkien, who went on to write one of the most significant novels of the twentieth century, the fantasy, *The Lord of the Rings*. Lewis was a constant companion on Tolkien's journey, giving enthusiastic support whenever the author flagged. But Tolkien played a key role in Lewis's development too, regularly discussing and disputing matters of philosophy with others in their pub discussion group, the Inklings. There came a day (night actually) when the critical moment arrived, during a 'long night talk' with Tolkien and others. Tolkien explained to Lewis how 'a myth is a story that conveys 'fundamental things' ... When the full and true story is told, it is able to bring to fulfillment all that was right and wise in those fragmentary visions ... For Tolkien ... Christianity's meaningfulness ... provided the total picture, unifying and transcending these fragmentary and imperfect insights ... A myth awakens in its readers a longing for something that lies beyond their grasp.'[39]

Tolkien's words provided Lewis with the connection he craved between rationality and imagination. At last he could embrace the realm of longing without awkwardness, as he found a convincing way to integrate the hard domain of reason with the yearning of the imagination. If ever a person experienced a *kairos* moment, surely it was Lewis that night! Through it he came to understand that 'rational exploration ... follows on from the captivation of the imagination through images and stories.'[40] Reflecting later on that crucial evening, he wrote, 'In the Trinity Term I gave in ... perhaps that night, the most dejected and reluctant convert in England.'[41] This development continued throughout his life. Over the next few decades, he persisted with his exploration of 'the relationship between reason and the imagination, between "the true" and "the real"[42] – in particular, the relationship between rational argument and the use of imaginative narratives ... From about 1937, Lewis seems to have appreciated that the imagination is the gatekeeper of the human soul' and he 'began to realise how fiction might allow the intellectual and imaginative appeal of worldviews to be explored.'[43]

Lewis is probably best known for his series of children's books, *The Chronicles of Narnia*. Written over sixty years ago, they remain hugely popular, having sold over 100 million copies in 47 languages.[44] In 2008, the first book of the series, *The Lion, the Witch and the Wardrobe* was voted the best children's book of all time.[45] What then is so powerful about the books? According to McGrath, 'they are about a quest for meaning and virtue, not simply the quest for explanation and understanding' and 'a marvellous way of exploring...questions – such as the origins of evil, the nature of faith, and the human desire for God'.[46] Perhaps he also effectively articulated the universal longings we all share, the 'liminality' that he first sensed as a young child and then grew, first to distrust, but then to embrace as a fundamental part of what it means to be human. As we have seen, this seems to be better expressed through story, poetry and song than in long treaties and essays of prose! (We will return to this theme of story in Chapter 8.)

The last word should go to Lewis himself. At the end of his autobiography he reviews that decisive *kairos* episode of his life and of course describes it in terms of Joy:

There was no doubt that Joy was a desire...But a desire is turned not to itself but to its object. Not only that, but it owes all its character to its object ... All the value lay in that of which Joy was the desiring...Inexorably Joy proclaimed, 'You want – I myself am your want of – something other, outside, not you nor any state of you' ... But this brought me already into the region of awe for I thus understood that in deepest solitude there is a road right out of the self.[47]

Lewis had come to view longing (Joy) as not the end in itself, but a means or signpost to something else – that to which the sign pointed, the source of the yearning. In this, he was not only anticipating the discoveries about wellbeing and life satisfaction opening up through today's research, but also expounding the experiences of many people down through the centuries – that true happiness comes not through the pursuit of happiness itself, but as a by-product of another kind of quest altogether, one that taps into the deepest longings of the human soul. These are longings for *connection* – to another person, to a place we can call home, to kinship groups to whom we can belong and to something beyond, as the antidote to lostness and loneliness.

Dimensions of longing – the need to connect

I wrote earlier that we all seem to have within us a strong intuition about what life should be like. When small children are playing it isn't long before someone cries out, 'It's not fair!' They don't generally need to be taught that something is 'just' or 'right' – it comes out spontaneously. And as we grow older, that sense of how things 'should be' only increases – about the world out there, but also my inner world 'in here'. No one needs to convince us that connection and harmony and are 'right' and so our struggle is with the opposite – disconnection, dissonance and a sense that all is *not* right. One of the most troubling features of the human condition is this sense of disharmony, separation and alienation that we all feel. It's an odd thing that even in the midst of a crowded room or busy street we can feel lost and alone. Here's the description of an experience I once had on a train journey:

> Travelling on a train, I'm looking out at the countryside. It's beautiful and yet – I don't know anyone round here. If I stayed here for some days or weeks, perhaps in a hotel, I might well feel lonely – wanting company whom I know. It makes me think, 'How friendly is this world anyway?' For many of us, there are times when it doesn't

feel very friendly or hospitable. In fact, it's rather cold and impersonal if you don't have family or friends. And even if you have, the time is coming when they will leave you, through travel or death. It's part of the existential angst[48] that so many of us feel but try to stave off through staying constantly busy and filling our lives with activity, noise and stuff. But it's there in the background. Is this a place in which to belong, or ultimately a foreign abode? Beyond all the stuff of life, even the beauty of the world, where can I know, be known, enjoy, come home to? Is there 'home' at all, or is it really rather bleak and alien? How do I find out? Who is to tell me?

Existential angst
- How do you react to this passage?
- What are your experiences of 'existential angst' or the kind of loneliness that you can't properly explain?
- What other feelings do you have about this?

Shakespeare, as he so often does, finds words to express this anguish when he writes the lines below in his play, *Hamlet*. Conditions (the 'time') in Denmark were 'out of joint', like a dislocated shoulder. Hamlet, the surgeon, would have to operate by both re-setting the bones and removing the diseased core, King Claudius.[49]

> The time[50] is out of joint—O cursèd spite,
> That ever I was born to set it right!
> Nay, come, let's go together.

This 'out-of-joint-ness' is another way of describing our feelings of disconnection and unrest. But often our default reaction is to find some kind of distraction, diversion or compensation to help us escape from our raw or distressing emotions. We especially look towards immediate, tangible, consumable comforts ('pleasure') – the usual suspects generally involve eating, drinking, seeking technology or finding pleasurable release. But the ache is still there. As the newspaper columnist, Bernard Levin once wrote:

Countries like ours are full of people who have all the material comforts they desire, together with such non-material blessings as a happy family, and yet lead lives of quiet, and at times noisy, desperation, understanding nothing but the fact that there is a hole inside them and that however much food and drink they pour into it, however many motor cars and television sets they stuff it with, however many well balanced children and loyal friends they parade around the edges of it ... it aches.[51]

But if a lasting solution to this experience is not to be found in the immediate or the superficial, where should we look? I believe the answer lies in our shared quest for meaning, which we began to explore in the last two chapters and is at the heart of all that we have been investigating in this chapter.

Summary

The sea always filled her with longing, though for what she was never sure.
Cornelia Funke, *Inkheart*

My library is an archive of longings.
Susan Sontag

In this chapter we have sought to follow the heart and not just the brain, encountering such questions as, why is it that we all experience such profound yearnings – for people, *the* person, and places? Why are these experiences so difficult to pin down? Why are our longings as painful as they are delightful? What is this nostalgia and homesickness and what does it all point to? One man who taught us a lot on the subject was C. S. Lewis, so we spent some time travelling with his hopes, desires – and joy. I believe it is significant that Lewis, in attempting to describe his most profound experiences, preferred to use this word, joy, rather than either happiness or pleasure.

In the next chapter we will be more brain-centred, but in a way that you may never have considered or contemplated. Prepare for a few surprises!

FOUR

TWO WAYS OF EXPERIENCING THE WORLD

The heart has its reasons of which reason knows nothing. We
know the truth not only by the reason, but by the heart.
All of humanity's problems stem from man's inability to sit
quietly in a room alone.
Blaise Pascal, Mathematician, physicist, inventor and writer

Allow me to introduce you to twin brothers, Larry and Ronny,
who are also colleagues in business. They are very attached
to each other and usually work pretty well together. They look
very similar, but they are not identical – there are some very
significant differences. In fact, they view life and the world so
differently that they are almost polar opposites. But they really
need each other, because one cannot flourish without the other.
On the one hand Ronny is incapable of speech – he's unable
to express himself in words since he has no voice. That makes
communication rather challenging. But there's more, much
more. He lacks the ability to think in a straight line – he couldn't
string a sentence together even if he had the words, because
all of life for him is one continuous experience. But he does have
emotion – lots of it. In fact, it can be quite overwhelming. And
in any situation he can see the whole picture very quickly. He
doesn't break things down into parts and build them up again,
as his brother does. He's got a fantastic sense of humour and
'gets' things immediately. He is empathic, extremely sensitive to
other people and able to sense their feelings almost before they
do! Other people love being with him. He loves to just *be*.

Larry, on the other hand, is very articulate. He can speak
very well, and he is logical – he can put a cogent and coherent
argument across very effectively. He is excellent at constructing
things. He loves technology and is very much at home in today's

digital world (his brother is *so* analogue!). He is the ultimate *do*-er. As a matter of fact, he is so impressed with his powers of thought, speech and action that he considers them to be the sum of everything – although he does seem to take himself very seriously. None of this touchy-feely emotional stuff for him (he does possess one emotion in fact – anger). He is therefore prone to being quite dismissive of Ronny, who clearly hasn't got what it takes to express himself – at least, not in the ways that really matter. So Larry often takes the public stage and rather likes it that way. After all, what is more important than thinking things through, coming to conclusions and then articulating them well?

The only problem is that it is only Ronny who is in touch with the world as it really is. Larry thinks he has everything figured out, but what he doesn't realise is that he inhabits an ivory tower of virtual reality, and in fact is dependent on Larry to feed in the reality 'out there'. But it's a double-whammy: Larry isn't in touch with the real world (and so he often comes to conclusions that don't tally with reality) but he thinks he knows best and asserts his view vehemently. He therefore has a propensity to dismiss what Ronny thinks and feels. He regularly ends up dominating the situation and Ronny is left out in the cold.

I wonder if that rings any bells with you? Well, the interesting thing is that these are real characters – and they live right inside your head!

Two views of the world

Of all the books I've read in recent years, one stands out in particular. It's 'The Master and his Emissary' by the psychiatrist and Oxford English don, Iain McGilchrist.[1] McGilchrist developed an interest in philosophy and psychology whilst at Oxford and went on to become a consultant psychiatrist, with a special interest in neuropsychiatry. The book itself was the culmination of twenty years of study, research and reflection. It has been called 'masterly' and 'magisterial' by others and when you pick the book up you can see why – it's not for the faint-hearted![2] It deals with the two hemispheres of the brain and the way in which (as McGilchrist understands it) their very different functions have influenced the evolution of human civilisation. That's a bold claim, but he goes into immense detail to explain his thesis.

The book is in two halves: the first is all brain science, reviewing over fifty years of research into the workings of left and right brains. The second section broadens the view out towards the last three thousand years of human history, proposing that the relative dominance of one or other brain hemisphere has determined the course of whole civilisations! Put that way, it sounds preposterous and far-fetched, but he makes a convincing case.

I've included it in this book because his conclusions have helped me to think through my own perspectives on the strengths and weaknesses of our culture and how we might respond. In this chapter I try to précis some key parts of his book and make some comments of my own, attempting to express the view of our own culture and society that I'm exploring in this book.

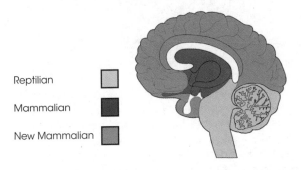

Reptilian

Mammalian

New Mammalian

It is a rather odd thing that our brains should come in two halves, and although most of us don't wake up asking that question, it's one that is worth pursuing. In fact all vertebrates have twin brain hemispheres but in humans they have become greatly enlarged and developed. The brain is an incredible organ - it has been estimated that there are in the order of 100 billion nerve cells (neurons) in the average human brain, with 100 trillion connections between them.[3] The brain is structured specifically in all three dimensions. Moving from bottom to top, the lower brain (the so-called reptilian brain) controls automatic functions like heart and respiratory rate; then comes the mid-brain (mammalian) which regulates emotions, memory and instincts; finally the higher centres, the cerebral hemispheres (new mammalian and especially developed in humans), govern not only motor and sensory control, but also conscious, voluntary thoughts and feelings.

The cerebral cortices also vary from back to front, with the vision centres at the back, areas controlling movement and sensation in the centre, and finally the frontal and prefrontal lobes. The prefrontal areas are much more highly developed in humans and through them we have the ability to go beyond instinct and sheer bodily functioning, to 'step outside' ourselves, giving us a sense of self, morality and insight. They are, from a physical perspective, what make us particularly 'human'.[4]

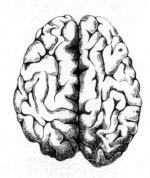

The final dimension of course is lateral, side-to-side. The human brain has two main divisions, the left and right cerebral hemispheres. At first sight, they look identical, but they are not – there are important differences. The right hemisphere is slightly larger, longer, wider and heavier than the left, although part of the left frontal area is larger – Broca's area, the speech centre. The right side extends slightly further forward than the left at the front, and vice versa at the back. Importantly, there is more white matter in the right than the left – important because white (myelinated) neurons transfer information across regions of the brain, rather than simply within local regions. The hemispheres rely on different neurotransmitter chemicals: the left on dopamine (the 'reward molecule'), the right on noradrenaline. There is surprisingly little connection between them; the corpus callosum, a bridge of nervous tissue linking them, with 300-800 million fibres, actually connects only 2% of cortical neurons. It appears to function in an inhibitory way, rather than potentiating.[5]

So why should there be such differences – and why have two hemispheres anyway? The answer, at least to the latter question, has something to do with the way in which we (and animals in general) pay attention to the world around us. For example, in order to feed, an animal needs to be able to focus in on its food, narrowing its attention, to grasp it and put it into its mouth. But at the same time, it needs another awareness, which is much broader and wider, so that it doesn't become another creature's breakfast! The former activity concentrates on one's own needs, but the latter is orientated to others, whether they be friend or foe: 'I need to use, or to manipulate, the world for my ends, and for that I need narrow-focus attention. On the other hand, I need to see myself in the broader context of the world at large, and in relation to others...Here I may feel myself to be part of something much bigger than myself. This requires less of the willfully directed, narrowly focused attention, and more of an open, receptive, widely diffused alertness to whatever exists, with allegiances outside of the self.'[6] The narrow focus is a property of the left hemisphere, whilst the right hemisphere enables a broad, vigilant attention. This understanding sets the scene for other aspects of the hemispheres' differences – they serve different purposes. McGilchrist takes it further:

> My thesis is that for us as human beings there are *two fundamentally opposed realities, two different modes of experience;* that each is of ultimate importance in bringing about the recognizably human world; and that their difference is rooted in the bihemispheric structure of the brain...I believe they are in fact *involved in a sort of power struggle, and that this explains many aspects of contemporary Western culture* [my italics].[7]

That's quite an assertion, but the rest of the book seeks to justify it. It should be said that although he takes his conclusions further than some, he is by no means the only neuroscientist to recognise the profound difference between the two hemispheres. In his fascinating book, *Mindsight*, the neuropsychiatrist Daniel Siegel devotes a whole chapter to the issue. He too makes big statements about the hemispheres: '*the left and the right sides of the brain present us with quite different ways of perceiving reality and of communicating with each other* ... The right brain is the seat of our emotional and social selves', whereas 'the left hemisphere ... lives in a kind of 'ivory tower' of ideas and rational thought compared with its more visceral and emotional right hemisphere counterpart' [my italics].[8]

Split-brain and beyond

The history of the study of hemispheric lateralisation goes back to the time of Pierre Paul Broca, who in 1861 identified an area of the left hemisphere that is responsible for speech – now known as Broca's area. The German physician Karl Wernicke developed understanding of language and the brain, but it was only in the 1960s that studies by Michael Gazzaniga and Roger Sperry on patients whose corpora callosa had been surgically severed ('split-brain' patients) revealed the extent of the hemispheres' differences. By flashing images of different objects to right and left eyes separately they discovered that the two sides of the brain perceived very differently and resulted in widely different behaviours.[9]

One striking finding was that the left hemisphere had a tendency to fabricate reasons for its behaviour (called confabulation), articulating plausible but completely made-up answers. This phenomenon is common in right-sided damage of the brain and is characteristic of the left brain.[10] So consistent was this finding that Gazzaniga came up with a term for the left brain's language centre – the interpreter – whose role it is to give a running commentary on everything going on within the person's consciousness, even when it has no access to what is *really* going on! In fact, *it is the right hemisphere that is in contact with reality 'outside'*, but because the left side has the voice it will always speak, no matter whether it 'knows' the truth or not. Because of the left hemisphere's apparent dominance cognitively and verbally, Gazzaniga and other researchers concluded that the right hemisphere was less significant than the left – the 'minor' or 'silent' hemisphere, with 'no specialized role in behaviour'.[11] More recent research has shown how important the right brain is, but the key point to note at this stage is that the *functions of the right hemisphere operate at a more subtle, implicit and even unconscious level* (as we shall now see), and so it is very easy to overlook and dismiss them.

Seeing the whole picture – or not

I'm now going to run through a number of details about the differences between the two hemispheres. It's quite a list, but do stay with me over the next few pages, because after that, I'll relate the experience of someone who actually lost the use of her left hemisphere! The story is breathtaking, so I'd suggest you try to absorb the more technical details that now follow – they will come into their own when the real-life narrative emerges afterwards.

The right brain is concerned with relationships between things and people.[12] We see the 'whole picture' with our right hemisphere; the left divides it up into parts and then tries to build up a composite based on assembling those parts. The well-known image of the Dalmatian dog (see diagram below) illustrates this. You can only see the dog as it emerges as a whole (right hemisphere); trying to put all the dots together won't help – you just end up with lots of dots (left hemisphere)![13]

The left hemisphere takes a more detached view of the world around – what McGilchrist calls *territory*, for which you have to see the land from above, like a map. The right hemisphere sees the world around as it actually is – it's seen as *terrain*, inhabited and lived in. Both perspectives are important – we need to detach from our reality to an extent, in order to make sense of it. But if we do that all the time we lose connection with that reality. 'The right hemisphere ... is 'on the lookout'. It has to be open to whatever it is that exists apart from ourselves, as much as possible without preconceptions, not just focusing on what it already knows, or is interested in.'[14] Because it is in direct contact with the real world, the right hemisphere can perceive new things, whereas the left hemisphere lives in a kind of 'ivory tower', in which it accesses what it already knows. This makes it able to predict future outcomes on the basis of its previous knowledge. However, it is not flexible, as the right hemisphere is; it 'takes a local short-term view, whereas the right hemisphere sees the bigger picture'. The right brain explores, the left grasps.[15]

The right hemisphere picks up indirect, implicit cues from its surroundings, whereas the left hemisphere operates literally, by labels or categories. For example, it can only tell what the season is by referring to the calendar, not by looking at the trees outside! It is unable to decipher metaphors (it would take the phrase 'it's raining cats and dogs' literally!) or the subtleties of humour – it doesn't 'get' the joke.[16] It has a utilitarian approach – it focuses on what is useful. This means that it is interested in man-made things, tools and the mechanical – it's at home with a mechanistic view of the world. It's interesting to note that even if we are left-handed we grasp things (physically and cognitively) via our left brain. The right brain on the other hand, through its capacity for empathy, is interested in the living and the personal. The right hemisphere recognises uniqueness and individuality; the left prefers categories and types.[17]

Emotional brain – or not

Because the right brain is all about connecting with the real world, its interest in others and relationships in general means that it is empathic. 'Self-awareness, empathy, identification with others and more generally inter-subjective processes, are largely dependent upon … right hemisphere resources.'[18] The right brain can 'get inside someone's mind' and put itself in someone else's place – it is our emotional and social brain. The right hemisphere has more connections with the limbic system in the mid-brain, which is closely involved with emotions of all kinds. When our right hemispheres are activated we are more favourably disposed to others and more open to their point of view. In contrast, the left is neutral emotionally and unconcerned about other people and their feelings.[19] Interestingly the left hemisphere reads emotions by focusing on the lower face, whereas the right interprets what the eyes are doing. We 'see into' a person's emotional state by focusing on their eyes (empathic focus of the right – 'It's all in the eyes'), but of course we speak through our mouths (verbal perspective of the left)! In fact the face generally is more of a right hemisphere world. This starts very early in life, as the infant interfaces with the mother long before (left hemisphere-dependent) speech develops.[20]

The right hemisphere regulates almost all emotions by both reading others' emotions and expressing one's own. The only emotion (strongly) connected with the left brain is anger. Without the right brain's function we become emotionally impoverished. For example, alexithymia is an inability to recognise emotions in oneself; such people are not able to relate to other people. The problem arises from the right hemisphere's inability to communicate emotion to the left side.[21] The right brain is deeply connected with the embodied self and sees the body as a whole. The left tends to see the body as an assemblage of parts. Following a right hemisphere stroke, the patient is often unable to recognise parts of their body as their own, whereas this never happens with a left sided stroke.[22] Although the speech centre is in the left brain, it is the right brain that is more concerned with meaning; the left is more interested in form and structure. In emotionally charged or deeply meaningful moments, verbal communication (left brain) often seems totally inadequate: 'I was lost for words' or 'words were useless in that situation – only a hug would help.' This is right brain, not left, territory.[23]

Music, mood and morality

The perception of music[24] is fascinating. Music is a holistic affair, not easily broken down into pieces. There is a deep connection between music and the body – again, reflecting right brain activity. After a left hemisphere stroke a patient may not be able to speak, but they can sing songs easily![25] Music is a kind of narrative and unsurprisingly only the right hemisphere can follow a narrative. The connection between right brain and music perhaps explains the way in which music can provoke a powerful emotional reaction (remember my experience during the ironing?). It taps into something very deep in us and it is no coincidence that our longings and spirituality are often better expressed through music.[26] The logical, rationalistic domain of the left brain struggles to grasp this, since it is literally 'beyond its understanding'.

'The left hemisphere is concerned with what it *knows*, where the right hemisphere is concerned with what it *experiences*.'[27] The left brain prefers certainty of knowledge, classified into abstract categories rather than concrete realities. It dislikes ambiguity, even to the point of dogmatically insisting on its view and abrogating to itself decision-making. Denial is a characteristic of the left brain. People with inactivated right brains tend to be over-optimistic about themselves and stick to their own viewpoints. The right brain is more comfortable with uncertainty, which explains why it is at home with humour, irony and metaphor, since ambiguities and unresolved situations are part of the fun![28] The left hemisphere takes a more optimistic ('happy') view of the future – although it may be falsely optimistic. The right is more in tune with sadness.[29] When we are effective in empathising with someone we are also able to experience more of their pain. Sadness, empathy and suffering are related. Psychopaths, who have no sense of shame or responsibility are found to have right frontal lobe deficits. The Greek word *pathe* means feeling; it is related to *pathos*, meaning suffering. Hence 'passion' can mean strong emotion or a feeling of immense suffering and pain. (Jesus' experience of dereliction on the Cross is described as his 'passion'.)[30]

> To be just is to be disturbed by injustice. Pain, suffering and the loss of pleasure, then, sometimes constitute who we are and what we value. They are essentially woven into our deepest commitments. As reasons flow from our deepest commitments, we will sometimes have non-instrumental reason to suffer.[31]

McGilchrist is blunt: *'Only humans with their left prefrontal cortex have the capacity for deliberate malice. But then only humans, with their right prefrontal cortex, are capable of compassion'* [my italics].[32] Our moral sense is mediated through our right brain, since it is linked to empathy, not rationality. Damage to, or inactivation of the right prefrontal cortex is associated with greater selfish behaviour, addiction and pathological gambling.[33] This is unsurprising when we remember the right brain's capacity to see another's perspective. We rely on the right brain for self-control and the ability to resist temptation. McGilchrist sums up the left brain's propensities:

> Denial, a tendency to conformism, a willingness to disregard the evidence, a habit of ducking responsibility, a blindness to mere experience in the face of the overwhelming evidence of theory: these might sound ominously familiar to observers of contemporary Western life. A sort of stuffing of the ears with sealing wax appears to be part of the normal left hemisphere mode. It does not want to hear what it takes to be the siren songs of the right hemisphere, recalling it to what has every right ... to be called reality. It is as though, blindly, the left hemisphere pushes on, always along the same track.[34]

Not just theory – a neuroscientist's direct experience

If you're wondering what to make of all this science ('Can it really be true that the two sides of my brain function so very differently?') you may be interested to hear about someone who actually experienced the functional loss of one side of her brain. Jill Bolte Taylor's story makes for fascinating and sometimes bizarre reading. She holds a PhD in neuroanatomy and so has an expert's understanding of the brain's structure and function (she went into neuroscience because she grew up with a brother who suffered from schizophrenia). In 1996, at the age of 37 years, she suddenly suffered a brain haemorrhage – a stroke – that affected only her left hemisphere. Her TED talk[35] and subsequent book[36] are intriguing and entertaining, but also very revealing about the way in which the hemispheres operate. What she speaks about confirms much of what writers like McGilchrist say, with the additional factor that she, as a brain scientist herself, experienced the very things they write about!

She awoke one morning as normal but within minutes experienced a piercing pain behind her left eye. She had suffered a catastrophic haemorrhage within the left side of her brain that proceeded to expand. Suddenly the familiar 'brain chatter' that we all experience stopped and she was plunged into inner silence. Progressively she was unable to speak or even string coherent thoughts together. 'Those little voices, that brain chatter that customarily kept me abreast of myself in relation to the world outside of me, were delightfully silent.'[38] At the same time she began to feel a 'growing sense of peace' within. 'As the blood poured in over my brain, my consciousness slowed to a soothing and satisfying awareness that embraced the vast and wondrous world within.' She lost her cognitive capacities, including of course her linguistic skills; but more than that, the normal linear sequence of events and experiences had disappeared as time stood still in an 'eternal now' moment.

She realised what was happening within her head but could not focus sufficiently to do anything about it. Looking for clarity she placed the phone in front of her, hoping that some helpful recollection would surface. Then she remembered a work colleague, though not his phone number. It took the next forty-five minutes to work out the required action 'by matching the squiggles on the paper to the squiggles on the phone pad.' Fortunately the colleague answered, but when he spoke 'he sound(ed) like a golden retriever!' She herself could not speak out the words in her mind. Nonetheless he must have grasped the gravity of the situation because before long help arrived.[39]

One of the striking aspects of her story is the profound

change in personality and self-perception that emerged during the loss of her left brain.

> My perception of my physical boundaries was no longer limited to where my skin met air ... this absence of physical boundary was one of glorious bliss ... Without a language center telling me: 'I am Dr Jill Bolte Taylor. I am a neuroanatomist ...' I felt no obligation to being her anymore ... I didn't think like her anymore ... She was passionate about her work ... She was intensely committed to living a dynamic life. But despite her likeable and perhaps even admirable characteristics, in my present form I had not inherited her fundamental hostility ... *I had spent a lifetime of 37 years being enthusiastically committed to 'do-do-doing' lots of stuff at a very fast pace. On this special day, I learned the meaning of simply 'being'* [my italics].[40]

She goes on to describe how her shift from the 'doing' left brain to a 'being' right brain was accompanied by a feeling of being no longer single and solid, but of being 'fluid'. *She was not now separate from others or the world, not isolated and alone, but connected to all that is.* Even her eyes could no longer see things as distinct. Everything blended together: 'I was not capable of experiencing separation or individuality.'[41] Although she had lost her left brain functioning she was still conscious. In fact faculties normally masked by left hemisphere domination were uncovered: 'I was like a newborn unable to make sense of the sensory stimulation in the physical space around me.'[42] She puts these feelings into words: 'I wanted to communicate: *Yelling louder does not help me understand you any better! Come closer to me. Bring me your gentle spirit. S-l-o-w down. Be kind to me. Be a safe place for me ... I am vulnerable and confused ... reach for me. Respect me. I am in here. Come find me.'*[43]

This strong desire for understanding and empathy continued through her hospitalisation. She herself became more empathic and although she could not understand other people's words, she was able to read their facial expressions and body language. If a nurse or doctor was attentive to her needs, she found that she became 'energized', but another person's lack of eye contact or touch scared her. There was complete silence inside her head and she could make no sense of sounds coming from without. She could not see three-dimensionally nor distinguish colours, nor form words – only pictures. But she experienced everything as 'radiat(ing) pure energy': 'With childlike curiosity, your heart soars in peace.'[44]

Recovery – and a dawning realisation about left and right hemispheres

She now began a long period of recovery, including brain surgery seventeen days after her stroke. She had to re-learn all the skills she had lost and in all, it took eight years for her brain and body to recover. She began to get in touch with thoughts and feelings that belonged to the left brain, like anger, frustration or fear. She found herself beginning to 'blame' other people or events for her circumstances as her left brain became stronger. But she also discovered that as she paid attention to what emotions feel like in the body her recovery was accelerated. Writing over ten years later, she declared herself to be 'completely recovered'.[45]

In the final chapters of her book she reflects on life since her stroke and how different it is from before. As she recovered more and more of her left brain capacities she began to wonder whether she really wanted *all* the characteristics of that personality:

> Would it be possible for me to recover my perception of myself, where I exist as a single, solid, separate from the whole, without recovering the cells associated with my egotism, intense desire to be argumentative, need to be right, or fear of separation and death? Could I value money without hooking into the neurological loops of lack, greed, or selfishness? ... *Most important, could I retain my newfound sense of connection with the universe in the presence of my left hemisphere's individuality* [my italics]?[46]

She speaks of her fear of losing her newfound right mind's set of values and resultant personality in order to recover her left brain skills. Like McGilchrist and others she describes the way in which many neuroscientists have down-played the role of the right hemisphere because of its lack of verbal and linear functions, depicting it as an 'uncontrollable, potentially violent, moronic, rather despicable ignoramus ... In contrast, our left mind has routinely been touted as linguistic ... rational, smart, and the seat of our consciousness'.[47] This tendency for the left brain to dominate the right had in fact been her own lived experience, when prior to her stroke, her left hemisphere's cells had been 'capable of dominating the cells of my right hemisphere', with a judgmental and analytical character. Her conclusion is stark:

> *There are two very distinct characters cohabiting my cranium, which think and perceive very differently, possess very different values and display very different personalities!*

Although in normal life, we experience one consciousness and personality, she believes that it is possible to discern the differences between right and left brain characters. In fact, we commonly speak about what therapists call 'parts of self': the head/heart split; our thinking/feeling selves; mind/ body consciousness; capital ego mind/inner authentic self; researcher/diplomatic minds; sensing/intuitive minds; judging/ perceiving minds. Her conviction: they are all rooted in the two hemispheres of the brain.[48]

Her concluding comments about her two 'minds' contrast the differences: the right brain is all about 'right here, right now'. It is not anxious or uptight; rather it is empathic, compassionate and accepting of others. On the other hand, the more serious left brain is preoccupied with details and schedule (lists, lists, lists), demarcating boundaries and making judgments about people and situations. However, this hemisphere is vital to her wellbeing because it makes life manageable. It is the tool for communicating with the world beyond. It gives a sense of identity – 'I am who I am and no other' – separating one individual from the whole. It is a great organiser, keeping everything in its place. It is the great do-er, constantly going through its 'to do' lists. It processes information much faster than the right brain, responding better to higher light and sound frequencies, which enable it to perceive sharp boundaries, recognise separation lines between nearby objects and detect differing speech tones. It is a great storyteller, interpreting events to us as they happen, even to the extent (as we have seen with Gazzaniga's split-brain studies) that it *blithely fabricates story lines to fill in any gaps of knowledge*:

> As my left brain language centers recovered and became functional again, I spent a lot of time observing how my story-teller would draw conclusions based upon

minimal information ... Throughout this resurrection of my left mind's character and skills, it has been extremely important that I retain the understanding that my left brain is doing the best job it can with the information it has to work with. I need to remember, however, that there are enormous gaps between what I know and what I think I know. I learned that I need to be very wary of my story-teller's potential for stirring up drama and trauma.[49]

Certain characteristics of her left mind she preferred to leave behind: the reverberating circuit loops that kept repeating negative thoughts and possibilities; and the potential for anxiety, meanness and verbal abuse. Interestingly, such thoughts provoked unpleasant sensations within her body, such as a tight chest, brow tension or headache. Her left brain stubbornness, jealousy and arrogance were things that she would prefer to let go of, and so she has developed a practice of 'stepping to the right', i.e. choosing away from the left brain's judgmentalism and into the more empathic right brain.

Throughout the book she makes reference to her 'right mind' and her 'left mind'. This seems to me to have two implications. First, the two 'minds' are separate entities with, as she puts it, separate personalities. Because she experienced the loss of one (therefore the presence only of the other) and then the recovery of that 'lost mind' she (unlike the rest of us) knows what it is to discern the difference between the two. After all, it took years for her left brain to recover; and she has been able to switch from one to the other ever since! The second inference is that 'she' (that is, the essential 'Jill') is not synonymous with either of her hemispheres. 'She' was and is able to access either or both of her 'minds', knowing what they each feel like, separately and together. Ultimately we are more than, deeper than our brain hemispheres. We will pursue this thought in Chapter 8.

Step to the right

Jill Bolte Taylor talks about 'stepping to the right' when she needs to move from anxious 'brain chatter' to a place where her inner equilibrium is restored as she lives in the moment. She has the advantage that she has experienced life in 'one mind' only, but we can perform the

---

same action anyway, by practising the following activities. Why not try them out and see what happens for you?

1. Take fifteen minutes to practise living in the present, rather than focusing on the past and future. Look around and enjoy what is actually happening, not what you imagine (and fear) might occur.
2. Go for a walk in a park or other natural habitat. Enjoy connecting with the real world and not just the one inside your head.
3. Become more aware of your body in this present moment. Sit quietly for ten minutes with your eyes shut and focus awareness on different parts of your body, starting with your toes and move up. Notice your breathing as you do it.
4. Tomorrow, cut down on your screen time. Engage with the world as it is 'in the flesh' and move out of the ivory tower of the virtual world.
5. Spend some time face to face with a real embodied person, not just mediated through a machine. Enjoy the real relationship, not a virtual one.
6. Take some time to enjoy a favourite piece of music or art.
7. Spend fifteen minutes with someone you like but whose views you don't share. Ask them to explain why they think the way they do and listen to their answer without interrupting. Then discuss with them how the conversation was for both of you.
8. Experiment with communicating non-verbally (pictures, metaphors and emotions) rather than words.
9. This week decide to discover something new. Tell someone later what it was and how it went.
10. Have a conversation with someone in which you ask genuine questions about them without shifting the subject onto you and your interests. Stay listening to the other person.
11. Make your next shopping trip a spending spree on other people and shared experiences, rather than on things for yourself.
12. Pray or meditate – develop your spiritual side.

Two distinct personalities

Bolte Taylor's bold assertion that there are actually two different personalities within our heads (remember Ronny and Larry?) may sound far-fetched, but it is also the view of no lesser figure than the Nobel Laureate who led the seminal studies on split brain patients in the 1960s, Roger Sperry:

> Everything we have seen indicates that the surgery has left these people with *two separate minds, that is, two separate spheres of consciousness. What is experienced in the right hemisphere seems to lie entirely outside the realm of the left hemisphere*. This mental division has been demonstrated in regard to perception, cognition, volition, learning and memory [my italics].[50]

The rather strange title that McGilchrist chose for his book (*The Master and his Emissary*) is based on a tale re-told by Friedrich Nietzsche, about a wise master who[51] ruled his domain with a selfless concern for his people. With an ever-growing realm however, he needed help from emissaries, to whom he delegated authority. The cleverest and most ambitious of these ministers came to believe that he could do a better job at ruling, seeing his master's kindness as weakness. So he disdainfully usurped the master's position, ruling in a tyrannical way and bringing the kingdom to ruin. This is an age-old story, describing the universal human condition.[52] We now have neuroscientific support for its veracity!

Left dominates right

> The intuitive mind is a sacred gift and the rational mind is a faithful servant. We have created a society that honours the servant and has forgotten the gift.
>
> Attributed to Albert Einstein[53]

McGilchrist concludes the first half of his book with a summary of how the left hemisphere claims dominance over the right hemisphere. The proper situation should be right brain pre-eminence:

> The right hemisphere has primacy and ... though the left hemisphere has a valuable role, its products need to be returned to the realm of the right hemisphere and once more integrated into that new whole, greater than

the sum of its parts … The right hemisphere is the primary mediator of experience, from which the conceptualised, re-presented world of the left hemisphere derives, and on which it depends … *The left hemisphere does not itself have life, such life as it appears to have com(es) from reconnecting with the body, emotion and experience through the right hemisphere* [my italics].[54]

The balance of power should lie in the right brain's favour, but in fact the left brain usurps that power. How does this happen? The reason is that the left hemisphere 'is most accessible: closest to the self-aware, self-inspecting intellect.' It has conscious thought (the right only has unconscious) and the power of argument through language, logic and linearity – none of which the right brain possesses. The right hemisphere's knowledge comes through experience and all at once – it has no sense of sequenced time. So when it needs to communicate that knowledge to another person, the other person needs to have shared the same kind of *subjective experience*. In contrast, the left hemisphere passes on *objective knowledge*, without the other person needing to have had any experience of it. This is a great advantage. The right brain has no speech, so that makes communication more difficult. More than that, any system founded on language tends to devalue and discount whatever cannot be expressed in language.[55]

So here's the summary: the right brain has the life and the connection with reality, but it is dependent on the left brain to think it through and express it verbally. When that all works properly, we can function in a balanced, connected and integrated way. The flow of data and perception should be as follows:

Right (in touch with reality) → *Left (categorising and expressing)* → *Right (living it all out in the real world)*

But the left brain has a tendency to take over, leading to a lop-sided view of the world and a propensity to distort reality (at the same time, arguing vehemently that its take on the world is correct!). It's not difficult to see how all those misrepresentations and conflicts develop in our lives and in society.

Now for the big picture

So far the focus has been on the individual and how the two sides of our brains perceive the world in fundamentally different ways. But now the vista widens dramatically – to the ways in which different cultures (civilisations, in fact) have lived. In the second part of his book (some 223 pages!), McGilchrist moves his argument on from the individual, to apply the 'battle of the hemispheres' to whole societies and civilisations. He summarises,

> I may sometimes have spoken almost as if (the two hemispheres) were personalities, with values and goals of their own ... That is not as big a distortion as might first appear: they are substantial parts of a living being, which certainly does have values and goals. However, we are now turning to look at the 'battle of the hemispheres' ... over long periods of history. It may seem that I am suggesting that there is some cosmic struggle going on behind the scenes ... Metaphorically speaking this is true.[56]

In a fascinating review of ancient civilisations, McGilchrist sees early Greek society as a balanced affair as far as the brain hemispheres are concerned. There was no distinction between body and soul: Homer (who lived before the eighth century BC) understood the body as 'indistinguishable from the whole person' and thought and feeling were thoroughly embodied. However, by the time of Plato (428-347 BC) the separation of soul and body had become clearly fixed – something that is still with us today. Plato distinguished between visible objects and invisible 'forms' (abstract patterns that lie behind the visible entities we can touch and see: classically the *form* of a 'table' underlies the imperfect *copies* that we see). He wrote, 'The stars that decorate the sky ... are far inferior, just because they are visible, to the true realities.'

The development of vocabulary reflected the change in perspective. For example, the verb, 'to see' was initially associated with viewing things in relation to each other but later came to signify an abstract understanding; and the root word for 'theory' emerged late – ultimately it was derived from the word for 'spectator'. In the sixth century, philosophy began to develop, which required a certain 'standing back' from lived experience (very much a left brained perspective). The Greeks invented the definite article, thus allowing separate identity to be established. Written language gained a new impetus in the seventh century BC, being increasingly scribed in a horizontal and left-to-right fashion (more characteristic of a left brained perspective), rather than a vertical and right-to-left mode, which disappeared altogether in the West. Numeracy and the use of money flourished. They are tools, which provide greater control (the left hemisphere is the hemisphere of control par excellence), but not necessarily relationship (as anyone can testify today!). McGilchrist summarises the impact of the later Greeks in this way:

> There is no doubt that it is ultimately the left hemisphere version of the world that Plato puts forward, for the first time in history; puts forward so strongly that it has taken two thousand years to shake it off.[57]

Personally, I'm not convinced that we have yet come anywhere near doing that!

Roman civilisation followed a similar pattern. Beginning with a balanced perspective, it later moved towards more rigid, systematic patterns of thinking and behaving, as the famous Roman justice system and a centralised bureaucracy emerged – pointers to an increasingly left brain-dominated outlook. Although Christianity brought new flexibility, that too joined the legalistic and dogmatic mainstream as Constantine institutionalised the faith. McGilchrist's conclusion: 'Once the left hemisphere started to believe that its dominion was everything ... then the empire that the hemispheres between them had created ... began to crumble.' [58]

The Renaissance saw a flowering again of balanced two-hemisphere life. Poetry, drama and music of the age exemplified the harmony of left and right brain. The bitter-sweet lines of poems and madrigals expressed the longings characteristic of right hemisphere perceptions.[59] I remember singing madrigals at school (yes, we boasted a Madrigal Group!) and one in particular impacted me with its poignancy and sense of longing. See how it affects you as you listen to it.[60] Here are the lines:

> Adieu, adieu sweet amaryllis.
> For since to part your will is.
> O heavy tiding
> Here is for me no biding.
> Yet once again
> Ere that I part with you.
> Amaryllis, amaryllis,
> sweet Adieu.

The Renaissance (spanning the fourteenth to seventeenth centuries) gave space for the unconscious, intuitive and implicit, seeing artistic creation as discovery rather than invention. An appreciation of the world's beauty pointed to something beyond. The rediscovery of the Classical past was not a 'fact-finding mission' (unlike the pursuit of empire across the world) but rather the rediscovery of wisdom and virtue.

However, the Reformation that followed it (from the sixteenth century onwards) was characterised by a search for certainty. As the nineteenth-century philosopher and theologian Friedrich Schleiermacher put it (speaking of both the Reformation and the ensuing Enlightenment), 'Everything mysterious and marvelous is proscribed. Imagination is not to be filled with … airy images.' The written word was elevated over visual representations (exemplified by the literal elevation of the preacher in the pulpit) as *sola fides*, 'justification by faith alone' became the Protestant cry. The *individual's* faith became the most important dimension of belief, eclipsing corporate expression. Again, McGilchrist sees the influence of the left hemisphere, with a 'preference for what is clear and certain over what is ambiguous; the preference for what is single, fixed, static and sytematised, over what is multiple, fluid, moving and contingent.'[61]

Into the modern age

All of this paved the way for the Enlightenment. Francis Bacon, credited by many with devising the scientific method, was nonetheless respectful of nature. But only a short time later René Descartes made the bold assertion that science would make humanity 'the lords and masters of nature'. Descartes was suspicious of the body and its perception of the world around it, regarding it as likely to lead to error and even madness. Only the intellect, with its rational deduction, was reliable ('I think, therefore I am') and his aspiration was to become 'a spectator rather than an actor'. He saw the body as functioning like a machine, whereas the mind was separate and non-material, not following the laws of nature.[62] His dualism connects with Plato's ideas, dividing the visible material world from the invisible mind or soul. The Enlightenment sought certainty and brought to birth the idea that rational, scientific advance would discover fully knowable answers to all questions.

But it was with the Industrial Revolution that the left hemisphere perspective made the biggest strides, with its pretentions of human power over nature, harnessing it for human purposes – the ultimate 'grasping'. Irritating individual idiosyncrasies were to be replaced by uniformity, with straight lines and regular shapes (which never appear in the natural world) as the norm. Technology, that is, inanimate tools and machines, replaced human workers. 'The world that the right hemisphere was to deliver became simply 'the world as processed by the left hemisphere". The 'management' and exploitation of the natural world, still with us today, began in this period and led to the Modern world as we know it.[63]

And so to the present day – or at least to the Modernity of the past century or two. The twentieth century saw huge changes in technology and industry, with a profound impact on society and personal life. As we saw in Chapter 2, the 'disenchanted world' of bureaucracy and impersonal civil life, with its social disintegration and breakdown in familiar patterns of life, was associated with the loss of the 'sacred canopy' of traditional explanations of the meaning of life. As mobility, the change of life's pace and social fragmentation accelerated, the old sense of attachment, rootedness and belonging dissolved. What was previously experienced as intuitive and implicit now became explicit; but this came at the cost of depersonalisation and alienation.[64]

The divide between mind and matter (or spirit and matter), triggered by Descartes, now became more evident. Left hemisphere approaches of control and mechanisation took centre stage. McGilchrist likens this to the schizophrenic view of life, with detachment from the body, world and community. Indeed, diseases of that type (including anorexia nervosa, multiple personality disorder and autism) have increased dramatically over the last two centuries. All have in common the experience of dissociation, a sense of being cut off from one's feelings and embodied existence, a lack of empathy and fragmentation of the sense of self. These conditions have features suggestive of right hemisphere deficits and left hemisphere dominance. Mental illness is now a major feature of Western life, with a growing sense of alienation and social isolation. McGilchrist concludes, 'A culture with prominent 'schizoid' characteristics attracts to positions of influence individuals who will help it ever further down the same path. And the increasing domination of life by both technology and bureaucracy helps to erode the more integrative modes of attention to people and things that might help us to resist the advance of technology and bureaucracy.'[65] This is a disturbing vicious cycle.

Contemporary culture and society, then, is a 'world of words, mechanistic systems and theories' – characteristic of the left hemisphere – in which sources of the intuitive and imaginative (e.g. the natural world, the body, art and faith) are 'deconstructed'. And of course the focus on the individual exemplifies a left brained view of the world, since the right brain sees the individual only in the context of others.[66]

McGilchrist concludes his tome with a focus on the *three great bastions of right hemisphere life: the body, the spirit and art.* They are the least amenable to the mechanistic world of the left hemisphere. The body is 'messy, imprecise, limited', whereas modern humans have 'become more cerebral, and retreated more and more from the senses.' The left hemisphere is also dismissive of religion, although 'when we decide not to worship divinity, we do not stop worshipping: we merely find something else less worthy to worship.' But all three (body, religion and art) have one thing in common – they are 'vehicles of love':

> For love is the attractive power of the Other, which the right hemisphere experiences, but which the left hemisphere does not understand and sees as an impediment to its authority.[67]

Moving from left to right

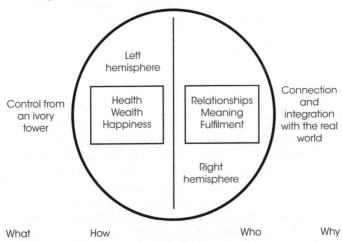

We can now return to our familiar two-sided diagram. In the light of this chapter's discoveries it appears to be a strikingly accurate picture of our brains' two hemispheres, since the emphases of each side of the diagram clearly mirror the perspectives of the two hemispheres. The left brain's focus is on utility and control, and it thinks instrumentally – if I can increase my effectiveness all will be well. So developing my health and wealth is a clear route to follow and will increase my happiness. Indeed, the left hemisphere *does* seem to be associated with positive emotions compared to the right side. It has long been known that left brain damage in patients is associated with negative mood, whereas injury to the right brain is linked with positive mood reactions. More recent research using brain imaging has shown that people with extreme left-sided brain activation (specifically their prefrontal regions) report more positive and less negative emotion than their right-activated counterparts.[68] So if we are looking for positive emotion the left hemisphere definitely has the advantage.

But as we have seen, this may come at the cost of reality, connection and meaning. Remember Roy Baumeister's studies on 'happiness' versus 'meaning' in Chapter 2? Their findings resonate convincingly with the understanding of the two hemispheres' perceptions that McGilchrist and Bolte Taylor promote. Baumeister's 'happy but meaningless life' pursues a self-absorbed direction. On the other hand the 'meaningful but unhappy life' is seriously involved in difficult undertakings, worries and stresses, thinks a lot about the past and future and engages in lots of deep thinking. It may be 'relatively unhappy', but it is nevertheless able to self-regulate well and is a giver more than a taker.

Our diagram is emerging then as a helpful tool based on both life experience and neuroscience. To understand happiness, wellbeing and lasting fulfilment we need to be aware of the way the brain functions, for it is both the instrument of perception as well as the means of knowing.

Finding the balance

If McGilchrist and Bolte Taylor have anything to say to us at all, it must surely be that maintaining a balance between our left and right brain functioning is essential for healthy and successful living. In particular our left hemisphere's propensity to dominate and displace the right hemisphere's attitudes and behaviour is some-thing we need to monitor and adjust.

So here's a question. When does the left brain's

---

vital function of defining, separating and making judgments and distinctions tip into judgmentalism, self-interest and dogmatism? What could you do to keep your left hemisphere engaged with and supportive of the right hemisphere's relational, connectional and others-focussed perspective? Here are some contexts:

- Can we change our inner thoughts and attitudes, especially towards ourselves: the patterns of thought that cycle through our brains, telling us that we are no good, or unable to cope?
- What about our attitudes to other people: the right brain wants to connect, the left brain stays separate and has a tendency to judge others?
- We all follow well-worn pathways of conversations, discussions and arguments: are we open to new approaches, or will we always stick with what we know (and are comfortable with)?
- Regarding people (and groups) who we don't know well: how do we break out of ignorance and prejudice and actually get to know people who are very different to us?
- Do we always want to be in control, or can we learn to let others take the lead?
- Do we have everything sewn up in our mindsets and worldviews, or is there something important we haven't yet discovered?
- Is there a group near you that you could join, to help you connect with people and attitudes outside your present comfort zone?

What are we to make of all this? Summary and concluding comments

I hope that you haven't been overwhelmed by the themes that have emerged through this chapter. For me, the combination of McGilchrist's weighty tome and Bolte Taylor's dramatic narrative paints a fascinating and comprehensive picture of a subject that for most of us is unfamiliar and perplexing. But it also makes sense of much of life. You may not have been convinced by McGilchrist's claim that the left hemisphere has achieved an unhealthy dominance in our age, but I find his arguments compelling and very relevant to our situation today. In fact, whether you call it 'hemispheric conflict' or the challenge of living a healthy life in the twenty-first century, we certainly need some help!

The issues raised by the material in this chapter are both extraordinary and challenging. They shine a powerful spotlight on how we perceive the world around us (and ourselves) and how we live out our lives as a result. I can think of no better way of summarising than to return to McGilchrist's words, quoted at the beginning of this chapter.

> ... there are two fundamentally opposed realities, two different modes of experience; that each is of ultimate importance in bringing about the recognizably human world; and that their difference is rooted in the bihemispheric structure of the brain...I believe they are in fact involved in a sort of power struggle, and that this explains many aspects of contemporary Western culture.[69]

This resonates extraordinarily well with C. S. Lewis's reflections, which we encountered in Chapter 3:

> The two hemispheres of my mind were in the sharpest contrast. On the one side a many-islanded sea of poetry and myth; on the other a glib and shallow 'rationalism.' Nearly all that I loved I believed to be imaginary; nearly all I believed to be real I thought grim and meaningless.[70]

It turns out that his intuitions were exactly right. What he called imaginary is in fact the basis of our relationships, longings, hopes and fulfilment. The rationalism he identifies should be secondary to that, but all too often it takes control and dominates our lives and lifestyles.

We experience life ... well, experientially, not theoretically. Although thoughts, ideas and concepts are vitally important, they do not override experience ('I am not my thoughts'). They interpret it (remember Gazzaniga's 'interpreter'?). They organise and order it. But they do not outweigh and supersede it. Experiential knowledge is a right brain phenomenon and such experience and such knowledge are at the heart of healthy relationships, which we will now investigate.

FIVE

HEALTHY RELATIONSHIPS I: HOW THEY WORK

No man is an island,
Entire of itself,
Every man is a piece of the continent,
A part of the main.
If a clod be washed away by the sea,
Europe is the less.
As well as if a promontory were.
As well as if a manor of thy friend's
Or of thine own were:
Any man's death diminishes me,
Because I am involved in mankind,
And therefore never send to know for whom the bell tolls;
It tolls for thee.

John Donne (my italics)

How would it be if all our relationships were healthy and fruitful; our family life was harmonious and our neighbourhoods places of friendship and hospitality; our national society majored on connecting disparate and isolated groups of people; and nations faithfully fulfilled every promise they made to each other?[1] What kind of world would that be, and how would it compare with the one we see around us now?

The poet John Donne wrote the powerful poem above four hundred years ago. It sums up much of what it means to relate healthily to others, and shows again (if we needed it) that we will not find happiness without fulfilling relationships. The thing about relationships is that when they go well, there really is nothing to compare with them. But of course the opposite is also true – when things go wrong, there's almost nothing worse. All of which goes to show how significant they are. We can't live without them and many of our longings centre on them (as we saw in Chapter 3), but their breakdown is the cause of some of the greatest pain known to humanity!

Many studies demonstrate the value of relationships. In fact, as psychologist Ed Deiner puts it, 'The links are so strong that many psychologists think that humans are genetically wired to need each other.'[1] This linkage is perhaps the clearest example of our need for connection that we encountered in Chapter 1. The benefits of healthy relationships operate at many levels. As individuals we become healthy as we grow social connections, but whole communities too are improved by developing strong links of trust and engagement.[2]

In fact, there is hardly an area of our lives that is not affected by the state of our relationships.

And almost nothing could be more relevant to our main topic – lasting happiness.

Of course, as we have already seen, one major tragedy of our age is that the very thing that enables us to flourish (our relationships) is under the greatest strain and is a cause of great unhappiness in our society. It is therefore well worth exploring what makes for strong and robust relationships and what we might do when they are damaged. Here's an exercise, to ease us into the subject:

What makes for a healthy relationship?
What goes towards nurturing and growing relationships that last a lifetime?

Make a bullet point list of some words or phrases. Ask someone else to do the same – then compare your notes.

As you look at the list(s), pick out one or two characteristics that strike you as most important.

Why did you select that one(s)?

Do you know anyone who lives it/them out? What is special about that?

How could you develop that characteristic in your life?

The brain and relationships – betweenness

Our ability to grow healthy relationships is dependent on the basic structure and function of our brains ('nature', if you like). This raw material is moulded and shaped by our early experience (all to do with 'nurture') and the interaction between the two sets our relational course for the rest of our lives. How it all develops is a remarkable story and I hope you will share my sense of wonder as we journey through it.

In the last chapter we explored the way in which our brains perceive the world around (and within) us, and discovered that our two cerebral hemispheres function very differently. The world of the left brain is linear (one-thing-after-another), virtual and broken into parts; whereas that of the right brain is all-at-once, real-life and connected, paying attention to all around it. One of Iain McGilchrist's favourite expressions is 'betweenness' – by which he means the way in which real things in the real world connect or relate to each other – and it is characteristic solely of the right hemisphere. The spotlight here isn't on the nature of the things themselves (the 'what-ness' of things), but rather the way in which they interact (the 'how-ness'). In McGilchrist's own words,

> The essential difference between the right hemisphere and the left hemisphere is that the right hemisphere pays attention to the Other, whatever it is that exists apart from ourselves, with which it sees itself in profound relation. It is deeply attracted to, and given life by, the relationship, the betweenness, that exists with this Other. By contrast, the left hemisphere pays attention to the virtual world that it has created, which is…ultimately disconnected from the Other.[3]

This relational 'betweenness' even operates at a cellular level in the brain. Says McGilchrist, 'when cell stations in the brain connect, the traffic is…not in one direction…Areas interact equally in both directions…The forebrain is overwhelmingly an arena of reverberating reciprocal influence'. So the norm is in fact relational, even at the micro level!

In this chapter we are going to investigate how relationships form and what is required to make them work well. Here's the summary:

It appears that the capacity to relate to other people is hard-wired into our brains and that such relating is at the heart of human flourishing. Relationships are primarily a function of the right brain, with its emphasis on implicit, unconscious, non-verbal processes. Emotions are essential to the development and nurture of all healthy relationships.

This is a bold claim, and so we should attempt to explore it to see if it holds true.

A relational and emotional revolution

For many years, psychologists and neuroscientists viewed the brain as a highly complex computer. *Behavioural* approaches understand human behaviour as conditioned by external influences, with very little involvement from innate or internal factors. Another perspective is *cognitivism*, which focusses on the way in which people perceive, think, remember and learn – cognitive behavioural therapy (CBT) is the best-known example of this approach. The brain, it is claimed, is just like a computer in the way it processes information. Artificial intelligence studies have developed from this discipline, aiming to create cognitive beings artificially. *Emotions* have not generally fitted in with this mechanistic perspective; they were even considered by some to be 'beyond the pale of scientific investigation'.[4] But today the scene is changing radically, for in recent years neuroscience has shown that emotions not only play a role in human experience and relationships – they are in fact primary.

Allan Schore is an eminent psychologist and behavioural scientist. He is at the forefront of what has been called the 'emotional revolution' in psychotherapy.[5] In fact, he goes further, describing the changes taking place in both neuroscience and psychology as a *paradigm shift*, as researchers and practitioners recognise that:

Relational, emotional and unconscious processes are more significant than rationalistic, cognitive and conscious dimensions in human interactions.

His conclusion is that this relational and emotional paradigm shift 'is altering the entire field of mental health'.[6] That is an extraordinary statement, given our cultural context, in which rationality and cognition still 'rule the roost' and emotions are still considered 'second cousins'. But more than that, the vital importance of emotions is now being partnered with both relational psychology (i.e. our psychology is not simply a matter of one person's thoughts and experiences, but rather the 'betweenness' of two people) and the findings of neuroscience (the buzz words are resonance, mirroring and neuroplasticity – we shall encounter them a little later). Here is Schore's verdict:

> Relational experiences, for better or worse, impact the early development of psychic structure and the emergent subjective self, and ... *these structures are expressed at all later stages of the life span.* I present interpersonal neurobiological models of attachment in early development ... and in the therapeutic change process. This work highlights the fact that *the current emphasis on relational processes is ... transforming both psychology and neuroscience* [my italics].[7]

Don't miss the point here. Schore is saying that the business of building healthy foundations in our lives and in repairing them later if they have gone wrong is all down to unconscious emotional processes and relationships. And of course, this 'paradigm shift' and 'emotional revolution' is centred around the brain's right hemisphere. Far from being subordinate to the left brain's cognitive and conscious processes, the right brain, with its implicit, unconscious and emotional operations, is central to all the activities of the personality, both in early life and throughout the life span. Based on decades of his own and others' research, Schore asserts:

> The development of the essential functions of the right brain over the life span is a central theme that runs throughout my work on development, psychopathogenesis and psychotherapy...*The highest human functions – stress regulation, intersubjectivity, humor, empathy, compassion, morality and creativity – are all right brain functions...*I am also suggesting that an expanded capacity of right and not left brain processing lies at the core of clinical expertise' [my italics].[8]

The capacity of the right brain to develop and sustain relationships continues throughout our lives and is vital if we want to repair what has gone wrong in our earlier experience. Schore refers to McGilchrist's mammoth treatise on the brain hemispheres (which we reviewed in Chapter 4), affirming its central tenets. He quotes McGilchrist, 'I believe that the representation of the two hemispheres is not equal, and that while both contribute to our knowledge of the world … one hemisphere, the right hemisphere, has precedence … and is alone able to synthesize what both know into a useable whole'.[9] Schore goes on himself to say, 'Over the last two decades a central theme of the body of my studies … has been that *the right hemisphere is not only dominant in infancy but over all stages of the life cycle*' [my italics].[10] This is weighty stuff. The side of our brains that some neuroscientists had described (to quote Jill Bolte Taylor) as 'an uncontrollable, potentially violent, moronic, rather despicable ignoramus' turns out to be responsible for the health and wellbeing of our relationships throughout our lives! The left hemisphere view of our brains is that they are super-computers, handling cognitive data and churning out thought and behaviour. In fact, our connection with other people is primarily mediated through the part of our brain that operates at a deeper, unconscious level than conscious cognitive thought, and emotions are at the heart of that relational connection. This is an emotional and relational revolution indeed!

How relational connections develop – attachment

> My eyes are not raised too high;
> I do not occupy myself with things
>   too great and too marvellous for me.
> But I have calmed and quietened my soul,
> Like a weaned child with its mother;
> Like a weaned child is my soul within me.[11]

I mentioned earlier that our inbuilt nature interacts with our nurture to determine the basic shape of our personalities and relationships. We have briefly explored the nature dimension – now we will look at the nurture aspect. The nurture in question takes place at the very earliest stage of our lives – the first two years. One theory – attachment theory – has, over the past fifty years, come to dominate our understanding of how we develop relational wellness – and frailty.

The father of attachment theory was the psychiatrist, psychologist and psychoanalyst John Bowlby. During World War II he began to work with children who had been evacuated from London and were therefore separated from their parents. He found that some of those who had been detached in this way showed signs of serious emotional disturbance. After the war he spent his time studying such children more fully. In the early stages of separation, after initial protest, the children would sink into a state of mourning and despair, which would then turn into detachment. The adult carers considered this helpful, since the children became less disruptive, but when the parents reappeared, the children would stay aloof and uninterested in anything the parents would say or do. The emotional damage was already done. At that time it was generally considered that sending children away for education was a good thing – it would 'toughen them up' – but Bowlby found that serious harm was being inflicted. From his extensive research, he developed his 'attachment theory', to explain the processes going on both within the child and the parent. These are inbuilt and begin to operate from the moment of birth. The tenets of his theory were as follows:

1. The infant or toddler has an innate need to seek and maintain proximity to the carer (attachment figure – usually the mother)
2. This carer is regarded as a 'secure base' (the term was applied later) from which to explore the unfamiliar world
3. The attachment figure is also the place to flee to (the 'safe haven') when danger threatens.

More recently the psychiatrist Daniel Siegel has helpfully summarised the dimensions of attachment (there are now considered to be four of them) in the following way – the infant needs to know that she is:

1. Secure (a secure base): she knows internally that all is well – an internalised sense of wellbeing
2. Seen: her carer is near and can see her empathically – not just with her eyes but her whole self
3. Soothed: when she is distressed, the carer will help with difficult emotions and situations
4. Safe (a safe haven): a safe place to return to, avoiding distressing situations[12]

The unexpressed questions in the child's mind are 'Is mum near? Is she available to me? Will she be there if I need help? Will she comfort me?' If the answer is 'yes', the child will be at ease, but if not, instinctive behaviour responses are triggered. It's rather like a thermostat that doesn't have to operate when the temperature is normal, but is activated if there is movement away from the set point. The behaviour isn't learnt, it's hard-wired into the system. 'Fear of abandonment is the fundamental human fear. It is so basic and so profound that it emerges even before we develop a language to describe it.'[13]

Over the following years, Bowlby and his coworker, Mary Ainsworth, worked to progress their understanding further. In 1963, in a series of classic studies, called the 'Strange Situation' experiments, Ainsworth demonstrated practically what until then had essentially been theory. She found that *securely* attached toddlers (the majority) used their mothers as a secure base, exploring happily in their presence. When the mothers left the room, after being initially distressed, they settled down in the presence of other adults. Similarly, on the mother's return they were readily comforted, having developed an expectation that when 'mum goes away she always comes back again'. However, another group of toddlers did not engage with their mothers and so these were labeled *avoidant*. A third group were preoccupied with their mothers' availability but angry or passive on her return and unable to be soothed – Ainsworth called this group *ambivalent*. The key difference observed between secure and insecure (avoidant and ambivalent) attachment was the reunion. A secure child's mother was able to soothe and deactivate the attachment system so that exploratory play became possible again.

These 'attachment styles', as they later came to be called, are now considered the basic types of behaviour that all young children exhibit (another style was later added, the *disorganised*, which is associated with chaotic and sometimes abusive parenting). Ainsworth further studied the mothers and found that each attachment style corresponded to particular behaviour in the mother. Mothers of securely attached infants were *responsive* to their needs – there seemed to be an emotional and intuitive attunement in the two-way communication. Mothers of avoidant babies however did not express the same concern – they were *dismissive* or controlling and would sometimes snub their children, refusing to respond to them. With ambivalent infants, the mothers behaved in an *inconsistent* fashion: sometimes they were attentive, but at other times they were distant and aloof. The key was in the mother's communication – or non-communication.[14]

Bowlby believed that infants develop 'internal working models' of relationships as they try out different behaviours, in order to achieve proximity to their caregiver. These models are honed by experience and become more fixed as the child grows. Unconscious core beliefs develop within the child, focussing on attitudes towards self and others and centering on key questions:[15]

1. The self:
    *   Am I *worthy* of love?
    *   Am I *able* to get that love?

2. Others:
    *   Are others *trustworthy*?
    *   Are they *willing* to help'?

The patterns of responses to such questions amongst the differently attachment styles look like this:[16]

Secure	Ambivalent
Self: I'm OK: worthy of love and able to get love Others: You're OK: trustworthy and willing	Self: I'm not OK Others: You're OK
Avoidant	Disorganised
Self: I'm OK Others: You're not OK	Self: I'm not OK Others: You're not OK

The unconscious answers that the child comes up with persist into the future and govern her view of herself and others throughout the rest of her life.

We all have an attachment style, although generally we are unaware of it. It determines what we think about ourselves and others, and significantly shapes our approach to relationships in later life – all because of our experience of parenting as a small child.

It bears repeating: our universal and deeply rooted need to love and be loved, expressed here in terms of attachments bonds, arises from our earliest moments in life. This understanding sheds light on those powerful longings that we explored in Chapter 3 – longings for intimate and lasting loving relationships for a person or a people.

Later, another key researcher, Mary Main, showed how *infants'* internalised attachment patterns are translated into *adult* attachment styles. She developed the Adult Attachment Interview (AAI), which enabled her to uncover hidden memories relating to attachment – as she put it, 'surprising the unconscious.' Just as the Strange Situation became a powerful tool in infancy, so too did the AAI for adults.

Main understood that many of these childhood memories were unconscious and so she focused more on people's *non-verbal ways* of communicating – the *how* rather than the *what* (parallel to McGilchrist's explanation of right brain functioning). Her conclusion: *the patterns of attachment in infancy determine how adults function in later life.* She coined the term 'attachment styles' for these patterns, and the relationship between early attachment experience and adult attachment style looks like this:

1. Secure attachment – *Secure* attachment style
2. Avoidant attachment – *Dismissing* attachment style
3. Ambivalent attachment – *Preoccupied* attachment style
4. Disorganised attachment – Unresolved or *Disorganised* attachment style

Take a moment to look through the questions asked of adults about their childhood experiences. How might you reply?

Adult Attachment interview [17]
Read through the following questions – what answers would you come up with?

[Take care: these questions may evoke some difficult or painful memories, so you may want to ask someone else to help you in this reflection. If they do raise issues, you may find a counsellor's professional support helpful]

What was your childhood like?

What was your relationship like with each parent? What adjectives or phrases come to mind?

Who were you close to as a child (that can include people other than your parents)?

When you were upset as a child, what did you do, and what would happen? Can you think of any specific incidents?

Why do you think your parents behaved as they did during your childhood?

Can you describe your first separation from your parents?

Did you experience loss as a child? What was that like for you and your family?

How do you think your overall early experiences affected your adult personality?

How did your relationships change over time?

If you have children, how do you think these experiences have affected your parenting?

When your child is twenty-five, what do you hope (s) he will say are the most important things s(he) learned from you?

Moments of meeting – intersubjectivity

There is no such thing as a baby —
if you set out to describe a baby, you will find you are
describing a baby and someone
Donald W. Winnicott[18]

Attachment theory proposes that all infants are born with a need to be close to another person. This is more than just 'helpful' – it is essential for survival, since human infants are not able to care for themselves, either physically or emotionally. But attachment does more than this – it also provides the foundations for other developmental processes. One such process is intersubjective relating or intersubjectivity, which is all about *knowing and being known by another person.* This interaction of two 'subjectivities' (two minds) is now becoming central to our understanding of how relationships develop.[19]

If attachment provides the context, then intersubjectivity delivers the connection.

This 'meeting of minds' is very deeply ingrained and we are born with the ability to relate to another person's mind. Forty-two minutes after birth, an infant intentionally imitates adults' facial expressions. At six weeks she imitates gestures that were shown to her the previous day.[20] Babies are able to read the intentions of adults nearby: 'we turn to other people to see what's in our mind and to find out what things mean'.[21] Here's what one expert says,

> Before language, there was something else more basic, in a way more primitive, and with unequalled power in its formative potential that propelled us into language. Something that could evolve in tiny steps, but suddenly gave rise to the thinking processes that revolutionized mental life. Something that (unfortunately) no fossil remains can show us. That something else was social engagement with each other. *The links that can join one person's mind with the mind of someone else—especially, to begin with, emotional links— are the very links that draw us into thought* [my italics].[22]

Babies learn about themselves and others by tuning into their mothers. *Attunement* is an aspect of intersubjectivity and it continues into our adult lives. It helps us to both resonate with another's feelings and communicate that sense back to them. This happens at a deep non-verbal level – remember that in the infant's case there are no words involved. When a parent mirrors her baby's facial expressions and sounds (all those funny noises we make at them) she is signalling back to the baby non-verbally that she understands her infant's emotions and can 'contain' her distress, even anticipating her intentions and wishes. This helps the baby to develop a sense of self that is accepted and understood, leading to healthy emotional development. The child of course is equally attuned – if the mother turns her gaze away from her newborn child even for a moment, the child becomes restless, but quietens immediately when that gaze returns.[23] So a beautifully choreographed 'dance' is going on between the two people quite unconsciously. One researcher, Daniel Stern, has a term for this – *interpersonal communion* – as one subjective experience is joined with another's.[24] Of course, all of this applies to every relationship throughout life.[25]

For reflection

As you reflect on your upbringing, what was your parents'/carers' principle way of acting towards you?

Would you say that they were more like a secure mother/father, or perhaps avoidant or ambivalent?

What was the impact upon you as you grew up?

As a result, to what extent did you develop secure, avoidant or ambivalent attachment patterns (of course we all have elements of secure and insecure styles – this question is exploring the dominant characteristics)?

How do you respond to the section on intersubjectivity? Would you say that you are well attuned to other people and their emotional states? How might you develop attunement more?

Looking to others – for better or worse

Interpersonal communion is a fundamental pillar of healthy relationships. Just like the infant, we are all looking for the gaze of intimacy from other person. We need others to mirror back to us what we are thinking and feeling. Neuroscientists have now found the basis of this mirroring – a network of brain neurons, called the *mirror neuron system*. We discern the minds of others and appreciate their mental, emotional and bodily condition through this framework. When someone yawns, we find ourselves doing the same thing. When we walk into a room where people are laughing it's difficult not to find ourselves smiling also – even when we have no idea what the joke is! But it goes beyond movements; our mirror neurons help us to sense *others'* emotional states as well – we 'feel their joy, or pain'. This is the basis of emotional intelligence and empathy – the ability to intuit what other people are feeling. There are in fact neuronal *resonance circuits*, which run from our (right) cerebral cortex down through our spinal cord, to networks of nerves in our body, especially around the heart and gut. That is why we have 'gut feelings' or a 'heartfelt sense' as embodied feelings. We really do have these intuitions, which connect us to our emotions, our bodies and those of other people we are with![26]

One consequence of this is that we all have an inbuilt

tendency to compare ourselves and seek others' approval. You probably have your own childhood memories. I remember looking automatically to my parents for support and sanction. In fact, part of my difficulties later in life could be traced back to my sense of non-affirmation from my father. Unconsciously, I was looking for affirmation from father figures (hospital consultants, other leaders or older men) that they could not give – or at least, were not required to give. I was still crying out on the inside for my dad's approval and encouragement. Even in my marriage, I would still look to my wife for reassurance. Nothing wrong with that, you might say, but there was a sense in which I needed to stand on my own two feet as an adult, and not look to another person for the strength that should primarily come from within. For all of us, our early experience has serious implications for whether we feel fulfilled in later life, since as children we are dependent on key adults to help us think about our own experience and enable us to fully make our own decisions.

Securely attached people, with healthy intersubjective capacities are of course able to interact effectively with other people. This means that they can cope with conflict in a constructive way and accept others' perspectives that are different from their own. Only when there is felt security in relationships can one afford a difference of opinion, knowing that it will not destroy the relationship. One therapist puts it this way, 'As research reveals new aspects of resonance circuits, *the sense of an overarching interpersonal oneness process grows more compelling*' [my italics].[27] This intersubjective togetherness or 'oneness' however, is not 'sameness'. There is a healthy 'betweenness' about the relationship, with space for separation and room for two minds – not a single homogenised merger. We'll explore that more in the next chapter.

It seems that we cannot overestimate the significance of early attachment and relational processes for our later emotional and relational functioning and wellbeing, as our genetically determined brain structures are sculpted by interpersonal experiences in infancy. This is perhaps one of the clearest examples of nurture impacting and shaping nature. But here's the point: if our ways of thinking, feeling and relating are established at a very early stage of our lives, this can clearly be for better or for worse. To the extent that our patterns develop in a secure and healthy way, we emerge as secure and balanced people; but that of course is never fully the case – we all develop to some degree damaged and distorted patterns of insecurity.

The good news, however, is that if attachment, attunement and intersubjectivity can enable us to develop well *in the first place*, they can also operate *later in life* to bring healing and restoration when early damage has brought pain and distress throughout our lives. As Wallin puts it,

> *Attachment relationships may also be the setting in which – whether in love or psychotherapy – our early emotional injuries are most likely to be healed.*[28]

There is great hope in this. If you did not enjoy secure attachment or empathic responsiveness in your early years, you can still find healing. As we will discover in the next chapter, your brain is 'plastic' and if you embrace consistent emotional support from other people, the neurons of your brain will begin to make new connections that endure permanently. But it is likely that you will need to retrace your steps back to source with the help of someone – a therapist or a loving, committed companion – who can be instrumental in undoing the damage.

So how does all this fit with our guiding diagram? From all we have considered, it is clear that it is the right brain that directs and enables our relationships and attachments, operating through its implicit and non-verbal processes. Our emotional connections are paramount and the meeting of minds that comes through intersubjective connection allows us to foster and cherish lasting and meaningful relationships throughout our lives – which of course lie at the heart of lifelong wellbeing.

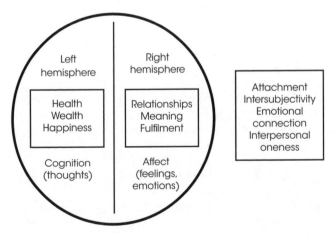

Summary and conclusion

We all enter the world utterly helpless, with an inbuilt need to bond, or attach, to other people. The relationship between carer and infant is fundamental to wellbeing, to such an extent that both persons can be seen almost as one (sometimes referred to as 'chother' or 'mochild'). Some have called this the 'human moment' and it remains a profound mystery.

In the 'dance' between carer and child, the infant receives the security, safety and soothing she needs to grow and develop. However, to the extent that the child is ignored, neglected or treated in contradictory ways relationally, she becomes insecure and uncertain of herself and others. Her attitudes and approach to others (her attachment style) become disinterested (avoidant), needy (ambivalent) or even traumatised (disorganised). These perceptions and behaviours become ingrained and persist throughout the rest of her life, but they can be re-programmed and healed through love and empathic attention over a period of time.

The proximity of attachment, then, provides the context for wellbeing, enabling intersubjectivity to deliver the connection. This inbuilt capacity allows us to know our own internal life as well as to connect with another person's feelings (i.e. empathy). But criticism, rejection and misunderstanding can become internalised within us, and consequently we may give up and cease to reach out in close relationships. Again, however, all is not lost, because with help, we can learn afresh healthy emotional and relational patterns.

What is extraordinary about all this research is the discovery that the patterns of our experiences of ourselves and others, continuing through the whole of our lives, are laid down in our very first weeks and months. At this stage verbal communication has not yet appeared – it is all non-verbal and unconscious.

This implicit, unconscious and non-verbal basis to relationships is immensely important for our understanding of how we perceive ourselves and relate to others …

… as we shall see in the next chapter.

The significance of right brain function for healthy relationships also emerges once more. The highest human functions –

intersubjectivity, empathy, morality and the rest – are all right brain functions; and this continues throughout our lives. Right brain deficits connected with insecure attachments underlie all psychological and psychiatric disorders.[29] The key connection for *all* relationships in fact (infant/carer, client/therapist or any other context) is a 'right brain to right brain' affair, lying at the heart of all reparative relationships. This brings us back to our initial summary statement:

> *It appears that the capacity to relate to other people is hard-wired into our brains and that such relating is at the heart of human flourishing. Relationships are primarily a function of the right brain, with its emphasis on implicit, unconscious, non-verbal processes. Emotions are essential to the development and nurture of all healthy relationships.*

This is a radical statement, and stands as a profound challenge to the markedly left brained emphasis of our twenty-first century Western culture. It is one of the propositions of this book that although a clear understanding of what makes for healthy living (including relationships) is available to all, our culture is actually orientated in a very different direction – a direction favoured by the left brain.

Having laid the foundations for healthy social relating, then, we are in a position to explore practical ways through which we may nurture and repair our relationships.

SIX

HEALTHY RELATIONSHIPS II: REPAIR AND RESTORATION

I am convinced that material things can contribute
a lot to making one's life pleasant, but, basically, if
you do not have very good friends and relatives who
matter to you, life will be really empty and sad and
material things cease to be important.
David Rockefeller, Banker[1]

Love is patient and kind; love does not envy or boast;
it is not arrogant or rude. It does not insist on its own
way; it is not irritable or resentful; it does not rejoice at
wrongdoing, but rejoices with the truth. Love bears all
things, believes all things, hopes all things, endures all
things. Love never ends.
1 Corinthians 13:4-8

How do we make relationships work? We've just explored the
basic mechanisms of relationship development and the ways in
which they can be damaged. Since lasting happiness cannot
develop without our giving attention to relational health and
repair, in this chapter we will look at ways to function well – and
some more reasons why we don't!

How humans work: being separate and together

How are your relationships? It's likely that some of your best
experiences have come through being with other people, but it
may also be true that your greatest pains have been relational
as well. That's certainly been my experience.

The more time you spend in a close relationship with
another person, the more aware you become of two equal
and opposite forces that inhabit us all. One is all about

'me', that is, separateness, individuality and personal autonomy – we need to be ourselves and not another.[2]

How often have you heard the rallying cry, 'be yourself' or the misquote of Shakespeare, 'to thine own self be true'? We need to know where the boundaries between 'me' and 'you' start and finish.

The other force is the very opposite – it's all about 'us'. We don't want to be alone; we want and need to be with other people; we want to be together, close to other people. It's very interesting that when tragedy strikes, our natural response is to reach out to others, to physically hold each other, to be together in grief.[3]

It's also true when we celebrate – it doesn't work very well to be alone when you're getting married, or you've passed an exam, or you've just rediscovered friends you haven't seen for a long time. Remember that quote from John Ortberg in Chapter 2: 'The yearning to attach and connect, to love and be loved, is the fiercest longing of the soul. Our need for community with people...is to the human spirit what food and air and water are to the human body'.

Both forces are essential. But they are also in constant tension with each other, pulling in opposite directions, and such tension always produces anxiety. We want and need to be individuals, treated with love and respect; but we also want to connect and feel we belong. However, we can't always do both at the same time. As part of an interrelated system of relationships we are constantly bumping up against each other. Your 'self' bumps up against mine and vice versa. I want something but you want something else. It's not surprising that all kinds of tensions arise and if we don't learn to compromise we will end up in destructive vicious cycles of conflict. We have a huge need for mature, unselfish ways of breaking out of such cycles.

Why we struggle

The psychiatrist Murray Bowen pioneered family systems therapy in the mid-twentieth century, and coined the term *self-differentiation* to describe the enviable state in which the 'me' force is in harmony with the 'us' force. If you are a person who differentiates him/herself you are able to:

1. Be clear about who you are ('define' yourself) and yet ... Stay in touch with others
2. Take responsibility for yourself, yet ... Be responsive to others

3. Maintain your integrity and wellbeing without ... Intruding on that of others
4. Allow the enhancement of another person's integrity and wellbeing without ... Feeling abandoned, inferior or less of a self
5. Have an 'I' and enter a relationship with another 'I' without losing your self and diminishing the other person's self.[4]

That sounds like a tall order, and yet it's a place we must come close to if we are to be able to both maintain our own sense of self and nurture others' wellbeing. Only those people who are able to differentiate themselves (i.e. know who they are as an individual and be comfortable in their own skin) are then competent to reach out to others in a healthy way. Says psychotherapist Steinke, 'We separate in order to unite ... Community means two unique people meet ... This is the fundamental idea conveyed by the word "relate". It bears the notion of "carrying back".'[5]

He goes on to explain that the need to be separate and distinct can become distorted, resulting in one of two common coping behaviours. On the one hand, we may distance ourselves from another person. We disengage and cut off emotionally. On the other hand, because of insecurity and the need to be close, we may over-attach and become enmeshed with the other – we fuse emotionally. In one case, there's too much separateness, in the other too much togetherness. The diagram shows how this works. When someone is functioning healthily, both forces are in balance, but anxiety will push the person in one direction or the other:[6]

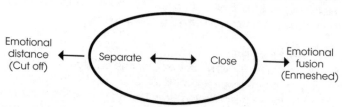

You can see immediately the parallel with attachment styles. Securely attached people are more likely to have a robust view of both themselves (a healthy sense of self differentiation) and other people (an equally healthy force of togetherness and engagement). Insecure attachments are liable to produce unhealthy tendencies. So, individuals with an avoidant or dismissing style will tend to distance themselves or cut off from others emotionally, whereas ambivalent or preoccupied people are likely to become emotionally fused or enmeshed.

How does this all work? Well, think of the most emotionally secure person you know. It's quite likely that they are good at relating to other people. They're not moody and unpredictable – they stay connected with others, without withdrawing emotionally from them. On the other hand, they don't get into enmeshed relationships (what the therapists call co-dependency). They are able to 'be themselves' in different contexts – they don't go round apologising for themselves all the time – and yet they are able to reach out empathically to others. They aren't over-intense, nor are they aloof and distant. They are proactive rather than reactive; that is to say, they initiate contact without rancour, and don't simply *react* to other people's emotional states. Their boundaries with people are neither too porous (merging with others) nor too rigid and inflexible. Sound a bit too perfect? Well, the ideal person doesn't exist, but perhaps the one you're thinking of is a little like that.

Being an stable individual yet connecting well with other people
- Is self-differentiation an impossible goal?
- Do you know anyone who seems to combine self-differentiation and connection in a balanced and stable way?
- What is it about such a person that you appreciate?
- How might you apply that to your own mindsets and behaviour?

How does this tie in with our consideration of the brain? Well, the need to be a separate and distinct individual relates to our understanding of the left brain's operation (the 'me' focus); whereas connecting with others reflects the right brain's approach ('us, together'). Remember Jill Bolte Taylor's experience of losing her left brain function? She lost her sense of separateness – she was even unable to 'clearly discern the physical boundaries of where I began and where I ended.'

On the other hand, her awareness of her connection with all around her was hugely expanded: 'I no longer perceived myself as a whole object separate from everything. Instead, I now blended in with the space and flow around me.'[7] It's clear then, from neuroscience, psychology and experience that both perspectives are vital, since an over-functioning of the left brain will lead to too much individualism (cut off), but excessive right brain activity brings fusion and merging.

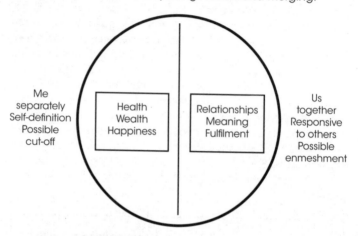

Me
separately
Self-definition
Possible
cut-off

Health
Wealth
Happiness

Relationships
Meaning
Fulfilment

Us
together
Responsive
to others
Possible
enmeshment

A personal story

My own tendencies are towards avoidance and cut-off. I have worked quite hard on myself over the years, especially since I became more aware of the significance of attachments in early life and emotional systems generally. But generally speaking when emotionally threatened or insecure, my default has been to distance myself from the person who is troubling me. I can feel the emotional pressure inside and the desire to move away (sometimes physically) to dampen down my emotional response. As I've reflected on my childhood, it's become clear that the way in which my father in particular acted towards me was significant in my emotional development. He was an austere person, a perfectionist and a stickler for correct procedure. He was not proficient at showing his emotions. (I remember my mum often saying, 'We're not a demonstrative family', although she had little trouble herself in expressing her own feelings!) For example, I don't remember times in childhood when he would either say, 'I love you' or give me a hug. That is classic avoidant behaviour and in his case it could be traced back to his rather lonely childhood. He was an only child, with an often-absent father who was in the Royal Marines and therefore more often away than at home. His mother was rather self-focussed and my dad had little respect for her as he grew into adulthood. He didn't trust his emotions much and after he met and married my mum he concentrated all his affections on her. I can't remember my very early years of course (when attachment patterns are mostly laid down), but I do remember learning to avoid situations that might provoke my dad's ire.

So my patterns of relating were already fixed by the time I left home and although I have an outgoing personality, I would find myself over-reacting to criticism or rejection. I met my (future) wife, Jill, at a point when I thought I'd nailed down my sensitivities (I was almost thirty by the time we married), but was deeply shocked when I realised, after we'd been living together for a few months, that actually I still had a long way to go! That was thirty-four years ago, and the journey still continues. Jill has tendencies towards an ambivalent attachment style, so our interactions developed along predictable and repeatable lines. She is an emotionally expressive person (what do rhinos do when provoked?), whereas I, with my avoidant tendencies, am much more of a 'hedgehog' (how do they react when poked?). So our typical conflicts have involved Jill expressing strong emotion with me retreating into my shell.

You will have your own propensities I'm sure – we all have. How we respond in social situations will depend in part on others' personalities, but much more is down to our own patterns of reaction and response. It's well worth reflecting on your inclinations and susceptibilities, since that will help you to discern where you need to change and grow.

Anyone who has achieved lasting happiness and contentment has acquired the capacity to spend time both alone and with others, without a sense of insecurity and inadequacy.

For me, it's still a journey, but one in which I know I'm going in a positive direction!

Your patterns

What are your principal patterns and reactions in social situations?

How do they compare with the patterns outlined above?

With regard to the less healthy patterns, what might you do to begin a process of change?

What might be the outcome of that change, for you; for others?

Mature and immature patterns of relating

We all enter adulthood carrying within us well-established patterns of thinking, feeling, behaving and relating to other people. These templates are so ingrained that we don't even think about them – they are 'normal' for us. But, as we've also seen, some at least are distortions and (mal)adaptations based on our less-than-perfect childhood experiences. Some of us grow up thinking that we are *not* 'OK'; that other people are *not* really to be trusted; or that life is stacked *against* us and other people have a better deal than us. The number of permutations is as diverse as we are individually, but many patterns are predictable, in a similar way to attachment styles.

Eric Berne was a psychiatrist and psychoanalyst who through his practice came to the conclusion that many therapists' approach to clients was too complex and inaccessible.[8] He therefore devised a methodology that helped people to both understand and cooperate with the professional. He referred to three 'ego states' as the basis of his system (an ego state is a pattern of thinking and feeling that keeps recurring within us and determines repeated styles of behaviour).[9] These states were the 'Parent' (compare Freud's 'superego'), 'Child' (like the 'id') and the 'Adult' (as 'ego'). Berne suggested that all of us possess these states, but that depending on our early upbringing, one or other of them manifests in response to social situations. The Parent ego state reflects thoughts and feelings stemming from parental figures – the parent is as it were, still speaking to us in our head. Other significant people also speak to us still, for example, teachers or other authority figures. Berne distinguished two types of Parents. One is the Nurturing Parent who exhibits care and support, but in a way that shows (s)he is stronger and more dominant than the person him/herself. The second Parent state is the Controlling Parent, whose critical voice disapproves and censures.

The Child ego state represents the young child's feelings and responses, carried over into adulthood. Since such a child has little understanding of emotional and relational ideas and vocabulary, her feelings are buried deep within her psyche without conscious understanding – they become the 'norm'. We all have a 'child within' who shows him/herself in certain circumstances. Berne identified two Child ego states: the first is the Adapted Child, who conforms to parental expectations, either by 'fitting in' or with anger or aggression (either obvious or passive). The second is the Free Child, who has escaped the influence of parents and expresses herself, sometimes inappropriately, as a spontaneous, less inhibited person. This can bring its own social difficulties of course.

The Adult ego state refers to attitudes and behaviours that accurately express the authentic or mature person, without all the overlay of Child or Parent. The Adult is able to perceive and respond to the real world in a responsible and appropriate way that enables others to act similarly. Verbal and non-verbal formulations (e.g. tone of voice, facial expressions, vocabulary and posture) fit well together and other people feel able to relate back in an appropriate way. The person is able to live out their lives, not in reaction to past negative influences, but in an authentic and autonomous way, yet responsive to others' needs and personalities (this all sounds very much like Bowen's self-differentiation).

How we interact: 'Am I OK – or not?'

Voices in my head
Of course, these voices are not audible, but the thoughts and feelings we experience consistently express the same viewpoint. Here are examples of such narratives:

Child voice
Victim role, defensive, deficit-focus – whiny, sarcastic tone, rolling eyes

Examples:
You don't care about me
It's your fault
Why don't you do something to help me?
I hate you

Parent voice

Authoritarian, aggressive, judgmental, directive – 'win/lose' mentality, punishing, threatening

Examples:
You shouldn't do that
Tough – suck it up!
That's a stupid thing to say
Why aren't you more like Charlie?

Adult voice

Non-judgmental, respectful, positive body language, sticks to the point, 'win/win' attitude, no hidden agenda

Examples:
I understand what you're (trying to) say
So how do you think that we can resolve this problem?
Have you thought of 'X' as a possibility?
We agree to disagree

We each possess all three ego states of course, but many people find themselves operating out of one or other by default. Berne goes on to explain how the different ego states interact – he calls these transactions (hence the term for his whole method: Transactional Analysis) and describes how we all play unconscious 'games' with each other. Some of these transactions are complementary, i.e. a stimulus that provokes an expected response: 'Isn't our neighbourhood going down in the world?' – 'Yes, the police aren't doing their job' (Parent, with Parent response). Others are 'crossed', when a stimulus meets an unexpected response: 'Did you pick up the milk on your way home?' – 'What do you think I am, your servant?' (Adult, with Child response). Still others reveal an ulterior or hidden agenda:

'So, you're not feeling very well?' – 'You've always wanted to take care of me, haven't you?' (Adult, with Child response).

A fun activity – with a serious dimension

You may find it fun to act out the different transactions with a few other people. Work out some scenarios (e.g. family, work, shops, neighbours, etc.) and then have two people act out two ego states. So for example, you might have a Controlling Parent with an Adapted Child, or Adult with Free Child. Enjoy the interaction and then talk together about what it felt like to operate out of one type of ego state, then the other. Perhaps have a third person observing, who then gives their perspective. But be aware that acting these states out may trigger some buried and hidden experiences and painful memories.

Berne expands these anecdotal scenarios into life scripts, portraying 'winning' or 'losing' characters, symbolised by 'OK' positions. There are four categories: 'I'm OK – you're OK'; 'I'm OK – you're not OK'; 'I'm not OK – you're OK'; and 'I'm not OK – you're not OK'. You'll notice that I have applied these positions to the four different attachment styles in the Chapter 5, since our experiences early in life determine in large part how we relate to ourselves and other people later on. Someone occupying the first position (OK/OK) is 'comfortable in their own skin' (securely attached) and sees good in others too. The 'not-OK/OK' position is referred to as 'depressive'; whilst the 'OK/not-OK' category is seen as 'paranoid'; and the 'not-OK/not-OK' position is described as one of 'futility'. It's not difficult to see resonance with ambivalent, avoidant and disorganised attachment styles here.

Transactional analysis therapy aims to help clients towards autonomy, transforming an unhealthy life script; to develop the secure 'I'm OK – you're OK' position; to move beyond playing games in relationships (the interactions between ego states that degrade relationships); and to help them take responsibility for their feelings and choices. This is clearly a challenge, since the patterns we have grown up with are thoroughly ingrained. But unless we are willing to seek to understand those patterns and initiate reparative actions, we will remain stuck in them for the rest of our lives.

Getting personal – again

Speaking personally again, because of my avoidant attachment style I have generally tended towards the 'I'm OK – you're not OK' position, which is something of a judgemental perspective! But there is another narrative within me. My 'Child' sometimes reacts to other people with excessive sensitivity: 'Take notice of me, don't be so harsh!' That has resulted over the years in a tricky combination of slightly bombastic approaches to people (I've been called 'Tigger-ish'[10] a few times in my life!) combined with a hyper-sensitivity to their responses! I've had to work on that and I think I've made progress, though there's some way to go! The challenge for us all is to give our Adult voice more scope – to 'turn up the volume' on that voice, whilst toning down on the Parent and Child voice. It's as if the Adult says to the Child, 'I understand how you feel – your needs are genuine and should be heard. But we're going to turn your volume down a little right now'. The Adult might also address the Critical Parent with, 'I know you feel very strongly that we should (not) do a certain thing, but there are other ways of approaching the situation.' This self-compassion is important if we are to make progress (the right brain's influence over the left brain's judgemental tendencies). We are often our own harshest critic and other people, if they are granted access to our deepest feelings about ourselves, may well respond with, 'Don't be so tough on yourself!' Daniel Siegel calls a whole chapter of his book, 'Our multiple selves'[11] and goes on to refer to his 'Checker' – the voice inside us that insists on checking for danger or trouble (just like Bolte Taylor's brain chatter).[12] I don't suffer from Obsessive-Compulsive Disorder, but my Checker often has me counting the number of spokes on a car wheel I'm walking by, or the number of storeys in a high-rise building! Many of us experience the voice of the Critical Parent, constantly telling us off for our thoughts, words or actions: 'Stupid boy', 'Why did you do that?' 'What were you thinking of to come out with such a ridiculous comment?' Becoming aware of the reasons why those voices exist is an important starting point for being able to deal with them. They are not villains in our head to be resisted at all costs (or followed slavishly), but they arise from patterns laid down years ago in childhood.

I have a number of strategies I use on myself:

1. When tempted to retreat into my Child and cut off, I say to myself, 'Don't cut off - stay with the person/people'.

2. Another version of the same thing is, 'Stay in your adult - don't revert to Child here'.

3. To my Child I might say, 'It's OK , you'll be alright - they're not out to get you!'

4. And of course I sometimes take Jill Bolte Taylor's advice, 'Shift to the right'.

Your inner voices

As you've read through the passage on Transactional Analysis, you have probably related to one or more ego states or 'inner voices' - after all, we all have them. So here are some questions to reflect on:

- What are the most significant inner voices that you contend with: Child? Parent? What kind of Parent, what kind of Child?
- What are your usual coping methods? Do they work? Why (not)?
- What could you do to begin to quieten the critical, negative voices and begin to increase the volume of your Adult voice?

Getting into drama triangles

One of Berne's students, Stephen Karpman, employed Berne's social transactional framework, or games, to develop a particular model, which came to be called The Drama Triangle.[13] Murray Bowen had earlier demonstrated how, often, when we feel insecure or anxious with someone, we seek to draw in a third person to bolster our perspective - we form 'triangles'. A notable example of this is gossiping, in which we talk to someone about a third person (in negative terms) and try to get them 'on our side' by denigrating the third party. Karpman described a triangle that illustrates the kinds of power plays we can get into and the roles we adopt to influence other people. It looks like this:

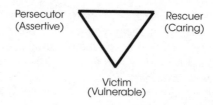

Persecutor
(Assertive)

Rescuer
(Caring)

Victim
(Vulnerable)

The Victim is rather like the Child in Berne's games – he doesn't take responsibility for himself and feels overwhelmed by events and feelings ('It's no good – I can't do anything!'). The Rescuer is always ready (like the Nurturing Parent) to jump in and take responsibility for the Victim ('Don't worry, I'm here – I'll do it all!'). The Persecutor however (like the Critical Parent) stands back, criticises or shames the Victim ('What's the matter with you – you're never able to do it for yourself!'). All three roles interact with each other and maintain a kind of equilibrium, but with unhealthy consequences for all.

Some years later another triangle was described as a way forward from this vicious cycle. Called The Winner's Triangle, it re-ascribes the three roles. The Victim now becomes Vulnerable, willing to recognise his vulnerability, but willing also to take responsibility and act into it. The Rescuer now is Caring, showing concern but encouraging the Vulnerable person to make their own choices and actions. The Persecutor becomes Assertive, choosing for themselves rather than for the Victim, and becoming assertive without punishing. All of us have tendencies in one direction or another – sometimes we play more than one role. But finding our way from unhealthy to healthy roles will help not only us, but others too, to find more positive ways to think and act. It's noticeable that what moves someone from a Drama Triangle role to a Winning role is the willingness *either to step back and give someone else room to take responsibility for themselves, or to step forward to take that responsibility.*

Your drama triangle

Do you ever take on one or more of the roles in the Drama Triangle? Which one(s)?

Thinking of one of those roles (perhaps the one that you're most concerned about), how might you move towards a Winner's Triangle role?

> Is there anyone who might be of help in this?
> What would it take for you to either give space for others to take responsibility for their actions, or to take that responsibility yourself?

You've probably realised by now that I find all these different theories and approaches fascinating. There seems to be profound overlap and integration across them. They add up to a convincing picture of how secure and insecure, healthy and unhealthy, constructive and destructive attitudes and relationships develop and operate through our lives. However, it may be as you read it through, that you feel a little intimidated and end up saying, 'Well, it's so complicated and involved that I don't see any way through for me – how can I change and what can I do?' There is some good news – we can change!

Our choices change our brains

You may remember in the Introduction that I quoted the research that demonstrates that 40 per cent of our subjective wellbeing (the psychologists' name for happiness) is determined by our own voluntary choices. Not everything in life is down to me, but these are – completely. And making the same choice every day will bring change – it has been calculated that it takes six to eight weeks to form a new habit.[14] If we choose the same thing, it will change us. Choices become habits and over time, habits change our character. Choice is real, but what and how we choose is the key – and once again, neuroscience has helped us to understand how that happens.

One of the most significant recent discoveries in neuroscience is something called neuroplasticity. It was once thought that unlike other organs of the body, the brain's structure is fixed. We now know that at both the micro level (the neurons themselves) and the larger level (the whole brain and areas within it) the brain is malleable and susceptible to change. Daniel Siegel coined the phrase, 'What fires together, wires together', by which he meant that when we repeatedly focus our attention, thoughts and actions in certain ways, brain neurons that were not previously strongly linked begin to work or 'fire' in a new and concerted way – and this changes the brain itself. He goes on to say, *'From our first days of life, our immature brain is ... shaped by our interactions with the world, and especially by our relationships.* Our experiences stimulate neural firing and sculpt our emerging synaptic connections. This is how experience changes the structure of the brain itself – and could even end up having an influence on our innate temperament' [my italics].[15]

So, although we are born with certain (apparently) fixed genetic characteristics, it turns out that our experiences really do mould those characteristics, especially in early life. Things become more set later on, but even then, change is possible. Even the expression of genetically determined processes is subject to influence, through something called epigenesis, whereby our experiences can alter the way in which the nerve cell's internal workings operate. *The key to change is how we focus our attention.* 'By harnessing the power of awareness' we can 'voluntarily change a firing pattern that was laid down involuntarily.'[16] This is the basis of the practice of mindfulness, in which we focus our attention towards the present moment, including for example, our breathing or the state of our body. Our attention moves from the brain chatter within our minds to something more calm and settled and in the process our brain is altered. Of course it's one thing to say that we can change, it's another to actually do it! Following are some encouragements to help us move in that direction.

The paradox of life – letting go

Grief and loss are both painful and inevitable. When we lose *things* we feel angry and irritated. But losing *people*, through death, divorce or other forms of rejection is much, much more grievous. This is the flip side of attachment – close relationships lead to our most powerful and meaningful experiences in life, but for that very reason, the pain is so much more excruciating when they go wrong or are lost. And the closer the relationship, the more aching and raw is the hurt. Yet loss and bereavement are inevitable. Throughout our lives we undergo losses and we are nearly always unprepared for them. Psychiatrist M. Scott Peck writes about the apparently permanent certainties that turn out to be only temporary possessions, which, like it or not, have to be relinquished sooner or later:

- The state of infancy, in which no external demands need to be responded to
- The fantasy of omnipotence

- The desire for total (including sexual) possession of one's parent(s)
- The dependency of childhood
- Distorted images of one's parents
- The omnipotentiality of adolescence
- The 'freedom' of uncommitment
- The agility of youth
- The sexual attractiveness and/or potency of youth
- The fantasy of immortality
- Authority over one's children
- Various forms of temporal power
- The independence of physical health
- And, ultimately, the self and life itself.[17]

We may lose our relationship with someone through death, but more commonly the connection becomes damaged, distorted and lost through some kind of relational breakdown – someone says or does something that causes us rejection, hurt and pain. When that happens, our natural response is to want either to put the maximum distance between them and us or to punish them in some way. As I intimated earlier, these responses have been called 'hedgehog' or 'rhino' reactions; they tap into feelings of avoidance or revenge – and the passive aggression of a 'hedgehog' is just as destructive as the more explicit anger of a 'rhino'. Our responses may be so strong that they can overwhelm us and affect almost everything we think about or do. What is more, although they may get buried for years (and therefore as far as anyone knows, including ourselves, have 'disappeared') they are in fact still alive and can surface at the most unexpected moments. Road rage or air rage are sudden and often violent outbursts of anger, triggered by apparently innocuous events, like someone 'cutting up' another driver on the road.

Alternatively, they may quietly fester within us, nurturing resentment and bitterness, both towards the perpetrator and other people. The toxicity spreads to other parts of our lives, infecting and affecting others in the process. To give you some idea of the magnitude of the problem, imagine those negative attachment ties that result from our feelings of anger and bitterness as ropes that bind the perpetrator to us. Wherever we go we carry the person with(in) us – *the paradox is that the very person we most want to forget is most present inside us!* It's a negative attachment that keeps us connected to them in spite of ourselves. They may have moved to the other side of the world, or even died, but their face, words and actions are still very much alive. Something needs to change and once again our choices are vital for that change. One way to do that is to forgive.

Learning to forgive

Perhaps one of the biggest paradoxes in life is that *the 'unnatural' act of forgiveness is the most effective way to liberate us from the effects of harbouring resentment and unforgiveness.* It seems to go against all our instincts to let go of that legitimate sense of righteous anger and desire to see the offender suffer. And yet research (and many people's experience) indicates that forgiveness *does* make a difference. As Sonja Lyubomirsky relates, 'forgiving people are less likely to be hateful, depressed, hostile, anxious, angry and neurotic. They are more likely to be happier, healthier, more agreeable and more serene. They are better able to empathize with others and to be spiritual or religious. People who forgive hurts in relationships are more capable of re-establishing closeness. Finally, the inability to forgive is associated with persistent rumination or dwelling on revenge, while forgiving allows a person to move on.'[18] Who would want to live in a state of anger, hostility and isolation? Who would not wish to move on from the pain of hurt and abuse? Yet the decision to forgive someone and let go of our anger can be the most difficult and demanding choice of our lives. This is an area of great sensitivity and should not be discussed lightly – in this book, or anywhere else! But forgiveness may be the key to open up the 'cage' in our inner lives that has been held shut for many years.

The psychiatrist Dr Everett Worthington has developed a model that can help us to practise forgiveness. He uses the acronym 'REACH' to summarise the five steps involved – I've paraphrased them as follows:

1. **Recall the hurt.** When we're hurt we often think that it's best just to forget it. But anger never truly dies – it's buried alive and goes on to fester. So recall the hurt as objectively as possible. Simply recognise that a wrong was done to you and that you are aiming for repair (not necessarily retribution).
2. **Empathise.** Empathy helps us to see things from someone else's point of view, feeling their feelings, recognising their pressures. So, write a brief letter to yourself, as if you were the other person. How would they explain the harmful acts?

3. **Altruistic gift of forgiveness.** As you seek to empathise, think about your own life. Have you ever hurt or offended someone, especially a person you love? Did the other person forgive you? If so, you have received the gift of forgiveness from someone else. How did that feel? Many people would say that they feel free – the chains have been broken. Can you now begin to apply that towards the one who has hurt you, and seek to set them free too?

4. **Commit to forgive.** After people have forgiven, they may later feel that they haven't *really* done it! They remember the offence and consider that they didn't really release the person. So make your forgiveness tangible – tell a friend or family member what you've done. Write a 'certificate of forgiveness', recording the date, time, place and action that you've taken.

5. **Hold onto forgiveness.** Whenever you doubt what you have done, remind yourself of the REACH process, look at your certificate and remind yourself that the painful memory of hurt does not negate the important work of forgiveness you've achieved. Focus on the positive achievements, not the pain.[19]

It's important to say that forgiveness is not the same thing as approval of what someone has done, nor is it excusing or justifying their actions. It is not about denying, pretending or 'forgetting' the serious nature of their act. Nor is it reconciliation – the wrongdoer might even be dead by now. The only person who benefits in the first instance is the one choosing to forgive. It is a choice to relinquish the 'right' to punish and thereby let go of the toxic effects within. Is this easy? Is it a superficial thing? Is it simply a matter of just turning the page? No. But it can open up new opportunities to live free of the down drag of resentment and bitterness.

Does forgiveness work?

Well, you only have to look at the faces and lives of people like Nelson Mandela, Martin Luther King or Kim Phúc[20] to get a sense that it might. But there have been a number of studies carried out to discover its effectiveness. One such study of 259 people offered six sessions on forgiveness to them.[21] Those who took the workshops and practiced forgiveness as a result were found to be less stressed four months later. Six months on, they reported a 70 per cent drop in the degree of hurt. They were also less angry, more optimistic and more willing to forgive in other situations. The Forgiveness Project[22] is full of inspiring stories of people who have chosen to move beyond their painful experiences. 'The Railway Man' is the story of Eric Lomax, who suffered brutal torture in a Japanese prison camp in World War Two but overcame his bitterness to reconcile with his former captor.

My own experiences are more modest. I haven't had to forgive huge offenses, but like us all, I have had to make decisions about whether to let go of anger, resentment and the desire to get back at people who have hurt or offended me. I remember times when people have misunderstood or misrepresented me privately and publicly. My default reaction has often been to retreat back (remember my avoidant tendencies?) into feelings of wounded pride and self-pity. But by choosing to let go of my righteous indignation I can say that I have definitely been able to move on from the stuck position of offence. The word scandalise (meaning to shock offensively) is derived from the ancient Greek word (*skandalon*) for a trap or snare, which by entrapping the unwary causes them to stumble or fall. When others offend us, we can often fall into such a trap. And in practice, whether we become offended or not comes down to our choices. It *is* possible not to be offended; it just takes a lot of maturity to resist the affronted feelings in the moment, or jettison them later on.

The ability to let go of painful memories and resentments is probably one of the most significant capacities we can develop. We are aided by a secure foundation in childhood and upbringing, but in adulthood we still need to choose our way into healthy attitudes and behaviours. One of the marks of a mature person is the degree to which they have consistently made such choices. Lasting happiness will not develop without these capabilities. In a way, we come full circle when we learn to let go – the infant has not yet learned to grasp and keep hold of much yet. The mature person has arrived at the place where (s)he holds all things with an open hand, able to release what (s)he cannot long keep hold of. In the words of Jim Elliot, who was martyred for his faith,

He is no fool who gives what he cannot keep to gain what he cannot lose.

Letting go
- How easy (or not) do you find it to let go of past resentments and hurts?
- Do you think that a process like the REACH course of action might help?
- Who do you know who might be helpful?
- Are there any other things you could let go of in your life?

Summary

In this chapter we have explored a number of perspectives, each of which gives us an understanding of how relationships work in practice. How we think about ourselves and others, and therefore how we behave, is profoundly influenced by our upbringing. We may have learned to cope by cutting off from or fusing with other people, and this is reflected in our adult behaviours. We may have tendencies to unconsciously control others, acting like their parent; or we may default to a childlike approach. We may have a propensity for victimhood; or an inner need to rescue others. These unconscious mindsets carry over into all our relationships, but discovering our own particular inclinations can help us to decide to change – and point us in the direction we need to go.

Towards the end of the film, *Good Will Hunting*, therapist Sean Maguire has a powerful encounter with troubled teenager Will Hunting.[23] Both have experienced abuse in their childhoods. As the intensity of their encounter grows, Sean repeats over and over, 'It's not your fault. It's not your fault. It's not your fault.' It's a very moving scene and the words are exactly what Will needs to hear. It may be that words like that are important for you too. It was not your fault that your parents divorced. It was not your fault that you experienced painful things as a child at the hands of others. It was not your fault that other people rejected or demeaned you.

But you can find healing. You can put it behind you, if you choose to do so. That may not be easy and it may take time. You will almost certainly need help from others. And you may also need to be willing to let go of attitudes and perspectives that you have held on to for so long that they have become part of who you are. But they can be relinquished, although it may be the most difficult thing you have ever done. Your lasting happiness may well depend on it.

SEVEN

DISCOVERING MEANING

What is the meaning of life?
I don't know. The computers are down[1]

Eat, drink, and be merry, for tomorrow we die[2]

The story of the American businessman and the Mexican fisherman

The story is told of an American businessman who was standing at the pier of a small coastal Mexican village when a small boat with just one fisherman docked. Inside the small boat were several large yellowfin tuna. The American complimented the Mexican on the quality of his fish and asked how long it took to catch them. The Mexican replied, 'Only a little while.'

The American then asked why didn't he stay out longer and catch more fish? The Mexican said, 'I have enough to support my family's immediate needs.' The American then asked, 'but what do you do with the rest of your time?'

The Mexican fisherman said, 'I sleep late, fish a little, play with my children, take siestas with my wife, Maria, stroll into the village each evening where I sip wine, and play guitar with my amigos. I have a full and busy life.'

The American scoffed, 'I am a Harvard MBA and could help you. You should spend more time fishing and with the proceeds, buy a bigger boat. With the proceeds from the bigger boat, you could buy several boats, eventually you would have a fleet of fishing boats. Instead of selling your catch to a middleman you

---

would sell directly to the processor, eventually opening your own cannery. You would control the product, processing, and distribution. You would need to leave this small coastal fishing village and move to Mexico City, then LA and eventually New York City, where you will run your expanding enterprise.'

The Mexican fisherman asked, 'But senor, how long will this all take?' The American replied, '15 – 20 years.' 'But what then?' asked the Mexican.

The American laughed and said, 'That's the best part. When the time is right you would sell your company stock to the public and become very rich, you would make millions!' 'Millions – then what?'

The American said, 'Then you would retire. Move to a small coastal fishing village where you would sleep late, fish a little, play with your kids, take siestas with your wife, stroll to the village in the evenings where you could sip wine and play your guitar with your amigos.'[3]

It's a fun story that carries a powerful message. The people in the tale breathe the same air, stand in the same location and speak a common language – but they are light years apart in their worldviews. And the significance of worldviews will emerge as the key theme of this chapter.

Given all we have explored so far, our original quest (the pursuit of lasting happiness) could perhaps be rephrased as a reaching out for something or someone to relate to; seeking answers to questions about who I am, who you are and what our experience of the world around us means; and how we might find true satisfaction and fulfilment in life. These questions express the heartfelt longing of the human soul both individually and as a society.

But can we go further? I believe we can – into the layers of thought, belief and consciousness that provide the foundations of our lives, but which we take for granted rather than reflect upon and perhaps even challenge. I'm referring to our cultural worldview, which though mostly unconscious, determines what we think, say and do throughout our lives. This goes to the heart of the way in which we perceive the world around us, and links with all that we have discovered about the hemispheres of our brains.

Asking the Big Questions

A few years ago a survey was carried out in the Coventry area of the English Midlands, aiming to discover something about people's 'big picture' questions, that is, existential issues that run deeper than everyday concerns.[4] The respondents had no declared faith and came from a number of backgrounds. The central question they were asked was, *'If there was one question you would want to have answered, what would it be?'* Their responses were intriguing and revealing. Everyone professed to having big questions that required answers, and those questions were later grouped into the following categories:

1. Destiny. What happens after we die? Where, if anywhere, are we going?
2. Purpose. What is the point of life? What values should I live by? Whose life and values might I take as an example to inspire me?
3. The universe. How did it start? Is it designed? Is it planned? Is it controlled in any way?
4. God. Does God exist? If so, what is God like? What, if any, viable relationship could there be between God and human beings?
5. Spiritual realm. Is there a spiritual realm? What form does it take? Does it have any relevance to me and my life?
6. Suffering. Why is there so much suffering in the world? What national and international issues particularly concern me? What can be done about them?

(Here's a question: what do you think left-brained answers to these questions might look like – and how might they differ from right-brained responses?)

These are big questions indeed, but the point here is that in early twenty-first-century Western society, questions that human beings have been asking from time immemorial are still very much on our minds (or at least they are when someone prompts us to consider them!). A similar picture emerged when the internet search engine Ask Jeeves published for its tenth anniversary the top ten 'Unanswerable questions' it had been asked over that period (out of over a billion questions).[5] An Ask Jeeves spokeswoman said, 'Even we have to admit that occasionally there is going to be a question where there is no simple answer so we're letting our users do it themselves.' And the questions? Well, they included, 'Do blondes have more fun?' 'What is the secret to happiness?' and 'What is love?' But right at the top, beyond 'Is there anybody out there?' came, 'Is there a God?' and 'What is the meaning of life?' It appears that worldview questions really are still at the top of people's agendas.

So what are we to make of these big issue questions? They perhaps aren't the sort of queries that we wake up asking each morning, and so we will have to delve a little deeper than we usually do in everyday life. What sorts of answers does our society generally come up with and what does that have to do with lasting happiness? We are into the domain of 'cultural worldviews'; so let's try to navigate our way through it all. There are a number of questions that arise:

1.   What do we mean by 'worldview'?
2.   What has 'culture' got to do with it?
3.   How does this connect with our primary concern – whether our Western culture promotes or undermines our quest for lasting happiness?

We'll look at the second question first and then move on to the other two.

What is culture?

'Culture is what makes you a stranger when you are
away from home.'
(Philip Bock, Professor of Anthropology)

Try this exercise:

Your cultural background

Think for a moment about the group of people among whom you grew up.

What were they like? I don't mean physically, so much as what sort of things they liked to do.

What did they consider important: priorities that should be followed (even to the detriment of other things) concerning politics, religion, approach to life, attitudes to people, work and society, and so on?

> How did those priorities determine how they spent their time, money and energies?
>
> What was more important – earning lots of money or spending time with family and friends?
>
> How did they regard people who were different from themselves? As aliens and foreigners, with strange and outlandish ways, or as interesting people, worth getting to know?
>
> What do you think of their attitudes now? Do you agree with them, or have your views changed radically?

These are all questions relating to culture – the attitudes, beliefs and behaviours of a particular group. One anthropologist has defined culture as 'the integrated system of learned patterns of behaviour, ideas and products characteristic of a society'.[6] We are not born with culture – we *learn* it from others.[7]

And we learn it quickly. Research indicates that children develop a firm understanding of their culture and language between ages three and five. Three-year-olds notice skin colour, even to the extent of demonstrating racial prejudice![8]

Culture has been likened to an iceberg: only a small amount is visible at first, but if you spend some time near it you will discover there is much more under the surface.[9] It functions imperfectly and sometimes in contradictory ways (we can see other people's flaws immediately but are curiously blind to our own!), but it works for most people, most of the time. It has to, otherwise it would just die out.

As we've already seen, humans are social beings, who generally prefer to live in groups, and in this context they have developed particular ways of thinking and acting. Such collectives, with their distinctive cultural attitudes, think in *patterns* and generalisations. How often have you heard someone say, 'Well, all men are …' or 'Of course, all Africans think like this…'? But despite the limitations, contradictions and imperfections, culture makes sense to its members: 'Well, it's obvious isn't it? Surely everyone thinks like that…?' It is not rationally evaluated – things are just *assumed* unconsciously: 'That's simply the way things are done round here.' Cultural behaviours and mindsets are followed as 'the only right way'

('How else would any sane person want to do it?'; or as a parent would say to a child, 'No, don't do it that way – this is how to do it!') and just as we are all naturally egocentric ('I am the centre of my universe'), as a group we are ethnocentric ('Our way is the right way'). It is also a holistic affair – it embraces and accounts for the whole of life. It is an *integrated* and interlocking system[10] – everything connects with everything else.

If you press on one part of an airbed, there will be a corresponding movement in another part of it. In the same way, interacting with one aspect of a culture always influences other parts (for example when well-meaning Europeans opposed the African practice of polygamy, it had the unintended consequence that the discarded wives ended up becoming prostitutes for lack of other opportunity to make a living in that culture). Change ramifies. And of course culture impacts our *thoughts, attitudes, relationships and behaviour* – frequently without us giving a moment's thought to whether we are really correct in our assessments!

Recently my wife was sitting in a south London café and couldn't help overhearing a conversation between two women. There had been a terrorist attack in London just a week or so beforehand, and one of the women was recounting some messages she'd received from friends in a rural part of the country. 'Of course', she said, 'What they don't understand is that we're different here in the city. We've got used to such events and are much more resilient than people in the provinces.' Perhaps her correspondents had simply been expressing concern and support, but the woman speaking was convinced of her superiority anyway!

All of us are impacted by our native culture. We tend to think, 'our way is the best way', but that may simply be because we haven't had the opportunity to discover how others do it! Our assumptions need testing but even in a multicultural city like London we generally stay inside our cultural comfort zones, keeping hold of what (and whom) we know. Our ethnocentric perspective is so deeply embedded that for most people it is an assumed non-negotiable, but it is also a classically left brained perspective: 'I'm the centre of my universe and my view is the one that counts.' Think again of the description of the left hemisphere's 'interpreter' and 'story-teller' from Chapter 4, which is capable of filling in the gaps outside reality. Remember too that the right brain is by contrast, open to novelty and is not as likely to defend its own viewpoint.

But we can take things further. Our cultural attitudes and behaviours are very deeply ingrained and you might think that they are the deepest foundations of our lives as a society. But they are constructed on something even more profound – something that is not even recognised in ordinary life because it consists of our assumptions and presuppositions about people, the world and the universe. What is it? Our worldview. Someone has described a worldview as being like a pair of spectacles that fit so naturally that we are unaware they are there. But they give everything we see a tint, a hue, a colour that is different to the one many other people see, even though they are looking at exactly the same thing. Why? Because they are wearing different glasses. We 'see the world differently' quite literally. A worldview has been defined as *the central assumptions, concepts and premises widely shared by a particular group of people and upon which they base their activities.*[11]

The key word is assumptions, because the elements of a worldview are simply presumed to be real and there is no conscious felt need to examine them. But anthropologist Paul Hiebert describes their crucial importance:

> Faced with a bewildering variety of experiences, people continually seek to find meaning in existence and to impose order on the world. They cannot easily face the chaos of suffering and death, nor the gap between things as they are and as people think they ought to be without the conviction that these mysteries are somehow explainable ... *To lose the faith that there is meaning in life and in the universe is to lose part of what it means to be human.* There are few fears so great as those which arise when our explanation systems fail us [my italics].[12]

He goes on to depict the 'explanatory models' we all carry in our minds: models *of* reality but also *for* action – they provide the blueprints, which interpret, integrate and guide our behaviour.[13] Without these blueprints, life would make no sense (literally, 'nonsense') and would become intolerable.

> *Humans are by definition, meaning-seeking beings and the embrace of a worldview, no matter how unconscious it is, is basic and essential for them.*

How culture works

So how does all that work in practice? Lloyd Kwast worked cross-culturally in Africa for many years and developed a framework for understanding the behaviours, values and underlying assumptions associated with any given society.[14] He viewed this framework, or model, as a series of concentric circles; or better, spheres operating within each other – like a Russian nesting doll, which consists of several dolls of decreasing size placed one within another. He imagined an alien from outer space, who has never encountered humanity before, arriving at a town near you and observing the behaviour of people. The alien asks what is going on, and why. What underlies the behaviour? In the process he uncovers the layers of determining factors and processes:

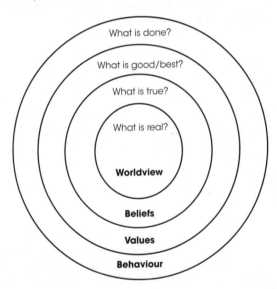

First of all, he notices that humans are behaving in particular ways. For example, every morning, they group together in moving objects that transport them quite quickly from more sparsely populated areas to places where there are lots of buildings. They do the reverse later in the day. Also, adults take smaller humans to buildings for a similar period each day. The small people move to rooms in groups and perhaps sit down in chairs in the same place every day. This is *what is being done – it is behaviour*.

The alien might then ask why such behaviour exists and conclude that humans choose certain behaviours rather than others (which they might otherwise select). Clearly they are deciding *what is best* in that context – there are *values that determine behaviour*. A value is simply something that is considered important, worthwhile or useful (i.e. it's 'valuable'). It therefore tends to be chosen above other possible but less deserving things and is shared by most if not all members of a cultural group. Those members are therefore helped to discover what 'should' or 'ought' to be done in many different situations. It helps to regulate society and encourages people to 'fit in' with accepted patterns of behaviour.

The next stage might be to try to understand why such values are considered important. This uncovers the *beliefs of the society*, namely the underlying fixed views on *what is true* about humans and their world. Such beliefs about who and what humans are may lead some people to take up weapons and kill others because they are infringing their codes of proper living (expressed through their values and therefore behaviour). Other people, because of their beliefs, may spend their whole lives amidst severe poverty, working to help others find a healthier and more hopeful life. Some (operating) beliefs are very influential, whereas others (theoretical) have little impact. For example, someone might believe that stealing is anti-social and selfish but not think twice about taking things home from the office and quietly 'forgetting' to take them back! In this case, values and behaviour do not match belief. Generally, however, beliefs determine both values and behaviour consistently and powerfully.

Finally, the alien might delve into the core of human action and belief by asking what underlies it all – *what is considered real* by a society of people? Such questions as, 'Who are we?', 'Where did we come from?', 'Why are we here?' and 'Is there any future for humanity and the universe as a whole?' are all *worldview questions*. They are not often consciously asked (in some cases, never!) but they lie at the heart of a culture and society – even deeper than the belief system, which as we have seen, includes some matters that do not make much practical difference to lived experience.

In many Western societies, there are now lots of different cultures, each with their distinct worldview. Behaviours may be shared (e.g. going to work or to school); values may be very similar (earning money in order to obtain a high standard of living; or getting a good education); but at the level of belief there is more divergence (what the fundamental basis of human life is, or what is just and true in the foundations of a society); and worldviews are fundamentally different (e.g. the nature of the universe, including life on earth and human beings; or the conviction that reality consists in more than the things we see and touch). People of differing cultures may (or may not) live peaceably side-by-side, but their worldviews are constantly in conflict. Because such worldviews are so fundamental to human life and thought – and yet so different – any one person cannot hold two conflicting worldviews simultaneously; rather, he will hold to one and reject the others.

Our worldview is the most fundamental context for meaning in our lives, since it gives us a foundation and framework for everything we experience. It addresses the most basic questions of life and by default gives us the answers – even if most of time we are unaware of both questions and answers, since they operate on an unconscious and unexamined level. The answers they provide are often incomplete and perhaps even contradictory at times, but they profoundly influence our attitudes, behaviour and life direction.

The philosophy and English literature professor James Sire offers us a number of worldview questions, including, what is prime reality; what is a human being; what happens at death; how do we know right and wrong; what is the meaning of human history and why do we need to know anything at all?[15] He adds, 'The fact is that *we cannot avoid assuming some answers to such questions. We will adopt either one stance or another.* Refusing to adopt an explicit worldview will turn out to be itself a worldview, or at least a philosophic position' [my italics].

What's your worldview?

You may never have given it a moment's thought, but here's a chance to reflect on your worldview – remember, everybody has one!

- How would you answer Sire's questions?
- What assumptions do you hold about the universe, the world, humanity and your own life?
- Why do you hold such perspectives?
- Where did you get them from?
- What impact do they have on the way you live?
- Are there any uncertainties or unanswered questions?
- How might you go about trying to address these?

Just in case you think that all this talk of worldviews is simply theoretical, here are some of our everyday sayings that unconsciously give away our worldview assumptions (you could probably think of others):

- Que sera sera, whatever will be will be
- I expect Auntie Flo is looking down on us now, isn't she?
- We're all just a collection of atoms, when it comes down to it.
- It's all written in the stars isn't it?
- We'd better just keep our fingers crossed!
- It obviously just wasn't meant to be.
- Don't worry, it'll all come out in the wash, one day!
- When you're dead, you're dead – forget all that pie-in-the-sky stuff!
- He's going to come back next time as a slug!
- All things work together for good.
- It's all coming together now – touch wood!
- She was just too good for this world.
- I sometimes feel that there's someone up there watching over us.
- Science has disproved God over and over again.
- There's a day of reckoning coming, just you wait and see.

So, how do some worldviews answer such questions?

Answers from the dominant worldview

Every culture, underpinned by its worldview, tells its own story – it is in possession of a narrative – and that story determines most of what is thought, said and done. Of course, the West is no exception and for many centuries, Europe's narrative portrayed its civilisation as the pioneer of a whole new way of life. It goes by many names, but, as we saw in Chapter 1, one of the most familiar is The Western Dream. It perhaps began with the expansion of nation states (some view Columbus' discovery of the Americas as the first stage), but accelerated with the Enlightenment, the Industrial Revolution, scientific discoveries and world domination through empire. The watchword was Progress[16] and it was applied to all aspects of life: political, economic, scientific and cultural. We are still following its trajectory and Western nations still monopolise many of these areas (although their prestige has become rather tarnished in more recent years).[17] The Progress

Story has been very resilient, but like many stories it has elements of myth to it. In fact, the Myth of Progress is precisely what some writers began to call it during the twentieth century. Throughout the nineteenth century, the myth trumpeted inevitable forward movement, through science and politics, until finally, all peoples would embrace it. That seems a little naïve now, but it took the traumas of the twentieth century to take the shine off the glossy tale.[18] However, in a somewhat more nuanced form, the myth survives as Western power, culture and commerce continue to advance.

Lying behind this narrative is a worldview, as we have seen, and it's probably fair to say that the default worldview in Western cultures is what some would call Naturalism or perhaps Materialism. It takes the view that everything that exists in the universe (including here on earth) is physical, material – matter. This perspective projects inevitable outcomes for humanity – and for you and me. So it is of more than passing importance to try to understand that viewpoint and those outcomes. Bearing in mind the kind of questions posed by Sire, Naturalism's outlook might be summed up in a number of statements:

1. Matter and energy is all there is – no other force exists.
2. Everything in life (and the universe) can be explained in material terms.
3. Humans are very complicated machines – consciousness and personhood are a function of physical forces (many of which we do not yet understand).
4. There is no ultimate future for the individual, humanity or the universe – death is the extinction of personality and individuality.
5. There is no overarching purpose or meaning in the universe.
6. Since only matter exists, there are no ultimate and objective universals such as truth, good or evil. Essentially, there is no 'ought' – only what 'is'[19]

(Here's that question again: is this more of a left-brained perspective – or right-brained?)

Expressed that way it looks somewhat dismal, and it all seems a long way from happiness, lasting or otherwise. But it's important to recognise that we are talking about worldviews, which run deeper than beliefs or values. These are assumptions and presuppositions, which are not commonly contemplated or examined – yet they form the foundation for most of what is accepted and promoted in our culture.

Some great minds of course *have* spent a lot of time contemplating them and have come to definite (if stark) conclusions. Jacques Monod was a biochemist, who was awarded the Nobel prize for his discoveries in genetics. He wrote in a book describing the chance nature of events in the universe, 'The universe was not pregnant with life nor the biosphere with man. Our number came up in the Monte Carlo game', later adding, 'Man knows at last that he is alone in the indifferent immensity of the universe, whence he has emerged by chance. His duty, like his fate, is written nowhere.'[20] Another Nobel Laureate, Sir Francis Crick (a molecular biologist) wrote, 'The Astonishing Hypothesis is that "You", your joys and your sorrows, your memories and your ambitions, your sense of personal identity and free will, are in fact no more than the behaviour of a vast assembly of nerve cells and their associated molecules'.[21] The philosopher Ernest Nagel put it more tersely, 'Human destiny is an episode between two oblivions.'

The inevitable conclusion of all this is that ultimately you and I are arbitrary splodges on an impersonal, finally meaningless canvas, where neither it nor we have any enduring purpose or consequence. This could not be better expressed than by Stephen Crane's short, simple and devastating poem:

> A man said to the universe:
> 'Sir, I exist!'
> 'However,' replied the universe,
> 'The fact has not created in me
> A sense of obligation.'

These are somewhat bleak conclusions, but they are no more than Naturalism's logical implications. The picture painted of the universe (and of humanity) is that of a great and complex machine and everything is ultimately explicable in mechanistic terms. In 1687, Isaac Newton described three laws of motion, which established a clear and rather neat perspective of how matter functions in the universe. Since then, especially with Einstein's Theory of Relativity, the Newtonian view has become somewhat modified. But the fundamentally mechanical view of the physical world has persisted – notwithstanding the discovery that at the very macro (galactic and beyond) and micro (subatomic) levels, few if any of these 'laws' seem to operate.[22]

Statements of faith

One essential consideration to keep in mind when thinking about worldviews is that *they are not empirically 'provable'*, in the sense that we moderns use the word (once again, a left-brained perspective that looks for completion and control). We talk about laws of science, which we can 'prove' (even that assertion is challenged in our day), but the more we move away from the explicitly material realm, via the emotional and relational into the assumptions and presuppositions of our worldviews, the less amenable to 'proving' they are. For example, we could not prove that matter is all there is in the universe, any more than we could disprove it – even if we could travel to the furthest reaches of the cosmos. If our method of verification is based on examining and measuring *material* things only (which is essentially all that experimental science can do),[23] we should not be surprised if we conclude that only *material* things exist. It's a bit circular. But worldview questions run deeper than our physical senses or even rational belief systems – they are at the level of consciousness and experienced reality (very much right brain territory). We therefore have to 'verify' them in a different way – and that way is more experiential and existential than empirical science enables. Monod, Crick and Nagel then, are straying into worldview terrain, not empirical science, in the quotes above.

There's a connection here with the way our two brain hemispheres perceive reality. We 'know' things or people in two very different ways.[24] On the one hand, we 'know' *facts* about things or people. If I show you a photograph of my wife, you will observe that she is of a certain height, size, hair and skin colour. I might give you some more *information* about her – when and where she was born, details of her family and perhaps of her career and lifestyle. You would begin to discover quite a lot *about* her. This is cognitive knowledge, something that the left brain specialises in. The philosopher Martin Buber called this an *'I/It'* relationship, in which the 'it' is an object – there is no personal connection. But if you really wanted to 'get to know her' you would need to actually *meet* her. But the kind of knowledge you gain of her would be very different. It would be the knowledge of *encounter*. This is not factual, but experiential. It cannot be encapsulated by objective data (it is by definition, subjective). It is your knowledge and can't be transferred to someone else. In fact, you may struggle to explain it to others ('Well, she's ... kind of like, well ... it's difficult to put into words ...'). The encounter is primarily an emotional affair and is all to do with right brain knowledge (remember Allan Schore and his right brained emotional and relational revolution, in Chapter 5?). Buber called this relationship *'I/Thou'*, a human personal connection where there is no object, just two subjects (just like the intersubjectivity from Chapter 6).[25]

So the assumptions and presuppositions of our worldview take us beyond 'empirical, provable facts' into a very different realm. We cannot prove our worldview through the left brain approach of tangible, graspable data. It transcends that domain. We hold it as a *statement of faith, a credo,* which we continue to believe without being able to 'prove' it to another person. I could *assert* that there is nothing more in the universe than matter, but I could not *prove* it by appealing only to the existence of matter. I could claim that there is no ultimate future for humanity or that there is no overarching purpose in the universe, but I could not establish it with certainty. The right brain approach has no difficulty in accepting that, since it is comfortable with subjectivity, ambivalence and uncertainty. The left brain is not.

Left brain in charge

The Hidden Spring

Tom Wright tells the story of a powerful dictator who ruled his land through a highly organised bureaucracy. Via this system he discovered that the water sources (mostly springs) had become unreliable and sometimes even dangerous. So he came up with an ingenious solution – to pave the land with thick concrete that would keep the erratic springs under control and meanwhile channel the water through a system of pipes. All went well for many years, with water delivered efficiently and well under control. But one day, without warning, water started bubbling up through the concrete from the springs that had never gone away. The whole landscape began to be disrupted, with water gurgling up through the neat man-made structures.[26]

The Naturalist perspective resonates emphatically with a left brained view of the world. Think back to the description in Chapter 4 of the way in which the left hemisphere perceives things. It processes everything in a linear, logical, analytical, abstract, systematic way and focuses on non-living, mechanical, technical elements, piecing together the whole from those parts (in contrast, the right hemisphere sees the whole picture all at once). It is at home with a machine model of reality, but uncomfortable with the awkward, messy and unpredictable real-life world.

In a section at the end of his book, McGilchrist describes what, in his view, a world dominated by the left hemisphere would look like.[27] Such a world would see greater abstraction, envisioning the world as a collection of concepts and 'things'. The mechanical would be *the* model for the living as well as non-living things – including humans. With machines, we can determine how much they can do, how fast they work and how precise they are. This, applied to the living world, would alter how we perceive it. Quantities and numbers would rule and technology would flourish. Consciousness would be altered as the mechanical and technological increased, producing an insistence on quantification.[28] Everything could be taken apart and put together again from its components.

Because of this, the world would be marked by fragmentation, comprising a collection of pieces apparently randomly thrown together. Functional processes, in a 'disenchanted' world, would replace our natural sense of wonder and mystery. This would result in a loss of meaning and of our understanding of the higher values – religion would be regarded as sheer fantasy. The impersonal would replace the personal, with a focus on material things at the expense of the living. It would be important to be in control – uncertainty would be troubling and death (so omnipresent in the real world, and the ultimate challenge to control) would be avoided as much as possible. We, like Descartes, would be more comfortable as spectators than as actors.[29]

It's important to emphasise that our post-Enlightenment view of the world has in so many ways served us well – materially. It has helped us to uncover some of the most extraordinary secrets of the universe, the world and humanity. It continues to make progress in treating and even curing disease. It has produced hitherto unheard-of wealth for many – although it also consigns others (and the planet) to a much less prosperous existence. But (and it is a big 'but') it has proved utterly inadequate to explain and promote the flourishing of those things fostered by the right brain: connection with the real world, other people and the sense of wonder and meaning in lived reality. In particular, as McGilchrist asserts, the last great bastions of right-brain superiority – the body, the natural world, art and religious faith – have suffered, and continue to suffer, under the left-brain-dominated world of the West.[30]

Nevertheless, the left-hemisphere-controlled worldview that still dominates our culture has proved itself remarkably resilient. Sire offers us two main reasons for this.[31] First, it gives the impression that it is honest and objective, since only observable facts are admissible. Secondly, it appears to hold everything together – it is seemingly coherent. It focuses on what we can perceive with our senses and our rationality and therefore we can trust its conclusions.

> *But it is the dimensions that it does not explain and deliver that leave us yearning for more.*

The Enlightenment was called as such because it claimed that human reason and rationality, supported by the scientific method, would bring light to the world and sweep away outmoded superstitions, ushering in the 'Age of Reason'. Humanity had finally 'come of age.' It's as if it says, 'Here's how everything works. We will now explain everything you need to know about the universe, the world and human beings. All questions will be answered. But if you come up with questions that require anything other than empirical science or rational thought, we will deem them to be 'non-questions', simply because it is impossible to discover rational answers – or even recognise the questions!'

It's time to revisit our guiding diagram. The main focus of this chapter has been the underlying materialistic worldview of a materialistic culture, which is entirely in line with a left hemisphere-dominated perspective on life. But it has come at a huge cost. Its inadequate, attenuated reach has left the implicit, non-rationalistic dimensions of our lives bereft, desperately seeking something more fulfilling.

One of the principal mainstays enlisted by the Western Dream

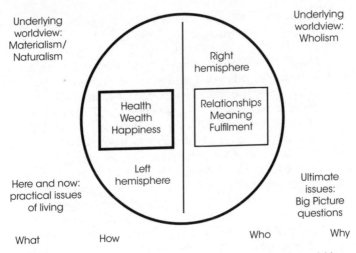

Underlying worldview: Materialism/Naturalism

Underlying worldview: Wholism

Right hemisphere

Health
Wealth
Happiness

Relationships
Meaning
Fulfilment

Left hemisphere

Here and now: practical issues of living

Ultimate issues: Big Picture questions

What · How · Who · Why

and the Naturalist worldview is science, so perhaps it would be helpful to explore that a little more. It has been, after all, at the heart of the Progress Myth and the successful narrative of the Western worldview.

The limits of science

Can science explain everything?[32] Essentially, science measures things and then develops rational theories, or hypotheses, to explain its findings. If we can't measure it, we can't construct those theories. Biology, for example, concludes from empirical evidence that human beings are very well adapted for life – we have evolved, developed and adapted certain characteristics through natural selection. Other features, less adaptive, would have led to us dying out. So we think and act in ways that have enabled our species to survive, reproduce and thrive. Social scientists take this further. They say that our social structures (kinship groups, institutions like marriage and family, etc.) have evolved as 'constructs' that have enabled humans to flourish.

That is all very well. But it's not really enough to get us leaping out of bed every morning with the cry, 'Wow – I'm well adapted, and my social constructs have enabled me, with others, to develop successful kinship and bonding!' We need something a little more personal and compelling to get us going, connecting and achieving.

McGilchrist picks up the dissonance ironically between our

lived experience and a sheerly technical perspective, linking it with left hemisphere values:

> Beauty...is a way of ensuring that we select healthy reproductive partners; bravery acts to defend territory in the interests of the gene pool; intelligence leads to power to manipulate the environment, and one's fellow creatures; holiness is an invention designed to promote cohesion of the group; and so on – the arguments will be only too familiar. Those who are not relying solely on their left hemisphere's construal of the world will detect the fraud instantly ... (O)f all the myriad sources of beauty in the world, sexual partners can only form a small part, and even there beauty is not the same as sexual attractiveness. It is just that they fail to convince: back to values – which ultimately lie beyond argument. *Rationality is, naturally, reluctant to accept the very possibility of a thing lying beyond rationalistic argument* [my italics].[33]

Science is very good at observing, analysing and theorising about human life. But some would say that it isn't great at taking us towards a deeper understanding of life. It can propose mechanisms that attempt to explain our lives. It can unpack and analyse – but it is perhaps better at taking apart and inspecting than putting together for a whole explanation. And we shouldn't blame it for that, since its focus is on the 'What' and 'How' questions that we encountered earlier (What tangibly is it we are dealing with here; how does it work?).

> *But it was not intended to tackle non-physical (i.e. metaphysical) questions of 'Who' and 'Why' (Who am I anyway, and why am I here – what is my purpose?).*

Other authorities may lay greater claim to that, for example, philosophy or faith.

There was a period in the early twentieth century when a philosophical movement called Logical Positivism declared that anything that could not be empirically and objectively proved (i.e. by science or rational thought) should be ruled inadmissible and thrown out of court (religion at the top of the list). But the movement fizzled out, because it became apparent that everyone had their own set of presuppositions and subjective perspectives and prejudices and so it was impossible to prove even the Positivists' own assertions! The emergence of Einstein's theories and Heisenberg's Uncertainty Principle has pretty much swept away such pretentions.

Science measures *quantities* (the left brain loves quantity). What science cannot measure is *quality*, for example, entities like happiness, love, hatred, truth or transcendence. These qualities happen to be among the deepest and most significant elements of life (the right brain loves quality). Though their *effects* can be measured and quantified (the words and behaviours exhibited by a happy person or by someone who claims spiritual experience), the qualities *themselves* lie beyond the reach of science. Questions such as 'Who am I?' 'Why am I here?' and 'What is the meaning of life?' cannot be answered by science and technology. They are existential issues, requiring radically different approaches, mediated primarily through the right hemisphere.[34]

An attenuated worldview

In our post-Enlightenment world the elevation of the 'what' and 'how' of Naturalism, with a corresponding reduction in the 'who' and 'why' of alternative paradigms, has had some interesting consequences. Here is Charles Darwin's experience.

> Up to the age of thirty or beyond it, poetry of many kinds … gave me great pleasure … Formerly pictures gave me considerable, and music very great, delight. But now for many years I cannot endure to read a line of poetry … My mind seems to have become a kind of machine for grinding general laws out of large collections of facts … *The loss of these tastes is a loss of happiness, and may possibly be injurious to…the moral character, by enfeebling the emotional part of our nature* [my italics].[35]

Vladimir Lenin is quoted as saying, 'I cannot listen to music. It makes me want to say kind, stupid things, and pat the heads of people. But now you have to beat them on the head, beat them without mercy.'[36]

Our Modern worldview can only take us so far towards fulfilment. It has little in it to meet the deep felt needs in human beings, for it is just too thin, attenuated, monochromatic, one-dimensional for the task. The word attenuated means, 'to make something thinner or weaker'.[37] Have you ever used Blu-tac? It is used to stick paper or card onto the wall. It has the texture and consistency of chewing gum and stretches out in a similar way if you pull on it (though a little more hygienically!). As the strands stretch out they become thinner and therefore weaker – they are attenuated.

That's the picture I carry in my mind as I think of the limitations and inadequacies of Naturalistic materialism. It addresses some questions (mostly those within the material domain), but comes up far too short on the others: emotionally, relationally, socially, communally, spiritually and existentially. It cannot see beyond the material horizon – in fact it refutes the very idea that there *is* anything beyond that. It cannot satisfy the longing of the human heart – it just doesn't have the equipment to do so. When the Enlightenment unceremoniously jettisoned all talk of the transcendent – anything that lies beyond 'plain sight' – it consigned a whole civilisation to a deliberately limited view of the universe. We are today in desperate need of a worldview that is broader and deeper and that addresses implicit as well as explicit issues. As Einstein once remarked, 'A perfection of means, and confusion of aims, seems to be our main problem.'

That makes today's discoveries and conclusions make very interesting reading, for example the commonly used expression, 'transpersonal' in psychotherapeutic practice,[38] or the discoveries of right brained perception and function. These do not necessarily 'prove' that there is 'something beyond' but they are subversive of the reductionistic assertions of deterministic materialism.

Summary

All societies are characterised by a set of attitudes and behaviours known collectively as culture. Cultures are holistic and embrace the whole of life, connecting and integrating all elements of the society. Cultural practices are underpinned by beliefs about people and the world, which in turn rest upon unconscious and unexamined assumptions and presuppositions, termed a worldview.

Every society tends to view its culture as superior to others, and of course Western civilisation is no exception. Its worldview understands everything that exists in material terms. This has much in common with a left-brained perspective and of course works itself out in all areas of life, promoting primarily material values and behaviours. Our culture cries out for something more, as we shall see in our final chapter.

EIGHT

FINDING OUR WAY

'Every ant knows the formula of its ant-hill,
Every bee knows the formula of its beehive.
They know it in their own way, not in our way.
Only humankind does not know its own formula.'
Fyodor Dostoyevsky

'Those who have a 'why' to live, can bear with almost any 'how''
Viktor Frankl

Introduction

'Are we nearly there yet?' was a question we often heard from the back of the car when our daughters were young, as we drove to another part of the country. The problem was that we had only been driving for thirty minutes and we all knew it would be hours before we got to our destination! So, like most parents, our creativity was tested to the limit to find fun ways of passing the time. How many things beginning with 'X' can *you* think of for 'I spy' as you drive down the motorway?

In the Introduction, I proposed a journey towards lasting happiness and wellbeing, and I wonder now what you've made of it. The family journey I just mentioned lasted just a few hours, but for most of us, getting to our destination in life is a trickier business. That question, 'Are we nearly there yet?' evokes some deeper reflections about what our lives are about. Not that we're very sure where or what 'there' is, but we do want to know something about the destination – or perhaps the better word is destiny.

As we've journeyed through this book we've explored the notion that we call happiness and seen that it can mean so many different things to different people in different situations. It's used a lot in our contemporary culture – perhaps overused to the extent that it loses a fair amount of its currency. Wellbeing perhaps gets closer to our goal of lasting happiness, but that turns out to be rather awkward to define.

We humans are creatures of longing and seem to desire so much more than we can obtain – but much of what we long for appears to stay just (or a long way) out of reach. This longing though has a connection with the part of our brain (the right hemisphere) that connects with the real world – what McGilchrist calls the 'Other'. A connection that we usually *do* achieve is with other people, though our capacity to do that depends significantly on our experiences in very early childhood. And the way we conceive ourselves, the world and the cosmos also profoundly impacts what we hope and dream for, and what we actually achieve in life.

That's a brief summary of the last seven chapters. In this concluding chapter I want to try to draw these various strands together and offer my own perspective on what makes for a life-well-lived – what enables us to discover lasting happiness. But first, that other metaphor from the start of the book – narrative or storyline.

Who doesn't love a good story?

I wonder what your favourite story is? One of mine is *The Lord of the Rings* by J. R. R Tolkien. It's one of the few books I've read more than once, so that probably tells you something about me and my predilections. (I've read it three times, which is no mean feat, since it's 1,077 pages long, if you include the Appendix! A friend of mine confessed a few years ago that he'd read it fourteen times – mostly when he was quite young!) Why do I like it? Well, it's a really good read and I found myself getting lost in all the plots, subplots and adventures. But more than that, although we all know that there aren't actually any hobbits around these days, it's what they represent that has always inspired me – their ordinariness and apparent insignificance and vulnerability, combined with their amazing warmth, courage and resilience. We can identify with them very easily and, in a way, they represent much of what is good about human beings.

We are all fascinated by stories and it seems that every culture engages in storytelling. Psychologist Dan McArthur has specialised in studying the significance of stories among different people. He believes that we all develop life-stories that integrate our past, present and future, 'to provide a life with unity, purpose and meaning.'[1] He equates our sense of identity with our inner story – 'a person's life story is 'inside' him or her'.[2]

So we carry within us a narrative that tells us both who we are (our identity) and why we are here (our purpose or meaning). It is rooted in both our personal history and the shared story of our culture.

Another psychologist, Robert Emmons, puts it this way, *'Humans are the only meaning-seeking species on the planet. Meaning-making is an activity that is distinctly human'*.[3] He has demonstrated that we develop goals, which come in four main departments:

1. Work and achievement
2. Relationships and intimacy
3. Religion and spirituality
4. Generativity (i.e. contributing to society and leaving a legacy)[4]

Interestingly, they don't all carry the same weight. People who prioritise achievement and wealth are less happy than those who focus on the other types.[5]

We all have a story to tell, and everyone's story is both unique and valuable. According to physician Lissa Rankin, telling our story to others is good for our health, since it lowers our levels of stress hormones and releases others like oxytocin and endorphins.[6] And Daniel Siegel reports that 'the best predictor of the security of our children's attachment to us is our ability to narrate the story of our own childhood in a coherent fashion.'[7]

Telling your story

Suppose you had to tell your story in only four minutes – what would you say?

What would be most important to include?

Would it be just a matter of facts (when and where I was born, where I've lived, the jobs I've done)…

Or would you include other deeper things, like…

- What has become most important in my life?
- How have I changed over the years – and why?
- Who has been most significant for me – and why?
- What kind of legacy will I leave behind?

When we tell our stories, we tap into all the different levels of our lives – the everyday *chronos* periods, the dramatic *kairos* episodes, relationships that matter to us and perhaps the deeper, meaningful dimensions of life. They connect very powerfully with much that we have explored in this book and certainly relate to lasting happiness. But stories come at very different levels, from the individual and personal right through to the communal and global.

Stories: Big picture and local

Of what story do you feel a part? Obviously, there's your personal story. Then there's your family's story – not just your immediate relatives (parents, siblings, children) but beyond that too. You may be aware of your grandparents' histories, although not many of us can go back much further than that, extending beyond living memory. There's also the community of which you are a part – traditionally that's been geographical (village, town, district), but today it may be more of a functional or occupational matter. But there's a story there anyway. And beyond that lies your nation's (hi)story; things that give you a sense of identity, that you're proud of – or maybe, not so proud. Then of course there is the human story, going back generations and millennia. And we are all part of that, although it becomes a little more distant and mind-boggling when we try to imagine life in far distant times – or countries (after all, there are over seven billion of us now!).

But there is further we can go – the big picture story of the world (4.5 billion years old) and of course the universe (13.8 billion years!). Just by existing, our universe creates a story (as do we all). We may not be able to say much about it experientially (life began 3.8 billion years ago, but humans have been around for only 200,000 years – occupying just 0.4% of the earth's timespan!) but we are discovering more of it year by year.

In the Introduction I proposed that every culture possesses a dominant narrative, a storyline that connects all the parts and gives meaning to the whole plot. Without its interpretation and explanation everything is simply a collection of random and perplexing events, lacking any overall meaning. Any narrative about our *lives* is likely to shape, even determine, how they should best be lived, so we do well to reflect on what such a narrative is about. According to culture-watcher Tom Sine, *'Whatever vision we embrace as the good life and better future determines what is really important to us. What is important to us directly determines where we spend our time and money'*.[8]

Narratives generally have a script, and the Western world's storyline has a very particular one, as we investigated in our Introduction. I suggested that it could be summarised with the words, 'health, wealth and happiness', but that many of us are not finding this mantra strong, deep or durable enough for all the dimensions of our lives. The problem is that it seems to be the 'only show in town'. That isn't necessarily true; there are other narratives – they just don't get much airtime!

The technical word for such a storyline is metanarrative, which is 'an overarching account or interpretation of events and circumstances that provides a pattern or structure for people's beliefs and gives meaning to their experiences'.[9] It's the Big Story that underlies other stories. We're back to worldviews again. We don't think about them much but they are the foundation for all that we believe and therefore how we live our lives. They matter. We looked at our culture's dominant metanarrative in the last chapter.

My contention is that although our culture's metanarrative explains some of what we are, think, feel, know and do, it falls lamentably short in those domains that mean most to us – relationships, meaning and the longings of our hearts.

However, anyone raising questions about these fundamental matters of life will not usually find deeply satisfying responses, other than that human evolution has produced such desires in order to propagate the species – a somewhat circular explanation! Remember McGilchrist's comments in Chapter 7 on the solely technical perspective of left hemisphere values? 'Beauty, for example, is a way of ensuring that we select healthy reproductive partners; bravery acts to defend territory in the interests of the gene pool – the arguments will be only too familiar. Those who are not relying solely on their left hemisphere's construal of the world will detect the fraud instantly'.[10]

In recent years, a further development has occurred, through what is called Postmodernism. But we will not find much comfort there either, because in the famous words of one of its founders, Jean-François Lyotard, 'I define postmodern as incredulity toward metanarratives'.[11] His reasoning was that metanarratives claim too much for themselves and that in any case they are exploitative and oppressive, because they marginalise and dominate other storylines. Postmodernism asserts that no one has access to ultimate reality 'out there' and so we should stick to our own local stories, giving equal significance to each one. There is undoubtedly value to such an approach but it should be said that 'local' narratives can be just as oppressive (think ethnic cleansing or apartheid) and Postmodernism is in fact another metanarrative that is anything but local, since it makes very totalising, if not domineering claims about the whole cosmos – and other metanarratives!

Mechanisms – or more?

I beg to differ, and propose that metanarratives are not only real, but are actually central to what it means to be a human being. To quote Emmons again, 'Humans are the only meaning-seeking species on the planet. Meaning-making is an activity that is distinctly human.' Just as we all possess a worldview, we also follow a metanarrative (although most of us wouldn't think of it that way), because the two are intertwined and perhaps are simply alternative ways of expressing the same thing. But if we are told either that the Big Story is simply impersonal materialism (Naturalism), or worse, that the question of whether there is a Big Story at all is a non-question (Postmodernism), it's no wonder that as a culture we are confused and anxious. It's very interesting that many of today's most successful novels, fantasies, dramas and films focus not on the Modern age, nor on the Postmodern, but on the *Pre*-modern age – especially the late Medieval period (why are shows like *Game of Thrones* so popular?). It's as if we yearn nostalgically (remember our longings in Chapter 3?) for a time when the narrative was less complex and confusing. The plot is clear (down-to-earth good versus in-your-face bad); the battles are straightforward (lots of swords and spears); and we know what a hero is supposed to be like (brave, with uncomplicated convictions). Even in futuristic science fiction stories, the plot and the characters' characters (if you see what I mean!) are actually much the same.

Incidentally, very few people I know live strictly and consistently out of a materialistic, naturalistic worldview. Many of us see human life, relationships, and issues of truth, justice and meaning, in practice, as based on more than a collection of atoms vibrating together. Although the party line remains that that is indeed the basis of everything, I suspect that elements of other more personal metanarratives are (un)consciously smuggled in, while still maintaining that there are ultimately no such things as personhood, morality and universals like love and hope.

Naturalism and its derivative Postmodernism make dogmatic claims about the universe, humanity and me. But just because one storyline dominates the horizon doesn't mean that it is the most appropriate one – the one that fits life, experience and the universe best. Still less that all our lives should be determined by it. *We can choose another if it works better.* Of course that will have significant implications for how we think about the cosmos, humanity and our own lives – our relationships, priorities and direction in life. But that's the point: metanarratives, big picture storylines and worldviews come as a package. You can't pick and choose – at least, not if you want to live a connected, integrated, wholistic life.

We need a more complete storyline

So, if the grand narrative we've lived under for many years isn't up to the job, we need to find something better – a framework, a mental model, a paradigm that takes account of all that we have explored and discovered in this book so far. We need a storyline that recognises that life satisfaction is not built simply (or primarily) on material health, wealth and pleasure, but also emphasises purpose and meaning. One that elevates relationships, attachment and intersubjectivity and is able to fulfil the yearnings of the human heart. A narrative that works for every part of life and prioritises right-brain mindsets, not just left-brain. A hermeneutic, interpretative framework that is big, broad, deep and wholistic enough to do the job that a worldview should accomplish.

> *The contrast is between utterly different worldviews. One is reductionist, that is, it breaks the whole into small parts and then builds up a picture from those parts. The other is wholistic – it starts with the whole picture (a story, in fact) and applies it to all situations. Once again, the handiwork of left- and right-brain perspectives is writ large!*

I suggest that such a framework needs to have at its heart two fundamentals:
1. Personhood: the relational dimension that addresses the *who* question.[12]
2. Purpose: the meaning component that satisfies the *why* issue.[13]

As a wholistic metanarrative, it has to attend to and explain not only the material realm, but also relationships and all the other human activities that give us satisfaction and keep us well. Think again of those extraordinary statements about relationships in Chapter 5: the intersubjectivity of minds in 'interpersonal communion'; the amazing connection between mother and child – so close that it is referred to as 'mochild'; the way in which a damaged and distorted personality can be healed through committed and attuned empathy; and the increasingly compelling 'sense of an overarching interpersonal oneness process' as our minds and bodies resonate together – not just within the individual person but also between people.

It must also go deeper still to satisfy the deepest human longings and give meaning and purpose to our lives. Remember from Chapter 3 the awareness we have of what life should be like, and yet as we attempt to fill the gaps with 'things' we are left with an ache that won't go away? The storyline must bring satisfaction and hope to our own individual lives; yet also span time and beyond to account for all that preceded us and will continue after we've passed out of the picture. It must attempt to account, not only for all the *good* in life, but also the *pain*, grief and sorrow that all of us experience. That's a tall order and only a worldview that integrates wholistically can do it.

You may remember the 'signposts for the journey' I wrote about at the end of Chapter 1, comprising those two words, connection and integration. We are in fact, deeply *disconnected* in our culture today and long to bring together the strands, themes and elements that are separated in our lives, to generate something whole and meaningful. Only a wholistic storyline can do this. I call it a 'hermeneutic of life' and it needs to be strong, broad and consistent enough to bear the strain of real-life living, with all its competing streams and strands. Yet it must also be able to connect with and integrate that dimension of life, which seems so often to evade us – the realm of the transcendent and trickier-to-grasp-hold-of domain (so amenable to right brain thinking) that many would call the spiritual.

Going against the cultural grain

If the views of McGilchrist and Schore are even remotely near the mark, then the focus for our attention should land more on the realm of real-life, relational, emotional, meaning-making and trans-rational living. To use expressions like trans-rational, or going deeper than the rational sounds strange to us, but that is the implication.

> *It means that experience, emotions and the imagination take primacy over rationality, cognition and intellect. This is so counter-cultural that we struggle to even entertain the idea that it could be true.*

In a culture that is heir to Plato and Descartes (remember his [in]famous phrase, 'I think, therefore I am'?), which elevates rational, intellectual, left-brained cognitive thought, it goes entirely against the grain. But relationship, meaning, longing and fulfilment are to be discovered from another source – the territory occupied by right-brain perspectives.

The saying, *'the unexamined life is not worth living'* is attributed to the Greek philosopher Socrates, after he chose death rather than exile or agreeing to silence his views. It's quite a strong statement: if you don't examine your life, it's not worth living it! Isn't that a bit too strong? I'm no philosopher, but I am convinced that to go through life without spending time reflecting on one's own life and that on planet earth in general, *is* something of a waste. It might simply be that we are lazy and we don't want to bother with 'deep' things. I've mentioned already the response of some people to my co-worker in developing the ideas behind The Happiness Course. But it may be subtler than lethargy and indolence. We may be reticent to delve deeper into our own or humanity's more profound secrets because we sure about what we will find and we're afraid of what it might do to us or require of us when we get there.

The deeper you journey into the issues of life the more meaning, purpose and explanation you require. What do I mean? Well, if you're eating an ice cream or enjoying the beach in summer, everything is fairly obvious and explicit – you don't need much philosophical insight! That's the Pleasant Life. Go a little deeper and appraise your job, relationships or general direction in life – well, that requires more contemplation and reflection. Welcome to the Engaged Life. But when you ask the really deep questions of life, like 'Who am I?' 'Why am I here?' and 'What's life really all about?' you enter much more challenging territory. The need to understand is there (you could call it longing) but the explanation demands more from us. And when you encounter pain, loss and suffering, the questions become loud, insistent and anguished cries – but the replies seem muted, even silent.[14]

Do you really want to explore the Meaningful Life? It will be more costly – but ultimately more worthwhile. Lasting satisfaction has many components to it, and some of them hurt.

How then to find our way?

The Hidden Spring

The most beautiful thing we can experience is the
mysterious.
It is the source of all true art and science.
He to whom the emotion is a stranger,
Who can no longer pause to wonder and stand
wrapped in awe
Is as good as dead – his eyes are closed.
Albert Einstein, *Living Philosophies*

In Chapter 7 I retold a parable first related by Tom Wright. It's about how pesky springs of water kept bubbling up and interfering with the well-organised systems of a very controlling dictator. What I didn't reveal at that point was Wright's interpretation of his allegory: 'We in the Western world are the citizens of that country. The dictator is the philosophy that has shaped our world for the last two or more centuries, making most people materialists by default. And the water is what we today call 'spirituality', the hidden spring that bubbles up within human hearts and human societies'.[15]

Despite Naturalism's best efforts to keep such spirituality tightly in check, the springs continue to gurgle. Various surveys have placed the number of people who call themselves 'spiritual but not religious' at from a fifth to over a third of the British population[16] - and of course that doesn't include those who would classify themselves as 'religious'. Wright continues, 'The scepticism that we have been taught for at least two hundred years has paved our world with concrete, making people ashamed to admit that they have had profound and powerful "religious" experiences'. The dominant worldview has declared, "We will pipe you the water you need … 'religion' will become a small sub-department of ordinary life; it will be quite safe, harmless in fact … Live as if the rumour of God had never existed. We are, after all, in charge of our own fate! We are the captain of our own souls".[17] But now the hidden springs have erupted and nothing can be the same again.

The writer Philip Yancey adds his perspective on spirituality.

'Many people ... still linger in the borderlands because they cannot set aside the feeling that there must be a spiritual reality out there. Maybe an epiphany of beauty or a sense of longing gives a nudge toward something that must exist beyond the everyday routine of life – but what?' [18] It is with such yearnings in mind that I offer the following.

An ancient yet modern way: Hebraic living

We all have a worldview or big-picture narrative, with all its presuppositions; so it's time for me to declare mine. My presuppositions are monotheistic, and specifically Judeo-Christian.[19] Theism is a belief in the existence of a god or gods and monotheism proposes just one God (with a number of characteristics) who is not only the creator of the universe but also sustains it.[20] The monotheistic worldview has a number of foundational tenets, just as any other does:

1. At the heart of the cosmos lies, not simply matter, but personality.
2. The universe is not eternal – personhood is. This personhood is the source and sustenance of all that is.
3. The universe, the world and humanity are not an arbitrary collection of meaningless matter, but a meaning*ful* and complex structure, made for purposes, both evident and as yet unclear
4. Human beings are not a random 'blip' or 'blop' of matter but persons, whose entire essence reflects the personhood of their maker. That shared personal nature means that people are able to share relationship with their creator
5. There is connection and integration to the cosmos and life on planet earth. Humans are not the centre of all that is, but on the other hand, they have profound inherent significance because they share the personhood and purposefulness of the person who is their source.
6. Relationship is at the core of existence, for the individual, for human communities and for the whole of the cosmos.[21] Everything is connected, whether in a human personal way, or across the universe. [22]
7. Wholistic wellness (summed up in the word *shalom*) applies to all domains, whether it's the whole of your life today, the whole of human life, or the universe as a whole.
8. The universe, the world and humanity, though made to

be whole and functional, have become distorted and dysfunctional. Humans experience suffering, grief and sorrow, but that is not the intention of the person who brought it into being – nor is it the end of the story.[23]

I appreciate that these are huge statements, which beg many questions. This is not the place to attempt to justify them all. They are no more or less 'scientifically provable' than the list of characteristics of Naturalism in Chapter 7; in either case, they lie much deeper than anything empirical science can 'prove'.[24] My intention is to lay out what seems to me a plausible and workable worldview that enables us to move beyond the limitations of our contemporary narrative. But I don't think you need to share my worldview to benefit from the principles and practice outlined in the previous chapters. On the contrary, I believe that they stand up in their own right – you don't have to be a member of any particular group to experience those benefits. We can flourish in life (i.e. find lasting happiness) as long as we follow the guidelines of relationship, meaning and fulfilment. But we will not necessarily discover a whole, joined-up and ultimately meaningful life without some reflection on our beliefs and worldview, to bring all the elements of our life together – connected and integrated.

So my final version of our now-familiar diagram looks something like this:

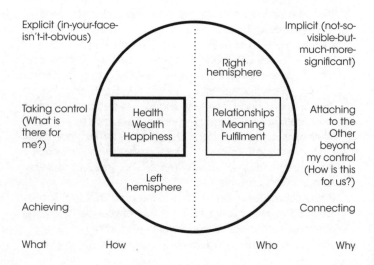

The difference between this final version of the diagram and all its predecessors is that the line between the two parts is dotted. It indicates that the separation, discontinuity and dichotomy is abolished and the two sides – whether expressed as material/non-material, separate/together, left/right brain hemispheres, or health and wealth/relationships and meaning – are brought together as distinct but integrated and harmonious parts of the whole. It must surely be possible to live a connected, joined-up, integrated and wholistic life, as our universal longings indicate. But we can only do this if we embrace a worldview that provides the foundation for such a life – not one that divides and separates mind/body, visible/invisible, physical/metaphysical, material/spiritual.

A wholistic perspective

Imagine a world...

What would life be like if all things were 'as they're supposed to be'?

Try to describe what that would look like....

- Personally
- Relationally
- Amongst your family and friends
- In your community
- In the world as a whole?

Why is it that we know what 'life as it's supposed to be' is like, anyway ?

There are two Hebrew words, which for me exemplify the wholistic nature of the Hebraic worldview. They are *tsedek* and *shalom*. The first of these is usually translated 'righteousness', which for most us is likely to conjure up images either of some pompous and dogmatic religious zealot, or an austere judge, passing down decisions on people who have little or no say in the matter! In fact, although the word does have ethical and judicial shades of meaning, in the first place, righteousness is *relational*.[25] It is derived from a word meaning 'straight', and our English word comes from the Latin translation 'rectitude', meaning a straight-edge. In other words, righteousness (or living right) involves a *relationship* with someone who is essentially *straight*, not bent or crooked – uprightness, if you like – and impacts every part of life. The word justice is derived from the same root word, straight. Justice is therefore all about straightness internally (another word for integrity, really) and externally (right relationships, both personal and communal).[26]

Shalom is usually translated today as 'peace', but it has a much broader and deeper meaning than that. It can be translated as 'health, welfare, safety, tranquility, prosperity, rest, harmony, and absence of discord'. The root verb *shalem* means to be *complete, perfect and full*.[27] Theologian Perry Yoder assigns *shalom* to three major areas of life.[28]

1. The first is *material* wellbeing and prosperity – the basic 'okay-ness' of our material and physical lives. The fundamental meaning is one of abundance, conveying the sense of being safe from threat and sound in our being.

2. Secondly, it is a *relational* word and expresses the state of affairs that develops when individuals, communities or even nations are in healthy and harmonious relationships. This 'okay-ness' of right relatedness includes justice and health-through-relationships. Its close connection with the relational basis of righteousness is beautifully expressed in the psalm, 'Love and truth meet in the street, *tsedek* and *shalom* kiss each other'[29]

3. Finally, *shalom* has to do with *ethical character* – integrity of attitude and action that makes living straightforward and rewarding. It's the opposite state of affairs to that in which we have to say, 'Well, it's all a bit tricky between us at the moment – you see, it's … complicated!'

(Notice that although this many-sided definition of wellbeing has *quantitative* aspects to it, its primary nature of one of *quality – especially regarding relationship, connection and integration*. It gives precedence to a right-brained perspective rather than a predominantly left-brained one).

So my working definition of *shalom* is:

Wholeness for the whole person in the whole of life, extending to the whole of the cosmos!

That's a pretty comprehensive definition! It's quite a contrast with the pessimistic words of health expert Allan McNaught, who we met in Chapter 2. His verdict on the definition of wellbeing is that 'the search for a generally accepted definition is fruitless, frustrating and ultimately impossible.' Perhaps this illustrates how a left-brained process of breaking something down into its constituents and then trying to piece it all together again is indeed 'frustrating and ultimately impossible', whereas a right-brained approach sees the whole picture and applies it to real-life contexts. Moreover, the scope and reach of *shalom* equates very closely with Martin Seligman's description of the Full life (also from Chapter 2), which is his attempt to bring together the Pleasant, Engaged, and Meaningful lives.[30] The difference though is that *shalom* goes much further than simply adding those different lives together. Rather, it describes the way in which *everything* in life can be connected and integrated wholistically (remember where we started in Chapter 1?), with my wellbeing linked with yours, the rest of humanity's, and ultimately with all things that exist! It even echoes the WHO definition of Health that we highlighted in Chapter 2: 'Health is a state of complete physical, mental, and social wellbeing and not merely the absence of disease or infirmity.'

The way things ought to be

A right-brained, wholistic summary of it all might be *the way things ought to be*. We all have a remarkably clear idea of what that looks like, whether it has to do with our own inner lives, our relationships or the world at large. It seems to be hard-wired into us, as if we intuitively recognise right-ness and wholeness when we encounter them. To try and show how *tsedek* and *shalom* belong together, here's an illustration. I enjoy coming back home after a trip away. But the safety and comfort that my home affords is dependent on two things. First, the structure of the house needs to be strong and secure – that's like *tsedek*, with its straight, robust and trustworthy security (who wants the wall to give way when I lean against it?). But secondly, I need to fill that structure with décor, furnishings, music and food – and people – so that I can feel 'at home'. That's what *shalom* is about. And when *tsedek* and *shalom* 'kiss each other' our yearning for 'homecoming' that we encountered in Chapter 3 is finally fulfilled.[31] What then, if C. S. Lewis's evocation of beauty as the 'scent of a flower we have not found, the echo of a tune we have not heard' was not simply sentimental wishful thinking, but a longing for something that is, after all ... real?

Just supposing that....

- This amazing cosmos we live in isn't simply some random, impersonal accident, but has purpose to it?
- All that yearns within us for hope, continuity and homecoming is real – we feel these things so deeply because they're connecting with something that really exists?
- These few decades of life aren't all there is – there's more beyond?
- There really is a 'home' to come to – somewhere to which our physical and family homes point?
- My personal narrative is integrated – all of a piece – with the big picture storyline?
- Our strong sense of justice and goodness points to a time when good finally triumphs over bad?

An integrated life

So, I've spoken about my grand storyline, my big picture narrative – the one that I find more convincing and relevant than the alternatives. You may well disagree. I don't mind. My purpose in this book is not to manoeuver you into agreeing with my underlying presuppositions, but for us to explore together pathways to healthier, more satisfying and sustained, joined-up living.[32] I hope that it has helped you to spend time reflecting on your own life and the foundations that underpin your everyday living.

I've used the word integration throughout the book because a life that consists of fragmented and disconnected parts is more likely to frustrate and confuse than bring us a sense of satisfaction and fulfilment. We sometimes talk of work-life 'balance', but that invokes for me the image of someone staggering around trying to keep all the parts of their busy life from falling apart, like balancing a precarious pile of books (which, for many of us, may well be the reality!). I think a better word than balance is *integration*, where we're not weighing one thing against another, almost like a competition, but where all the elements work together. I remember as a doctor treating patients who were so ill that the different organs of their bodies had ceased to function in an integrated way, perhaps because of severe infection or other trauma. Without rapid and drastic intervention the patient could not survive. The different parts of our bodies need to function together – heart, blood vessels, brain, bones, all working in harmony, integrating their various activities. It's called homeostasis and it keeps our whole beings in a healthy state. And if that's true physically, it's also true for the other dimensions of our lives.

So I'd like to offer a simple but profound image or metaphor, which may help you to bring about that integration. I call it 'The Tree of Life', or if you prefer, 'The Wellbeing Tree'.

Tree of life

I live in an inner London borough, which sounds rather urban and built-up. It is, but I am very fortunate to have a beautiful park at the end of my garden. Amongst its many striking features is the large number of trees of varying kinds and sizes. Watching them change from season to season has given me a real love for them. The thing about trees is that they give so much to us. Around the world, they provide shade, residence, fuel, food, oxygen, medicine, water, soil security – they even regulate the weather! The list goes on and on, and unless one actually falls on you, they have almost no negative effects. But they are also a very instructive metaphor. It's been a while since I studied any biology, but if my memory serves me well, there are three basic parts to a tree. In English, it works quite well: roots, shoot and fruit!

The *roots* are essential for the tree's life – it can't survive without them. They absorb water and nutrients from the soil and pass them on to the rest of the tree. But they do more – they give a solid and secure foundation to a plant that might climb tens of metres into the air. Even when storms batter the tree, it stays rooted in the ground. Generally, the roots go down and out as far as the branches go up and out, enabling them to spread far and wide. But the other key point is that by and large they are *hidden* – no one sees them and everything goes on under the surface.

From the root system grows the trunk of the tree (what I'm calling the *shoot*, because it fits well poetically). This is the key supporting structure of the plant since it bears the whole weight of branches, foliage and fruit. It therefore needs to grow *strong and straight*. If it doesn't it won't be able to sustain the load laid on it. Through it flows the whole life of the tree and year-by-year it expands so that the tree can develop and produce more fruit. It's not particularly glamorous, as the leaves and blossom are, but it is the strong, supportive and resilient part of the plant, on which everything else rests.

Above and beyond the trunk lie the branches, which extend upwards and outwards, giving the tree its characteristic size, shape and colour. A tree in full blossom is an amazing sight and at that point no one looks any more at the trunk, or even the branches (and they never get to see the roots anyway). It's the leaves, bloom and *fruit* that now interest everyone – the very *visible* outcome of all the unseen work beneath. Yet without the roots and the shoot, none of it would exist. All the parts of the tree have a function and those functions are crucial for the plant to flourish.

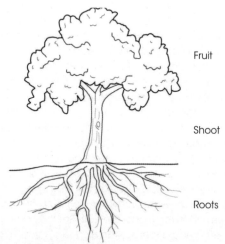

Fruit

Shoot

Roots

And now for the application...

You can probably see where I'm going with this – and perhaps also why it's such a powerful illustration of life and wellbeing. Just as the tree's health depends on its *roots* for health, so too we need an underground system to sustain us.

It is that which is invisible to others that either gives us strength and stamina, or saps and pollutes our vitality – it's our root system that matters. What we tap into in the unseen places will inevitably flow into the more visible, public spheres of our lives.

What is your *root* system like? What (or who) do you turn to when you need resourcing? Will that sustain you through the tough times? The soil around a tree's roots is crucial. If it is healthy, it will provide all kinds of nutrients to bring life and fruitfulness to the tree; but if it is polluted and toxic the poison will inevitably spread to the whole of the tree. Health professionals speak of 'mental hygiene' to describe how we keep our minds fit and healthy in parallel with our bodies. What we invest in during the routine times (when the pressure isn't on) will in due course reveal itself in our external lives, for good or ill. Road rage results from unseen, buried anger that suddenly and violently breaks out very publicly. Of course, the opposite is true too – spending time cultivating healthy, positive traits will stand us in good stead when the pressure comes.[33] Lasting happiness or fulfilment arises out of a healthy inner life nurtured throughout a lifetime.

The *shoot*, or trunk of the tree is more visible than the roots – it represents our lives 'on show.' As we've observed, it is totally dependent on the roots for stability and for life, but it has purposes of its own. The trunk has to stand up straight – otherwise the whole tree will collapse! And as we've seen, the word 'right' or 'upright' is derived from a word meaning 'straight'. So, for us, 'living (up)right' involves developing the inner strength and resilience that enables us to stand straight and resist the inevitable stresses and strains of life that would otherwise knock us over. Many of us struggle to maintain that 'straightness'. We bend into to others' criticisms and pressures or to the critical voice within us that we encountered in Chapter 6; or perhaps cave in to the social mores around us that undermine our personal integrity. The secret is to nurture the kind of character traits that will enable the 'straightness' to emerge – traits like patience, perseverance, forgiveness, honesty, generosity and hope. Another way of describing this 'straightness' is the 'self differentiation' that we explored in Chapter 6.

In a sense, the whole purpose of the tree is to bear *fruit* – to reproduce. That's a striking image for our lives too. Just by being alive, we all have an impact on the world and on other people (see the next section). Many of us would not see ourselves in that way, but if we were to ask our family, friends and work colleagues what our influence has been on them, we might be more than a little surprised! Very often, those verdicts aren't voiced until we die, when the speeches that others make about us are filled with gratitude and appreciation. If only they had said it when we were alive! I'm always struck by what people say on the news when they talk about colleagues or loved ones after a tragic death: 'They were always kind and thoughtful ... they'll leave a hole in our lives that can never be filled ...'. I wonder, had they expressed this to them at a point in their lives when they could receive it directly – and live in the good of it? Our lives will produce fruit, whatever we think about ourselves. The question is, what *kind* of fruit will it be – health-giving or toxic?

In a way, you could view the tree metaphor as our familiar circle diagram turned clockwise by 90 degrees. The outer, more visible aspects of health, wealth and happiness equate to the visible fruit and branches of the tree. But dig deeper beyond the trunk or shoot of the tree and you arrive at the hidden but vital roots. These are equivalent to the more profound relational and meaningful dimensions of our lives. They are the source and resource for all that is visible, but are more implicit and hidden than the observable components.

Leaving a legacy

We underestimate our impact on other people. Edmond Locard was a pioneer in forensic science (he was called the 'Sherlock Holmes of France') and played a key role in establishing fingerprinting in criminology. He used to say that *'every contact leaves a trace'*, meaning that no matter how light the touch, we will always leave some mark behind.[34] Speaking of the contact that a criminal makes, which is later picked up forensically, he writes,

> Wherever he steps, whatever he touches, whatever he leaves, even unconsciously, will serve as a silent witness against him. Not only his fingerprints or his footprints, but his hair, the fibres from his clothes, the glass he breaks, the tool marks he leaves, the paint he scratches, the blood or semen he deposits or collects. All of these and more bear mute witness against him. This is evidence that does not forget.

What a powerful testimony to the way in which our words,

choices and actions leave behind a legacy, which outlives us, perhaps by many years! So, again, it's worth asking, what is the fruit of your life? What will be left behind after you have moved on? What will be your legacy? You would probably need to ask other people what they think – it's difficult to grasp it for yourself. We talk these days of our 'carbon footprints', but what about our 'life footprints'?

Your legacy

My working definition of 'heritage' is that which has been passed down to us (e.g. English Heritage is a charity in the UK, which manages historic sites that have been passed on from previous generations), whereas 'legacy' is perhaps what we pass on to others ('He left a legacy of millions of pounds to his children').

- What heritage did you receive from others?
- What kind of legacy will you leave behind you?
- 'Every contact leaves a trace.' So, what kind of 'contact' do you make with others each day? What kind of trace is it leaving?

I call the metaphor the Tree of Life because that seems to be appropriate for our wellbeing. It's not original of course – it comes from the beginning of the Bible, where it represents the source of life and hope for human beings.[35] But you could equally name it The Wellbeing Tree, because it means pretty much the same thing. There are other parallels between trees and our lives, and here's one. If the tree is to flourish all its parts and systems must work together. For the roots to function without reference to the trunk would spell catastrophe, as would the branches separating their life from the main trunk. The tree exemplifies *wholistic, integrated living* and that applies to everything in nature. But we humans often live disconnected, fragmented lives, in which (as we saw in Chapter 1) our material, physical compartments have little connection with the emotional, relational or spiritual aspects of our lives. Lasting happiness or flourishing will not develop without us finding ways to integrate all the parts of our being.

More applications

There are many other ways in which the tree metaphor can be applied. Following are some that link with dimensions we have already considered in earlier chapters.

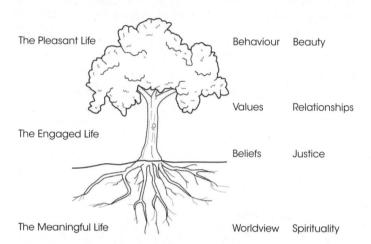

The Pleasant Life   Behaviour   Beauty

Values   Relationships

The Engaged Life

Beliefs   Justice

The Meaningful Life   Worldview   Spirituality

Just as the *roots* of a tree lie unseen beneath the surface, so too does the source of our lives. They aren't on show most of the time, but in a way, they are the most important part of our lives. They represent our *worldview* – that which makes our lives meaningful. We are wise to give that thought and attention, for if it gives way the whole structure collapses. That word 'source' is a significant one. Just as a river has a source, providing all its resources (both words have the same origin, the Latin verb, *resurgere*, 'to rise again, spring up anew';[36] to 'resource' of course means to 'source again'), we too have a 'source'. It provides not only physical, material resources, but also emotional, relational and spiritual supplies too. It's well worth reflecting on what they are and how to access them. For me, the ultimate source is spiritual.

Out of our *worldview* (what is real) emerge our *beliefs* (what is true), like the *trunk* springing out of its root system and becoming more visible. You might equate both our worldview and beliefs to the Meaningful Life. We face the world with our beliefs, engaging with it as a whole and with other people – our Engaged Life. On this basis we live according to *values* that we and most other people in our culture follow. Our consequent *behaviour* flows from those values and beliefs.

For many of us those behaviours form part of the Pleasant Life.

Tom Wright has identified four areas of concern in our culture: the quest for spirituality, the longing for justice, the hunger for relationships and a delight in beauty.[37] He suggests that they all point beyond themselves and we hear them as if they are echoes of a voice that comes from just around the corner, out of sight.[38] I find a link between them and the tree metaphor. The 'Hidden Spring' of *spirituality* that we encountered in Chapter 7 is like the roots of a tree, or the source of a river, or the foundations of a building. It is the source of life and without it all seems dry and barren. Out of this grows *justice* or right(eous) ness (remember that the two words share the same Latin root meaning of straightness). We cannot achieve justice without inner straightness – in other words, integrity – since (up)rightness is all of a piece with justice.[39] Like the tree trunk it must grow straight and true – otherwise the whole structure will collapse. Further, we cannot attain to healthy *relationships* without justice, but if the trunk is strong and straight, those *relationships* will flourish, like the foliage of a tree – they cannot long survive duplicity and dishonesty. The outworking of truth and openness of relationships will in turn bring *beauty* and fruitfulness, just like the blossom and fruit of a tree.

Your Tree of Life
Roots
- What has given you rootedness in your life?
- What's the soil like – what are you surrounded by that either sustains or stunts you (e.g. supportive relationships and trusting community; or cynicism and bitterness)?
- What would make you vulnerable to being uprooted – and what prevents that happening?

Shoots
- Do you have a straight or crooked 'trunk' ('straight' might include characteristics such as integrity, faithfulness or authenticity; 'crooked' might involve selfishness, arrogance or cynicism)
- What do others say about your character?
- How might you improve your 'mental hygiene'?

> **Fruit**
> - What does a 'fruitful life' look like?
> - Suppose someone was to take a bite from the 'fruit' of your life (via your words, attitudes, actions, etc.). What would that 'taste' like and what long-term effect would it have on their lives (toxic or nutritious)?
> - How could you become more fruitful?

Conclusions

Fifty years ago, Paul Simon wrote the song, 'America'.[40] In one verse he tells his girlfriend that he's empty and aching, but he doesn't know why. And all those people driving down the toll road seem to be just as lost – they're looking for America too.

Can we find lasting happiness? I believe the answer to that question is a definitive 'yes', but we need to decide what sort of happiness we are talking about. If it's primarily a matter of material health and prosperity, then Western society has much to offer – or at least to aspire to. The in-your-face and isn't-it-obvious world of the material (and the brain's left hemisphere) presents itself as the only real and valid way of living and flourishing. Could there possibly be anything else as important or relevant? Well yes, actually, there could. It's less explicit and obvious, but it turns out to be more profound and lasting in the long run. It's the not-so-visible-but-much-more-significant domain of interpersonal connection, deeply rooted community and an overarching and transcendent life purpose – the world of the right brain. Yet this is the very sphere that is under severe pressure today.

The contention of this book is that our prevailing culture promotes an incomplete material utopia because it is based on an impoverished worldview that is itself entirely materialistic. This leaves many people longing for more than that offered them by a society that advocates happiness primarily in economic and material terms. An alternative storyline is urgently needed.

The longings of the human heart are only satisfied by a vision that resonates with the deepest hopes and dreams we all carry within us. When Martin Luther King gave one of the most famous speeches of all time in Washington in 1963, he did not simply list a number of grievances that black people had.[41] He couched his message in terms of a story, a vision – a dream. He painted a picture. And what was he dreaming of? Relationship. Community. Reconciliation. Hope. Direction. Purpose. *Shalom*. As social scientist Jean Elshtain put it, 'His speech would never have seized the nation if he had stood before the Lincoln Memorial and stated, 'I have a preference. I have a personal preference today.'[42]

There is a direct link between longing, story, vision, dream and fulfilment.

We long for life 'as it should be'. But our contemporary (meta) narrative cannot deliver that wholistic vision, which transcends (but includes) the limited, partial vista of twenty-first-century culture.

Our experience of hopeful nostalgia and deep aching for home is not simply some random artifact. Our yearning for what I'm calling *shalom* is not arbitrary or anecdotal. I believe C. S. Lewis was right to suggest that our present experiences of things such as beauty are not the ultimate end, but rather 'the scent of a flower we have not found, the echo of a tune we have not heard, news from a country we have never yet visited.'[43] Martin Seligman (not a religious person, as far as I know), speaking of the Meaningful Life, declares, 'It consists in attachment to something larger, and the larger the entity to which you attach yourself, the more meaning in your life.'[44] I couldn't have put it better myself. And that 'larger entity' is in my view, a person, since it is only persons who can create, discover and experience the most important dimensions of life – relationships and meaning.

The writer and speaker Rob Bell contrasts the two conflicting worldview perspectives via a kind of dialogue.[45] One person, aware of 'something more' in life, attempts to explain his viewpoint: 'I just sense…'. The other replies, 'Do you have any evidence? Any proof? Any photos? Anything you can test in a lab?' 'No.' He ends up having to use words like 'sense, feel, trust, believe…' Two vastly divergent worldviews are at play here. One asserts that 'this is all there is – it's all we can prove or know empirically.' The other is in the awkward position of being definitively convinced, yet unable to do more than talk about nudges and hints and senses and beliefs. Experience and encounter seem inferior to solid, empirical rationality. And yet, as we have seen repeatedly with left versus right brain perceptions, the audacious claim emerges that the 'inferior' is more connected to reality – despite its inability to articulate and rationally describe all it knows. For its knowledge is that of experience and connection and the Other, not the ivory tower of virtual and disembodied rational knowledge.

This book is called *Lasting Happiness*. It seems reasonable to conclude that *only those things that are both good in themselves and enduring will bring us lasting happiness*. So, what is good that lasts? Not 'stuff' – by definition, it is short-lived. Even our careers will transition into retirement. And we usually discover late in the day that the temporary things we first relied upon do not persist indefinitely. Solid relationships, a life well lived, transcendent and purposeful living, a legacy passed on to others – these are surely more durable. So here's the key question: in your life, what is good that is going to remain after the transitory matters have faded?

It seems that Edward Hallowell was right. The two elements of a successful life consist of connecting and achieving.[46] We need both to be fully human. But the foundation and heart of it all is not the achieving part, for any achieving without connection is in the end an empty chalice. Connection is at the centre of being human and the persons and principles with whom we choose to connect will determine the course of our lives and result either in lasting happiness or lasting unhappiness. If the deepest human longing is to 'come home' to a person, a people and a place called home (summed up in the words relationship, meaning and fulfilment) the question remains, who is there to come home to, with whom do we journey, and what is that destination of home ultimately all about?

I'll end with this extract from an interview with an eighty-five year old woman from the hill country of Kentucky[47] (what do you think, does it resonate more with the left brain – or the right?).

If I had my life to live over

If I had my life to live over, I'd try to make more mistakes next time. I would relax … I would be sillier than I have been this trip. I know of very few things I would take seriously … I would be less hygienic. I would take more chances. I would climb more mountains, swim more rivers and watch more sunsets. I would eat more ice cream and fewer beans. I would have more actual problems and fewer imaginary ones.

You see, I am one of those people who live seriously and sanely, hour after hour, day after day. Oh, I have had my moments, and if I had it to do over again, I'd have more of them. In fact, I'd have nothing else. Just moments, one after another, instead of living so many years ahead of each day. I have been one of those people who never go anywhere without a thermometer, a hot water bottle, a gargle, a raincoat and a parachute. If I had it to do over again, I would travel lighter … I would start barefoot earlier in the spring and stay that way later into the fall. I would ride more merry-go-rounds. I'd pick more daisies.

THE HAPPINESS COURSE: MAKING THE JOURNEY

I began this book by inviting you on a journey towards lasting happiness. You'll probably agree that the route has had plenty of twists and turns along the way. In fact our whole life is something of a journey, which certainly has many ups and downs. We all have a unique story to tell and it's been a privilege for me to listen to many of them as people have shared their own story in The Happiness Course. Our stories are not all about constant unbridled happiness and as I've hinted at before, it isn't necessarily 'happiness' that emerges at the end. It may be something much deeper, even if it is mixed with less positive emotions. Here's a part of my story with The Happiness Course.

A short history

For many years I led a church community in southeast London, whose orientation was very much outwards, towards our local community. We experimented with a number of initiatives, seeking to serve the people of whom we were a part. One year, I remember taking a three-month sabbatical[1] after several years of working, to give space for thought, reflection and study. Such times are really valuable because they give an opportunity to ponder your life and work. The many 'lists' favoured by our left brains (Jill Bolte Taylor's brain chatter) are quietened, giving our right hemispheres a chance to hear the deeper and quieter voices that usually get drowned out by everyday concerns.

That was definitely my experience and I emerged from the sabbatical with a phrase ringing in my head. It was all to do with how our group might connect with and serve others more effectively. It went something like this: 'Whatever else we do, we need to be relevant. We need to 'scratch where people are itching'!' Not very erudite perhaps, but it summed up what I felt then, and still feel. Interestingly, I discovered that others had had similar thoughts, and so out of the discussions that followed a community initiative emerged. It was called 'Healthy Brockley', which was a play on words, since we were situated in Brockley, part of the borough of Lewisham – and of course 'broccoli' represents something very healthy!

It's not difficult to picture where people are 'itching' in Lewisham: housing, employment, financial issues, stress, anxiety and depression, relationships, parenting – the list is long. But how we 'scratch' is another matter. We were not a particularly large group but we did have talents and abilities. And so the Healthy Brockley initiative developed across three dimensions. First, we held a number of Healthy Brockley Days in the primary school where we normally met, running a mini-festival, with all kinds of activities, ranging from bouncy castles and free smoothies to face painting and ballroom dancing! We invited all the neighbours round and the school was full of local people throughout the afternoon. We also hosted many of the local community groups and societies to set up their stalls. A significant number came and it was very gratifying to see how all these groups were able to connect with local people. It felt as if we were being community connectors.

The second aspect of the initiative consisted of several community activities, ranging from lantern-making at Christmas, Red Nose Day and The Big Lunch celebrations, to summer fetes and children's events. Any excuse to be out there engaging with others. The third facet was down to me. I began to run a number of courses for the community, including relationships, parenting, money- and stress-management courses, as well as opportunities for life coaching for individuals. Most of these courses were sourced from other organisations, and I 'cut my teeth' through running them – with some success.

Through the Healthy Brockley initiatives, we linked up with someone whose job it was to run health and wellbeing programmes for the NHS. This introduced me to the emerging discipline of Positive Psychology. As I read about the research and interventions that were developing, studying how gratitude, nurturing relationships, forgiveness, volunteering and many other activities promoted happiness and wellbeing, my immediate response was, 'These people are doing the work for us!' Together with a colleague I then began to put together a four-session course that drew on such work. We called it 'The How of Happiness'. Through a local council grant, I then began to run pilot courses – and was amazed by the response I received from participants. They were eager to discover ways of growing their wellbeing, but more, many seemed desperate to find out how their lives could become more meaningful. They seemed like people struggling in a desert, frantic for water. It wasn't so much material, physical issues that troubled them, but rather the emotional, relational and meaningful dimensions of life.

In this way, The Happiness Course emerged – as the pilot course came later to be named. As I began to take the course to different contexts, first in London and then beyond, I encountered a similar response: 'This is really important – tell us how we can access more of it!' I was struck by the strongly felt need amongst many people for something that went beyond the materialistic diet that we are fed day after day. It was as if they were saying, 'We're hungry – we need something more than what we're offered'. In particular, the focus on finding ways to nurture relationships and discover meaning and purpose surfaced as most important for many.

Over the past eight years or so, I have run the course scores of times, in community centres, youth clubs, schools, children's centres, businesses, NHS contexts, parent/toddler groups, churches, homes – the list goes on. I have taken it to Europe and even to Africa! My experience in all these settings is similar: human beings are essentially the same wherever they live, and all of us want to experience some degree of happiness, success, healthy relationships and a sense of meaning and purpose.

Today, I work for much of my time with the charity Livability, as part of their Community Engagement Team. Livability took up the course and now trains church members to run the course themselves locally. At the same time I also continue to run the course in the many other contexts mentioned above.

What does the course look like?

The four-session course is a tried and tested approach based on scientific research and real life experience that people can apply in their daily lives. Its aim is to facilitate a journey, starting from the relatively superficial experience of pleasure, via the perception of success and the challenges and joys of relationships, to the deeper mysteries of meaning and purpose. The course may be short, but the journey goes far and deep!

There are four sessions. The first, *A Happy Life* starts off with questions that most of us are interested in: 'What makes you happy?' 'What is happiness anyway?' 'Are we happy today, and if not, why not?' In this session, we explore some of the factors influencing all our wellbeing, and how we might respond to them.

The second session, *A Successful Life*, asks a different question – not, 'What makes you happy?' but, 'What exactly is the Good Life?', or a life well-lived? Our Western societies tend primarily to give a material answer, but there is often a downside to this response. We probe a little deeper into 'success' and ask whether there are more fulfilling ways of spending our lives.

Relationships always figure prominently in any discussion on happiness, so our third session, *A Relational Life*, explores this aspect. Why are relationships so important to us, and why are they so challenging? What improves them and how can we develop healthy relationships? What part does forgiveness play? What about relationships in our communities? The journey has now taken us to some profound and taxing areas of life!

The final session is called *A Meaningful Life*. It builds on the previous sections, but goes deeper still. What is most important in our lives and what gives us meaning and purpose? We arrive at questions about who we are, why we are here, and what we might do with the rest of our lives. We don't presume to give all the answers to these questions, but we do try to encourage people to ask themselves about areas of their lives that often remain unexplored.

Features of the course

First, there is *learning:* information is given about happiness and wellbeing, both personal and societal. Many people find this information new and surprising.

But the primary aim is not so much to impart information as to facilitate the participants in their *own journey*. This is the second dimension: how is your own wellbeing and how can it grow? Questions arise as the course proceeds, such as, what makes you happy? What and who have influenced you over your life journey? How can you grow in character? What are your relationships like, and how might they develop more healthily?

There is also a *corporate* dimension. Even though participants spend just four sessions together, a rapport quickly builds and many find themselves sharing at quite a deep level as time goes by. It is therefore important to promise confidentiality from the start. This gives people the confidence they need to be open in what they share with others.

Finally there is a *longer-term* dimension. At the end of the course, many people ask if they can carry on meeting. A fifth session has therefore been developed, offered at around three or four weeks after the main course finishes. This gives everyone an excuse to meet up again, but also to both review how they have grown and changed and to give an opportunity for some mutual coaching for extended development.

Happiness – the Next Steps: the follow-up course

There is often a call to take things further, so a four session follow-up course, called 'Happiness – the Next Steps', has been constructed. The first course aims to help people reflect more deeply on their lives, reassess their life's direction and plan constructive ways forward – in other words, to grow in happiness and wellbeing. So, taking that as its starting point, the second course picks up each session's themes and takes them further. So The Happy Life now becomes The Unstressed Life, The Successful Life becomes The Well-lived Life, and so on. This is how the sessions pan out:

1. **In Control – or Out of Control? (The Unstressed Life)**
    Unpacking the three levels of happiness (Pleasure, Engagement and Meaning) we aim to show how each level works. What is helpful about them and how can we all deepen our happiness? Stress is the great happiness-buster, so what can we do to relieve stress in our lives?

2. **Frustrated – or Fulfilled? (The Well-lived Life)**
    Can I find success in the whole of my life, not just the physical and material? What does such 'whole-of-life' living look like? Will I look back on my life in the future and conclude that it was fruitful? Why does gratitude have such amazing power? And can I manage to live my life according to my key priorities?

3. **Communication – or Conflict? (The Harmonious Life)**
    What are the ingredients for a healthy relationship? What are the barriers? How do I communicate more effectively? Why is listening so powerful? Can I bring balance to my strained relationships?

4. **There must be more to life than this! (The Deeper Life)**
    We're often in such a hurry that we don't discover the deeper keys to life. So we end the course by exploring what

it means to live out a full and whole life, and how we can find fulfillment for the longings within. Finally we discover how to set a direction for the rest of our lives.

How does it work?

Both courses can be run in a number of different ways. Typically each session comes at weekly intervals (e.g. Tuesday mornings, Friday evenings, etc.). This enables participants to reflect on what they have learned and experienced and put into practice the outworkings of the reflective exercises – there is even 'homework' to take home and work on. (This is *not* academic! It consists of further reflections to help people think through important aspects of their lives and begin to establish new and helpful patterns).

But there are other ways of timing the sessions. The first two sessions can be run together, say, on a Saturday, with the remaining sessions coming on the following Saturday. This packs the course into just two weeks, and gives participants a rich experience for longer in a given day. I have even run the course over two consecutive weekdays, which is a little intense but keeps the focus going well. But my favourite context is a weekend retreat, in a delightful country setting, where for 48 hours, people can take time over the sessions and pass the rest of the time walking amongst nature!

The sessions are very participatory, with plenary periods interspersed with opportunities for personal reflection, and pair- and group-work. It is not all thinking and discussing, since there are hands-on group activities as well. Group members receive handouts, which are really worksheets to make notes on and help to process what they are experiencing. At the outset, I emphasise that no one is under pressure to contribute or share anything that would make them feel uncomfortable. In practice, of course, a good rapport develops within the group and there is plenty of discussion. The sessions last for anything up to two hours – which sounds like a long time but I often find that I have to bring proceedings to a conclusion myself because there is so much interaction going on!

Frequently asked questions

1. **Will you guarantee to make me happy?** That rather depends on what is meant by 'happy'! Most people who complete the course tell me that it has helped them, that they understand better how to make helpful changes in

their lives, and that it gives them practical ways to make those changes.

2. **Why is each session as long as two hours?** The sessions are not simply lectures in how to be happier! They involve a lot of personal reflection, pair and group discussions, exercises that develop wellbeing – and quite a lot of fun! I generally find that as the course progresses, most people want more time, not less!

3. **I find the information surprising – how do I know it's reliable?** The data is taken from reputable sources and surveys. The research is accessible via books and articles.

4. **What about the science?** The growing, well-respected area of psychology known as Positive Psychology concentrates not on fixing things that are 'wrong' with people's minds, but studying how to help us all flourish. Scientists are presenting credible research findings that uncover which factors are directly linked to happiness. This latest research tells us that happiness is strongly linked to our personal and community relationships.

5. **I don't want to share too much personally.** No one is required to say or share anything with which they are uncomfortable. If anyone feels awkward about disclosing anything about themselves, they are completely free not to do so. What I find though, as the course develops, is that people do share about themselves. But it's important to emphasise that anything said in the sessions is kept confidential to the group.

What people say about the course

At the end of each course, participants complete an evaluation form, giving their perspectives on how the course has gone, their learning and expectations for the future. There is also space for them to expand on their reflections, and many of the comments are really inspiring. Here is a selection [my italics]:

> Great – a fascinating, interesting, informative, meaning-ful course. It gave me more light and direction.'
>
> 'It has opened my eyes to things which I never thought of as consistent with happiness before.'

'Thank you, I have taken loads of notes from you which I will reflect on in changes to my life. You explained these views very very well. Like a life coach. Thank you, Andy.'

'I will be more aware of my personal choices and will try to concentrate more on making the difference. Thanks for making me feel welcome.'

'It made a very big difference. I'll think more carefully about the decisions that I make and I'll always keep in mind how these decisions can affect others.'

'It made me consider how to make myself more happy by just appreciating simple things in my life. It made me think about deeper things that matter in life.'

'Brilliant. Wow! Well done! I'll be passing on my learning to others. Thanks very much.'

'Thank you Andy for a very varied course, lots of different teaching methods, a gift to everyone who attended.'

'It has changed my life.'

Summing it all up

I've run the course many times now. It has enabled me to reflect a lot on the issues of wellbeing and satisfaction in life. I've listened to many people's joys, anxieties and life perspectives. Although I didn't plan it this way, the course seems to divide into two sections. The first (Sessions one and two) focus on what happiness is, its different components and the aspects that our society prioritises (mostly positive emotions and pleasure). The limitations of that become apparent – it's as if these first two sessions clear the ground in preparation for the later sessions.

The second section consists of the last two sessions. Session three receives the most approbation, since it digs deeper into how we connect (or not) with others. I remember one time, running through the part that encourages us to forgive people who have hurt us. One woman in her seventies left the group in tears. Later she came back, saying that she hadn't been offended, but the memory of her divorce thirty years ago had started to surface. Another woman responded, 'Yes, I never knew that it was possible to forgive. Thank you for giving us practical ways of doing that.' Finally, Session four raises questions about who we are and what our lives are really all about and people often report that they have been able to process important issues from the past and set goals for the future.

So if I were to sum up what the course is about and the key lessons from it, I would put it this way. There are two ways of approaching life. The first is primarily about 'getting'; the other prioritises 'giving'. They are very different, and the research definitely favours the latter in bringing greater wellbeing and life satisfaction. Here's how they go:

Getting...

1. A Happy life: through *pleasure and fun.*
2. A Successful life: comes through *stuff and status.*
3. A Relational life: you'll get it as you get the *(wo)man and satisfaction.*
4. A Meaningful life: consists of the *latest experiences.*

All these bring happiness and satisfaction – up to a point. But ultimately they lead to a sense of frustration and incomplete fulfilment. So, is there more?

Giving...

1. A Happy life: comes through *giving thanks* for all the good we have received
2. A Successful life: paradoxically, we find success as we *give away* (time, talents, even money, through a generous spirit)
3. A Relational life: to find fulfilment in relationships we must be willing to let go rather than grasp – we need especially to *forgive*
4. A Meaningful life: the paradox continues – we receive most in and from life, not as we keep as much as we can, but as we *give back* to others

Evaluation: Results

Here are the results of the evaluations of some recent courses:

1. Were your **expectations** met? **96%** say 'yes'

2. How useful did you find the course **materials**?
(10: very; 0: not at all) **7.9**

3. Which parts were **most valuable**?
32% say 'relationships'

4. Which parts were **least valuable**?
63% say '**none**'

5. To what extent would you agree with following statements (10: very; 0: not at all):
I better **understand** things that affect my happiness **8.2**
I feel better **equipped** to develop my happiness **8.1**
The course has **changed** my outlook on life **7.8**

6. Would you like to attend a **follow-up** course?
88% say 'yes'

KEYS TO MOVE US TOWARDS LASTING HAPPINESS

I'm not a big fan of lists of things to make you happy. They always seem too reductionistic, like a recipe for success or a template for joy, or some such thing. However, some attitudes and perspectives really do seem to make a difference to our wellbeing. They range from the obvious-and-why-don't-you-just-do-it via the challenging-but-achievable to the profound-and-totally-demanding-but-utterly-fulfilling! As we've seen, that requires more of us than just practising a few exercises every day. So here are some of my suggestions. I'm using as a framework the four words I applied to the guiding diagram throughout this book: what, how, who and why.

1. Learn to handle the 'What'

Our society majors on the tangible, explicit, material dimensions (the 'what') of life. The pressure to overdose on them is enormous, so learning to handle them healthily and responsibly goes a long way to growing wellbeing in all domains of our lives.

Cover the bases with the basics: Some practices are foundational and apparently obvious, but it's amazing how many of them we simply ignore or neglect. We have no excuse these days for not knowing about the enablers of physical health. Remember for example, the list of very doable activities we encountered in Chapter 2: sleep, exercise, a balanced diet and daylight.

Take delight in the (apparently) small and everyday matters of life: That cup of coffee, glimpse of morning sun, smile from a friend, kindness of a stranger, beauty of autumn mists, bravery of emergency services that you saw on the news when disaster struck...The list is endless. Savour and enjoy the good things you encounter every day.

Appreciate and enjoy what you have, rather than hankering after what you don't have: We spend so much time wishing we had more (and are daily encouraged to think that way by the culture in which we live) that we often fail to appreciate what we *already* have. The fact that you have a body (I remember a friend once telling me that she woke up every morning, saying, 'Thank you God for my arms'!), a home and possessions is a cause for celebration, not complaint. It all depends on how you look at your experience, from either the perspective of 'deficit' (focusing on what I lack) or 'abundance' (what I have). So take a moment now to list all the things you can call your own and express your thankfulness for them in some way (perhaps by taking a few minutes to talk to someone about them).

Manage our materialistic culture: The ubiquitous nature of materialism means that we are saturated with messages telling us that we need 'more'. Finding a stronger alternative narrative (one that arises from our deeper Who and Why perspectives) will help us to resist the outworkings of this insidious storyline. Paradoxically, loosening our grip on stuff will enable us to view materialism for what it is, and substitute a more sustainable and satisfying lifestyle in its place.

2. Grow in the 'How'

Practice inner hygiene: While physical health is important, it isn't the only 'hygiene' we require. Health professionals talk of mental hygiene and that's a helpful term. We all possess well-worn negative mental mindsets, so acting into them will help us experience more inner stillness and contentment.

So 'stepping to the right' (see Chapter 4), giving precedence to our right brains over the ceaseless chatter of our left brains, will help us to develop those calmer mindsets. Mindfulness has shown itself to be an effective approach, but there are many other simple ways to bring tranquility within, for example, putting the electronic screens away, relying less on technology and more on our direct, unmediated experiences of people and the world around, and practising empathic listening towards other people. Gratitude and an attitude of appreciation towards the good we have received are especially powerful agents of wellbeing.

The capacity to make choices, as we've seen, is amongst the most significant of human attributes. We are all capable of making positive, healthy choices, which actually change our brain structure and function. Making the same choice daily over two months will establish a habit enduringly, which in due course will radically shape our character – i.e. the kind of people we become. So decide today what choices you are going to make regarding your material priorities, mental condition and people-concerns. If necessary, call on others' help to make those choices stick.

Character development is more important than skill or technique. So growing authenticity and integrity in work, relationships and life generally will provide a strong and solid platform for the whole of your life. Developing such foundations will in due course cultivate wholeness and fulfilment. The psychoanalyst Donald Winnicott coined the term 'true self', as distinct from a 'false self'. He saw the false self as a defensive façade, behind which people hide their pain and anger, but which leaves them feeling dead and empty. In contrast, although cultivating our true or authentic self involves taking the risk of becoming vulnerable towards other people, ultimately it creates lasting health and satisfaction. How can you grow such a true, real self?

Facing life's issues and challenges, rather than running away from them, will in the long run bring us hope and fulfilment. That is by no means easy, but it is much more likely to steer us towards health and healing. In particular, that uncomfortable and confusing place of 'not knowing' which often leads us to act in ways we later regret, can be the point at which we grow and change for the good (another *kairos* moment). We struggle with a relationship and are tempted to abandon it. We experience failure and rejection, and therefore decide to jump ship instead of sticking with the pain of disappointment and finding a way through it. We lose someone close to us and start to walk down a pathway of emotional desensitisation and inner withdrawal. Or we just choose internally to become cynical about life, rather than staying vulnerable but still open to hope. Staying with the not-knowing may paradoxically become the gateway to restoration and hope. As the children's song goes, we can't go over the deep, cold river or under the narrow, gloomy cave – we simply have to go through them![1]

3. Prioritise the 'Who'

Prioritise people over things: Not many people on their deathbed lament the millions they never earned or the university degrees they never obtained. Most people say that they wished they'd spent more time with family and friends. Pursuing healthy relationships will cost you time, energy and perhaps material luxury, but it will bring you a very different kind of reward – wellbeing today and fulfilment tomorrow.

Become the kind of person other people want to be with: This has a lot to do with character development as outlined above. Someone who has nurtured their authentic true self (along the lines of self differentiation described in Chapter 6) is likely to be able to sustain strong and lasting relationships. Focusing on other people and their joys and sorrows is an effective route to maturity in ourselves. This of course does not mean that we deny or neglect our own needs and desires – it simply places us in a position to limit self-focus and opens us up to robust and healthy mindsets and behaviours.

Finding someone you can trust to share yourself with is probably one of the keys to life satisfaction – even though the pathway will involve pain and frustration. Such a person of course doesn't have to be perfect, but they do need to be willing to listen (not just keep giving you advice), empathise and be on your side. Of course, it's also worth asking the question whether you are like that towards others!

Paradoxically, with relationships, as with so many other things in life, letting go is often the pathway to greater possession. Parents who freely release their children and friends who are not possessive of others are more likely to find their relationships maturing and flowering than those who cannot let go. This is what it means to be generous of heart, a giver rather than a taker. Forgiveness is perhaps the deepest and most significant outworking of it, but everyday acts of kindness also cultivate an attitude of open-heartedness.

Finding a place and people to belong to is not necessarily a top priority in our individualistic culture, but the experience of corporate social connection is one of the keys to wellbeing. 'It is not good to be alone'[2] is primal and primary testimony to the need for and power of community. If you are isolated, you are at significantly greater risk of physical, mental, emotional and existential disease. So making the choice to connect with others *will* make a positive difference to your happiness. Just one encouragement however – choose your connections thoughtfully and carefully.

4. Discover and live out of the 'Why'

The Holocaust survivor Viktor Frankl wrote, 'Those who have a "why" to live can bear with almost any "how".' Our 'why' is probably the most important part of our lives, for without it life literally becomes meaningless. And yet many of us would probably say that we don't really know where to start with it. Here are some pointers.

Don't make happiness your central life pursuit: Life is full of paradoxes. This is one of them. The more we chase happiness the more it eludes us. So find something deeper and more lasting as your number one pursuit in life. Happiness, or more likely, contentment and satisfaction will follow.

Reflect on your life: the philosopher Socrates is credited with saying that 'the unexamined life is not worth living.' In the rushed life that so many of us live today, there seems to be no time to just 'be' and give time for reflection. But we lose so much that way, especially concerning the long-term and the big picture of our lives. So take some time off (preferably amongst nature, away from the routine of home and work) and give yourself time to reflect, contemplate and meditate on what is deeper and more implicit. What are your long-term hopes and dreams? How would you like to be remembered? What or who could guide you to find out?

Decide on your life priorities: Somebody once said that the main thing in life is to keep the main thing as the main thing. But what is your 'main thing'? How might you decide to put 'first things first'? What *are* those first things anyway – your most important life priorities? Matthew O'Reilly is a paramedic working in New York. In a video talk he speaks about the three sayings that he has heard repeatedly from dying people.[3] They are, the need for forgiveness; the desire for remembrance by someone else; and the craving for meaning, for significance – that their existence matters. Let's not wait until we're on our deathbed before we give those necessities some consideration.

Work out your life's vision: Some people find talk of 'vision statements' something of a turn-off, but the principle of having a vision for your life is a good one. The futurist Tom Sine writes, 'Whatever vision we embrace as the good life and better future determines what is really important to us. What is important to us directly determines where we spend our time and money'.[4] Something will inevitably fill our vision whatever we do, but if we do not take the trouble to ponder it, someone else's vision (most likely our prevailing culture's) will probably take centre stage. So take some time to think through what you most want your life to be and do.

Find answers to life's big questions: For me, the top three are 'Who am I?' (Identity); 'Why am I here?' (Purpose); and 'What should I then do?' (Destiny). I can't think of anything more important than discovering answers to these questions. I believe there are answers to be found. But many of us don't feel we have the time or the inclination to look for them – until grief and loss ambush us and force us to engage with them. But why wait until you encounter such a crisis? Invest time and contemplation in discovering answers to the question 'why.' You may be surprised by what you find.

Find an integrating framework to your life: We all need a framework that joins and holds together the many separate dimensions of our lives. As we've seen throughout this book, the context that our culture provides is largely inadequate for that. So find a worldview, a narrative, a hermeneutic that connects and integrates all those disparate elements – one that addresses and answers the what, how, who and why questions of your life.

NOTES

Introduction

1. 30 October 2017.
2. Thomas Hardy, *The Mayor of Casterbridge*.
3. A narrative is a storyline that connects fragmented elements and gives meaning to the whole plot. It interprets and explains events that might otherwise be random and confusing. It's important to add, though, that you don't have to subscribe to my worldview to gain benefit from the different principles and practices referred to throughout the book.
4. Viktor E. Frankl, *Man's Search for Meaning* (Rider: 2004), pp. 12-13.
5. Philippians 4:11-12.
6. Michelle McQuaid, 'Do Happiness Interventions Really Work?'. Interview with Sonja Lyubomirsky http://www.huffingtonpost.com/entry/do-happiness-interventions-really-work_us_58bce 9b7e4b02b8b584dfda2
7. This was brought home to me memorably when I was a medical student. Our group of students had just examined a patient and one reported back to the consultant, 'I think there's a query query ??mass in the abdomen, sir' (meaning that he thought he might have felt a lump, indicating the possibility of a tumour). 'Query query mass?' came the reply. 'What kind of diagnosis is that? I can't operate on a query query mass, young man! Either there's a mass there or there isn't!'
8. The description that follows of life in Qatar is taken from Matthew Teller, 'Has wealth made Qatar happy?', *BBC News Magazine* (April 2014) http://www.bbc.co.uk/news/magazine-27142647.
9. Wikipedia, 'Karoshi' https://en.wikipedia.org/wiki/Kar%C5%8Dshi.
10. Rupert Wingfield-Hayes. 'Why does Japan have such a high suicide rate?', *BBC News*
11. http://www.bbc.co.uk/news/world-33362387
12. Sonja Lyubomirsky, *The How of Happiness* (Sphere, London: 2007), pp. 20-22.
13. I remember one time when I ran this exercise in The Happiness Course, someone who had suffered quite severe depression for many years became very upset at hearing that genetics was significantly responsible. However, as we continued to discuss the matter, she suddenly blurted out, 'Wait a minute – it's not my fault! Or at least, 50% of it isn't!' It was a major breakthrough for her to realise that she need not berate herself so harshly for her experience.
14. It might seem from all this that only *kairos* moments have meaning and the *chronos* periods (much more common in life) are merely 'fillers'. This is not so, for every moment has meaning of some kind. But *kairos* events have what might be called an epiphanic quality, a sudden realisation or discovery around which there is meaning, that *chronos* occasions don't usually provide. We'll see more of this in Chapter 3.

Chapter 1

1. I don't know who wrote this piece, but it does seem to summarise how many things work today! I found it at https://www.devrant.io/rants/605665/hello-gordons-pizza-no-sir-its-googles-pizza-so-its-a-wrong-number-no-sir-google Thank you to whoever first wrote it.
2. John F. Helliwell, Richard Layard and Jeffrey Sachs, 'World Happiness Report' http://world happiness.report/wp-content/uploads/sites/2/2017/03/HR17.pdf , p. 20.
3. George Arnett, 'What makes the UK a good place to live and work?' https://www.theguardian.com/news/datablog/2013/nov/05/what-makes-uk-such-a-good-place-to-live-oecd
4. https://www.weforum.org/agenda/2016/08/foreign-aid-these-countries-are-the-most-generous.
5. https://www.irishaid.ie/what-we-do/how-our-aid-works/where-the-money-goes/
6. Ben Marshall, 'How does the rest of the world view Britain?' http://www.newstatesman.com/staggers/2012/12/how-does-rest-world-view-britain; Ipsos MORI, 2012's strong overseas impact for the UK. https://www.ipsos-mori.com/researchpublications/researcharchive/3094/2012s-strong-overseas-impact-for-the-UK.aspx
7. Expat Insider InterNations Survey Report 2016, p. 121-123, https://inassets1-internationsgmbh.netdna-ssl.com/static/bundles/internationsexpatinsider/pdf/expat_insider_2016_the_internations_survey.pdf
8. https://en.wikipedia.org/wiki/Jeremy_Bentham.
9. John Kenneth Galbraith, *The Dependence Effect*, in the *Affluent Society* (Houghton Mifflin, Boston:

1952), pp. 126-131. http://sites.middlebury.edu/econ0450f10/files/2010/08/galbraith.pdf

10. Tom Sine, 'Mustard Seed versus McWorld' (Monarch, Oxford: 1999), p. 123.

11. Perry Romanowski, 'A Cosmetic Industry Overview for Cosmetic Chemists', Chemists Corner http://chemistscorner.com/a-cosmetic-market-overview-for-cosmetic-chemists

12. Fifty-eight countries have universal health care – most are in the developed world. In a ranking of 37 European nations, England comes fourteenth, Scotland sixteenth and Ireland twenty-third. See Wikipedia, 'Healthcare in Europe' https://en.wikipedia.org/wiki/Healthcare_in_Europe.

13. Ian McGilchrist, *The Master and his Emissary* (Yale, New Haven: 2009), pp. 97-98.

14. Martin Seager, 'Bad science and good mental health', *Therapy Today*, September 2012, p. 12.

15. Lilian Anekwe, 'Pharma contributes £32 billion to UK economy', Pharmafile (2015). http://www.pharmafile.com/news/197926/pharma-contributes-32-billion-uk-economy;

16. rish Pharmaceutical Healthcare Association, 'Contribution to the Irish Economy', http://www.ipha.ie/alist/contribution-to-the-irish-economy.aspx

17. Nimnuan C, Hotopf M, Wessely S. 'Medically unexplained symptoms: an epidemiological study in seven specialities' *J Psychosom Res.* 2001 Jul;51(1):361-7. http://www.ncbi.nlm.nih.gov/pubmed/11448704

18. 'Life expectancy at birth, England and Wales, 1841 to 2011' http://visual.ons.gov.uk/how-has-life-expectancy-changed-over-time.

19. 'Irish Life Tables' http://www.cso.ie/en/media/csoie/newsevents/documents/irishlife.pdf; Life expectancy improves in Ireland http://countryeconomy.com/demography/life-expectancy/ireland

20. 'The UK, Germany and France: GDP over history' http://www.edmundconway.com/2015/02/the-uk-germany-and-france-gdp-over-history/ 'Gross domestic product at current market prices of the United Kingdom (UK) from 2000 to 2015 (in million GBP)' https://www.statista.com/statistics/281744/gdp-of-the-united-kingdom-uk-since-2000/

21. Health & Executive http://www.hse.gov.uk/statistics/causdis/stress/stress.pdf; Stress Management Society http://www.stress.org.uk/Stress-at-work.aspx

22. 'Employee Engagement Safety: A Literature Review', Kingston University http://eprints.kingston.ac.uk/4192/1/19wempen.pdf; 'The Global Burden of Disease Study: Implications for Neurology', Menken et al, http://archneur.jamanetwork.com/article.aspx?articleid=776117

23. Katie Silver, 'One in three "sick notes" for mental health, says NHS' http://www.bbc.co.uk/news/health-41124238 The Royal College of Psychiatrists called the figures 'alarming'. Most disturbing was the finding that more sick notes for psychiatric problems were being issued for longer periods of time than other types of illness.

24. Anxiety UK, 'Frequently asked questions', https://www.anxietyuk.org.uk/get-help-now/anxiety-information/frequently-asked-questions/

25. Michelle Roberts, 'Quarter of 14-year-old girls 'have signs of depression'' *BBC News*, 20 September 2017 http://www.bbc.co.uk/news/health-41310350 It is worrying because half of all cases of adult mental illness start by the age of 14, and so mental health issues that manifest in early life tend to continue into the whole of adult life

26. Menken et al , 'The Global Burden of Disease Study: Implications for Neurology' http://archneur.jamanetwork.com/article.aspx?articleid=776117

27. *Talkback*, magazine of the Mental Health Foundation, June 2017 https://www.mentalhealth.org.uk/sites/default/files/talkback-june-2017.pdf

28. Luciana Berger, 'How Can Ministers Claim to Be Promoting Patient Care When the Wellbeing of Those Who Provide It Is Suffering So Badly on Their Watch?' http://www.huffingtonpost.co.uk/luciana-berger/mental-health-junior-doctors_b_8477434.html

29. John Cacioppo, 'The lethality of loneliness' at TEDxDesMoines, https://www.youtube.com/watch?v=_0hxl03JoA0

30. Relate and Relationships Scotland, 'You're not alone: the quality of the UK's social relationships' https://www.relate.org.uk/sites/default/files/the_way_we_are_now_-_youre_not_alone.pdf

31. Jennifer O'Connell, 'Feeling lonely? You're far from alone' https://www.irishtimes.com/life-and-style/people/feeling-lonely-you-re-far-from-alone-1.2924443

32. Economic and Social Research Council, 'Mental health and social relationships' (2013) http://www.esrc.ac.uk/news-events-and-publications/evidence-briefings/mental-health-and-social-relationships; Sonja Lyubomirsky, 'The How of Happiness' (Sphere 2007) p139-151

33. Campaign to End Loneliness, 'Summit on tackling loneliness in older age' (2012) http://www.campaigntoendloneliness.org/wp-content/uploads/downloads/2012/03/15.03.12-Summit-on-Tackling-Loneliness-Report.pdf

34. 'Can the NHS help tackle the UK's obesity epidemic?' http://www.nuffieldtrust.org.uk/blog/can-nhs-help-tackle-uk%E2%80%99s-obesity-epidemic?gclid=Cj0KEQiAsP-2BRCFi4Lb2NTJttEBEiQAmj2tbdqii26UDAwBPjH5-VmSsf5Qk6CsV79THl23tIpWxLwaAg5r8P8HAQ

35. The Young Foundation, 'Sinking and Swimming: Understanding Britain's unmet needs', http://youngfoundation.org/wp-content/uploads/2012/10/Sinking-and-swimming.pdf

36. Lucinda Vardey, *A Simple Path: Mother Teresa* (Penguin: 1995). http://www.goodreads.com/quotes/139677-the-greatest-disease-in-the-west-today-is-not-tb

37. Tania Lombozo, 'Is Happiness a Universal Human Right?', http://www.npr.org/sections/13.7/2017/03/20/520803361/is-happiness-a-universal-human-right

38. BBC News, 6 March 2017.

39. Shawn Achor and Michelle Gielan, 'Consuming Negative News Can Make You Less Effective at Work', https://hbr.org/2015/09/consuming-negative-news-can-make-you-less-effective-at-work

40. Graham C.L. Davey, 'The Psychological Effects of TV News', http://www.psychologytoday.com/blog/why-we-worry/201206/the-psychological-effects-tv-news

41. Owen Gibson, 'Shopper's eye view of ads that pass us by',https://www.theguardian.com/media/2005/nov/19/advertising.marketingandpr

42. The idea is that a frog immersed in water, which is then very slowly heated to boiling point, will not jump out, but die, since it is unable to detect the gradual rise in temperature. See https://en.wikipedia.org/wiki/Boiling_frog. The experiment may be apocryphal, but the metaphor is a significant one!

43. Tim Kasser, 'What psychology says about materialism and the holidays', American Psychological Association (Dec 2014) http://www.apa.org/news/press/releases/2014/12/materialism-holidays.aspx; Tom Sine, 'Mustard Seed versus McWorld' (Monarch: 1999), pp. 122-123; Robert Emmons, 'Thanks' (Houghton Mifflin, Boston: 2007) pp. 149-150.

44. Christine Schoenwald, 'Why giving up Facebook will make you way happier, says science', http://www.yourtango.com/2015283529/why-giving-up-facebook-will-make-you-way-happier; 'Online networking harms health', http://news.bbc.co.uk/1/hi/uk/7898510.stm

45. Jenny Kleeman, 'I'll go to school on two and a half hours' sleep': why British children aren't sleeping', The Guardian (4 March 2017), https://www.theguardian.com/lifeandstyle/2017/mar/04/go-school-two-half-hours-sleep-british-children-arent-sleeping; Panorama, 'Sleepless Britain', BBC 1, 6 March 2017

46. Lydia Nuzum, 'Pitt study indicates presence on multiple social media platforms linked to depression, anxiety', http://www.bizjournals.com/pittsburgh/news/2016/12/20/pitt-study-indicates-presence-on-multiple-social.html

47. Quoted by Sally Brown, in 'How we live now', Therapy Today, June 2017, p. 8.

48. 'Online networking harms health', http://news.bbc.co.uk/1/hi/uk/7898510.stm

49. Sherry Turkle, 'Reclaiming Conversation: The Power of Talk in a Digital Age' (Penguin, London: 2015). A very helpful summary is found at Jill Suttie, 'The Place of Talk in a Digital Age', http://greatergood.berkeley.edu/article/item/the_place_of_talk_in_a_digital_age?utm_source=GGSC+Newsletter+%232-+November++2015&utm_campaign=GG+Newsletter+%232++-+November+2015&utm_medium=email

50. Sherry Turkle, 2015

51. The crucial importance of face-to-face contacts is one of the most deeply rooted foundations of the human psyche and provides the basis for all interpersonal relationships, as we will see in Chapter 5.

52. The basis for this will become apparent in Chapter 4, as we explore the workings of the two hemispheres of the brain.

53. Adapted from Schalk Cloete, 'Law of Diminishing Returns', https://oneinabillionblog.com/summary-2/collapse/law-of-diminishing-returns/

54. Jody Delichte, 'Does money make us happy?' http://positivepsychology.org.uk/pp-theory/happiness/101-does-money-make-us-happy.html; Tim Worstall, 'British National Happiness Plateaus Despite Improving Economy', http://www.forbes.com/sites/timworstall/2016/07/08/british-national-happiness-plateaus-despite-improving-economy/#5a74c00628ba

55. If there was a direct relationship between happiness and money, you would expect to see a straight line, from bottom left to top right.

56. Brian Halweil and Lisa Mastny (project directors), 'State of the World 2004: A Worldwatch Institute Report on Progress Toward a Sustainable Society', Linda Starke, Editor (W.W. Norton & Company, Inc.: 2004) http://geraldguild.com/blog/2012/05/23/happiness-as-measured-by-gdp-really/comment-page-1 The graph is for the USA, but similar patterns exist for other Western countries, including the UK.

57. Elizabeth W. Dunn, Lara B. Aknin, Michael I. Norton, 'Prosocial Spending and Happiness: Using Money to Benefit Others Pays Off', http://cdp.sagepub.com/content/23/1/41.abstract

58. American Psychological Association, 'What Psychology Says About Materialism and the Holidays' (2014). http://www.apa.org/news/press/releases/2014/12/materialism-holidays.aspx

59. Mark Easton, 'Map of the Week: Trust and Belonging', http://www.bbc.co.uk/blogs/thereporters/markeaston/2009/01/map_of_the_week_trust_and_belo.html

60. John Bingham, 'Britain the loneliness capital of Europe', The Telegraph, 18 June 2014. http://www.telegraph.co.uk/news/politics/10909524/Britain-the-loneliness-capital-of-Europe.html

61. Alexandra Topping, 'One in 10 do not have a close friend and even more feel unloved, survey finds', The Guardian, 12 Aug 2014, http://www.theguardian.com/lifeandstyle/2014/aug/12/one-in-ten-people-have-no-close-friends-relate

62. Putnam, R. D., Bowling Alone: The collapse and revival of American community, (Simon and Schuster: 2000), p. 331.

63. Mark Molloy, 'What's the secret to happiness? Scientists may have found the answer', The Telegraph, 23 May 2016, http://www.telegraph.co.uk/good-news/2016/05/21/whats-the-secret-to-happiness-scientists-may-have-found-the-answ/

64. 'Patient Info, Complementary and Alternative Medicine', http://patient.info/doctor/complementary-and-alternative-medicine#ref-2; Ian D. Coulter and Evan M. Willis, 'The rise and rise of complementary and alternative medicine: a sociological perspective', Med J Aust 2004;

180 (11): 587-589. https://www.mja.com.au/journal/2004/180/11/rise-and-rise-complementary-and-alternative-medicine-sociological-perspective#7

65. Cancer Research UK, 'Why people use complementary or alternative therapies' http://www.cancerresearchuk.org/about-cancer/cancers-in-general/treatment/complementary-alternative/about/why-people-use-complementary-or-alternative-therapies

66. Science direct, 'Rise in popularity of complementary and alternative medicine: reasons and consequences for vaccination', Vol. 20, Supplement 1 (15 Oct 2001), p S90-S93. http://www.sciencedirect.com/science/article/pii/S0264410X01002900

67. Edward M. Hallowell, *Connect* (Pantheon, New York: 1999), p xii.

68. http://www.dictionary.com/browse/integrate

69. https://www.merriam-webster.com/dictionary/integrity

70. I prefer to use the word 'wholistic' rather than 'holistic' because it derives from the word 'whole' – precisely the term that best sums up the kind of life implied by words like wellbeing, and is the destination many of us are seeking. Also, 'wholistic' has become linked with particular worldviews in popular parlance and that serves a different interest than the one I am espousing in this book.

71. http://dictionary.cambridge.org/dictionary/english/integrity

Chapter 2

1. Examples include: Ravi Chandra, 'Six keys to happiness', *Psychology Today* (2011), https://www.psychologytoday.com/blog/the-pacific-heart/201106/six-keys-happiness; Joel Gascoigne, '6 simple things you can do every day to be consistently happy', Buffer Social (2013), https://blog.bufferapp.com/6-simple-things-i-do-every-day-to-be-consistently-happy

2. Actually, one recent article that bucks the trend is 'The 7 Habits of Happy People' on the Pursuit of Happiness website. It lists the following as helpful for our wellbeing – and all of them resonate well with my understanding: relationships, acts of kindness, exercise and physical wellbeing, flow (engaging in a challenging but satisfying activity), spiritual engagement and meaning, strengths and virtues and a positive mindset (optimism, mindfulness and gratitude) See http://www.pursuit-of-happiness.org/science-of-happiness

3. See http://tlc.ku.edu

4. 'UK among "world's worst" sleepers', BBC News, 28 October 2016, http://www.bbc.co.uk/news/uk-37798383

5. Paul T. P. Wong, 'Three kinds of happiness: hedonic, eudemonic and chaironic' http://www.meaning.ca/archives/archive/art_pp_lecture_series_8_P_Wong.htm

6. We will come across this gift of joy in another context in Chapter 3.

7. Pronounced 'Cheek-sent-me-high'.

8. Seligman, Parks and Steen, 'A balanced psychology and a full life' *Phil. Trans. R. Soc. Lond.* B (2004), Vol 359, p. 1380

9. Christopher Peterson, Nansook Park and Martin E. P. Seligman, 'Orientations to Happiness and Life Satisfaction: The Full Life versus the Empty Life', *Journal of Happiness Studies* (2005), Vol. 6, pp. 25-41.

10. 'Engagement' is perhaps a rather awkward term, but it's difficult to find a better one. One alternative might be 'investment', since it emphasises the importance of our actions, activities and involvements. We 'invest' in our job, relationships or pastimes, rather than sitting back and simply 'enjoying' a pleasure. 'Involvement' also points to the need to step into an activity, rather than staying as 'consumers'.

11. Martin E.P. Seligman, 'Authentic Happiness' (Nicholas Brealey: 2002), pp. 118-119.

12. www.authentichappiness.sas.upenn.edu/testcenter

13. Seligman (2002), p. 14.

14. Martin E. P. Seligman, 'Flourish' (Nicholas Brealey: 2011) pp. 16-24.

15. Carol D. Ryff , 'Happiness is everything, or is it? Explorations on the meaning of psychological well-being', *Journal of Personality and Social Psychology* 1989, Vol. 57, No. 6, 1069-1081.

16. Emmons (2008), p. 17.

17. 'WHO definition of Health', http://www.who.int/about/definition/en/print.html

18. Nevin Mehmet, 'Ethics and Wellbeing' in *Understanding Wellbeing*, Anneyce Knight and Allan McNaught (eds.), (2011), p. 39.

19. Remember that those people who serve us through health and social services are not there to be our friends. They are paid to do the job of serving us. They may or may not be 'friendly' but generally we have to look elsewhere to find our long-lasting friends.

20. Allan McNaught, 'Defining Wellbeing', in *Understanding Wellbeing*, p. 10. Several definitions of wellbeing are given in Chapter 1, pp. 7-22.

21. McNaught, p 11.

22. Diana Divecha, 'Are Boundaries Overrated?', 22 April 2016. 'http://greatergood.berkeley.edu/article/item/are_boundaries_overrated?utm_source=GG+Newsletter+April+27+2016&utm_campaign=GG+Newsletter+April+27+2016+&utm_medium=email

23. Robert Waldinger, 'What makes a good life? Lessons from the longest study on happiness' , https://www.youtube.com/watch?v=8KkKuTCFvzl See also: Tanya Lewis, 'A Harvard psychiatrist says 3 things are the secret to real happiness' http://finance.yahoo.com/news/harvard-psychiatrist-says-3-things-164000284.html

24. Grant Study, https://en.wikipedia.org/wiki/Grant_Study
25. Mental Health Foundation, 'Doing good does you good' (2012) https://www.mentalhealth.org.uk/publications/doing-good-does-you-goodp 19
26. John Ortberg, 'Everybody's normal till you get to know them' (Zondervan: 2003), pp. 13-22.
27. We need to be careful here, however. There is a sense in which it is healthy to be autonomous and independent. Over-dependency on others is unhealthy and prevents us from becoming our authentic selves. But the opposite is also true – if we cut off too much from others (i.e. become over-independent) we lose the healthy two-way interaction that is required for us to become mature emotionally and relationally. It's a balance between 'being myself' and connecting with others, but as a society we have tended to veer too far in the direction of independence. Perhaps mutual inter-dependence is the best way. We will return to this theme in chapters five and six.
28. We are surrounded by messages urging each of us to 'do my own thing', 'be true to myself', 'have it my way', etc. This can encourage an exaggerated sense of entitlement, without too much reference to the needs of others.
29. We will examine this theme of how man-made systems trump real-life humanity and natural living much more in Chapter 4.
30. Wikipedia, 'Jean Vanier', https://en.wikipedia.org/wiki/Jean_Vanier
31. R2W Films, Summer in the Forest, See http://www.summerintheforest.com
32. See: http://dictionary.cambridge.org/dictionary/english/meaning; http://www.dictionary.com/browse/meaning?s=t; 'The Oxford Paperback Dictionary' (OUP: 1979).
33. https://www.britannica.com/topic/anomie
34. https://en.wikipedia.org/wiki/Max_Weber
35. Peter Berger, The Sacred Canopy (Anchor Books: 1967), p. 22.
36. We will explore this notion of 'homelessness' more in Chapter 3.
37. Roy F. Baumeister, Kathleen D. Vohs, Jennifer L. Aaker, Emily N.Garbinsky, 'Some key differences between a Happy Life and a Meaningful Life', Journal of Positive Psychology, 2013, Vol. 8, Issue 6, pp. 505-516.
38. This cultural basis of meaning explains why cross-cultural experiences can be so confusing, as I mentioned earlier. We will return to the importance of culture in Chapter 7.
39. We will pick up these contrasting perspectives again in Chapter 4.

Chapter 3

1. Carson McCullers was an American author of fiction, who explored the spiritual isolation of misfits and outcasts.
2. C.R. Snyder, Shane J. Lopez, Jennifer T. Pedrotti, 'Positive Psychology: The Scientific and Practical Explorations of Human Strengths' (Sage, Los Angeles: 2011), p 117
3. C. S. Lewis, 'The Weight of Glory', in Theology, Nov 1941 http://www.verber.com/mark/xian/weight-of-glory.pdf
4. Remember the distinction between chronos and kairos in the Introduction? Here is an example of chronos living that attempts to sideline the kairos moments – beware! It also relates to our consideration of the left and right sides of the brain in Chapter 4.
5. Online Etymology Dictionary, 'Long' http://www.etymonline.com/index.php?allowed_in_frame=0&search=long
6. Iain McGilchrist, The Master and his Emissary (Yale University Press: 2009), p. 308. The distinction between wanting and longing bears a more-than-passing-resemblance to Baumeister's tropes of Happiness and Meaningfulness that we encountered in the previous chapter.
7. This is once again anticipating all that we will consider in the next chapter.
8. See Chapter 5 for more on this.
9. The song was first released in 1965 on the album Help, https://www.youtube.com/watch?v=Ho2e0zvGEWE
10. Alex Richardson, '"Yesterday" is best song of the century', Independent, 2 April 1999. It's perhaps not surprising to find that the song was followed in popularity by Hoagy Carmichael's 'Stardust' (a ballad about loss and separation), 'Bridge over Troubled Water' (Paul Simon) and 'Candle in the Wind' by Elton John, respectively. All possess the same poignant quality. http://www.independent.co.uk/news/yesterday-is-best-song-of-century-1084749.html
11. Connie Francis, 'I Will Wait For You', https://www.youtube.com/watch?v=Mi57d50pCUw
12. Martin Garrix and Dua Lipa, 'Scared To Be Lonely', https://www.youtube.com/watch?v=e2vBLd5Egnk
13. 'Jerusalem, the Anthem, with simultaneous lyrics', https://www.youtube.com/watch?v=MKRHWT6xdEU
14. 'Into the West', from the film, Lord of the Rings (with lyric), https://www.youtube.com/watch?v=shdiTRxTJb4
15. Judy Garland, 'Over The Rainbow', https://www.youtube.com/watch?v=1HRa4X07jdE
16. Ofra Haza, 'Jerusalem of Gold - Yerushalayim shel Zahav' – with English lyrics,https://www.youtube.com/watch?v=JH8gtdDA5x0
17. Please note that by quoting this song I am not making any political point – Jewish joy over Jerusalem in 1967 was matched in equal measure by pain amongst Palestinians. Rather, the song illustrates powerfully how often we long, not just for another individual, but also for a group of people to whom we feel deeply attached and towards whom we experience an intense

feeling of belonging. Palestinians, just as deeply affected by the fate of Jerusalem in the Six Day War, also wrote songs, with the same passion as those of the Jews'. One of the most popular is 'The Flower of the Cities', performed at that time by the singer Fayruz. Its lyrics convey a people's fervency and pain in much the same way as Shemer's song. See https://www.youtube.com/watch?v=lYKnQ9814T8

18. 'Memory', from the musical *Cats*, https://www.youtube.com/watch?v=4-L6rEm0rnY
19. John Mayer, 'Something's Missing', https://www.youtube.com/watch?v=gWl7b9YA-T4
20. John Yorke is a renowned TV writer and producer. His recent book, *Into the Woods* (Penguin: 2013) explains how stories work and why we tell them. In it, he outlines the key elements of any story: protagonist, antagonist, inciting incident, desire, crisis, climax and resolution.
21. Expatiate means to speak or write about in great amount and detail.
22. https://www.azlyrics.com/lyrics/keane/sunshine.html
23. I presume that Rohr is not an expert on the subject of attachment, which we will look at in Chapter 5, but his comments about 'the body of our mother' strongly echo all that is discussed there.
24. Richard Rohr, *Falling Upward* (SPCK: 2012), pp. 88-89.
25. Henri Nouwen, *From Fear to Love: Lenten Reflections on the Parable of the Prodigal Son* (The Henri Nouwen Legacy Trust, Doubleday Religion: 2009) pp. 8-9.
26. There is apparently no direct English translation for *hiraeth*, although it can be likened to 'homesickness tinged with grief or sadness over the lost or departed. It is a mix of longing, yearning, nostalgia, wistfulness, or an earnest desire for the Wales of the past'. See https://en.wikipedia.org/wiki/Hiraeth
27. P. B. Baltes, Freund and S. Scheibe, 'The Psychology of Sehnsucht – an expose', http://www.diss.fu-berlin.de/diss/servlets/MCRFileNodeServlet/FUDISS_derivate_000000001714/03_theo.pdf , p 2.
28. https://en.wikipedia.org/wiki/Gem%C3%BCtlichkeit According to this article, other qualities of *gemutlichkeit* include wellbeing and social acceptance, which again point to our desire for wellbeing and community.
29. Compare this with Rohr's 'looking back and looking forward'; both are talking about the Big Picture of our lives. Unless we can connect with the whole picture we end up living anecdotal, unjoined-up lives.
30. S. Scheibe A. Freund, 'Approaching Sehnsucht (Life Longings) from a Life-Span Perspective: The Role of Personal Utopias in Development', *Research in Human Development*, 5(2), 121–133, 2008
31. Alister McGrath, *C. S. Lewis: A Life* (Hodder and Stoughton: 2013).
32. McGrath, pp. 15-16.
33. The quotations that follow are from Lewis's autobiography, *Surprised by Joy* (William Collins, 1955), pp. 18-20.
34. Lewis, p. 20
35. Lewis, p. 20. Lewis lived and died long before the current interest and research into happiness and wellbeing, but his distinction between Pleasure and Happiness on one hand and Joy on the other is worth noting, in view of all the research findings we have been investigating in previous chapters. It also anticipates what we will consider in the next chapters, particularly regarding the importance of sadness, grief and other 'negative' emotions.
36. McGrath, p. 64.
37. McGrath (p. 263), quoting Lewis, makes a clear and strategic distinction between 'imaginary' (something falsely imagined, with no basis in reality) and 'imaginative' (something our minds produce which points beyond 'to something greater than itself, struggling to find images adequate to the reality').
38. Lewis, p. 138. Lewis knew nothing of twenty-first century brain science, especially of lateralisation of the hemispheres of the brain. But this statement reverberates profoundly (and agrees) with discoveries about the very different workings of the left and right hemispheres of the brain, as we will see in Chapter 4.
39. McGrath, p. 150.
40. McGrath, p. 153.
41. Lewis, p. 182.
42. We will encounter this vital distinction between the 'true' and the 'real' (and the deeper nature of the 'real') again in Chapter 7, in our consideration of beliefs and worldviews.
43. McGrath, p. 174.
44. https://en.wikipedia.org/wiki/The_Chronicles_of_Narnia
45. http://www.thebookseller.com/news/narnia-voted-top-kids-book
46. McGrath, pp. 268, 264.
47. Lewis, p 176.
48. Existential angst: a sense of anxiety, dread or panic that comes as you contemplate life's biggest questions – you wonder whether your life has meaning or not. Other words that are used to express this feeling include *weltschmerz* ('world weariness' or 'world pain') and *ennui* (originally, 'boredom' but more relevantly, 'weariness and dissatisfaction'). A short but informative article about this is, 'How to Tell Whether You've Got Angst, Ennui, or Weltschmerz', by Arika Okrent: http://mentalfloss.com/article/58230/how-tell-whether-youve-got-angst-ennui-or-weltschmerz
49. Hamlet, Act 1, scene 5
50. Clearly, time is used here in a *kairos* sense.
51. Quoted in Nicky Gumbel, *Questions of Life* (Kingsway: 1993), pp. 13-14.

Chapter 4

1. Iain McGilchrist, *The Master and his Emissary* (Yale University Press: 2009).
2. If you find the book too daunting, a very helpful twelve-minute video can guide you through the main principles: https://www.youtube.com/watch?v=dFs9WO2B8ul
3. 'Neurons and synapses' http://www.human-memory.net/brain_neurons.html; Wikipedia, 'The Human Brain' https://en.wikipedia.org/wiki/Human_brain Some authorities claim that there are more connections between neurons in one human brain than atoms in the Universe!
4. The frontal lobes in the relatively intelligent dog occupy just 7% of total brain volume; in the lesser apes that rises to 17%; but in humans the figure is 35%. See McGilchrist, pp. 20-21.
5. McGilchrist, pp. 17,23, 33.
6. McGilchrist, p. 25.
7. McGilchrist, p. 3.
8. Daniel Siegel, 'Mindsight' (Oneworld: 2010), pp. 107-8.
9. Throughout the body, nerve fibres from one side of the body cross over in the brain to reach the opposite side of the brain. So for example, nerves from the left foot or left eye make their way to the right hemisphere.
10. McGilchrist, p. 81.
11. Muriel Deutsch Lezak, 'Neuropsychological Assessment' (Oxford University Press: 1995), p. 59.
12. McGilchrist, pp. 50-51.
13. Iain McGilchrist, 'Tending to the world' in *Mind in Architecture: Neuroscience, Embodiment and the Future of Design*, Sarah Robinson and Juhani Pallasmaa (eds.)(The MIT Press, Cambridge Massachusetts, 2015), p. 102.
14. McGilchrist, p. 21, 38.
15. McGilchrist, pp. 40-44.
16. McGilchrist, p. 49.
17. McGilchrist, pp. 51, 54-55.
18. J. Decety and T. Chaminade, 'When the self represents the other: A new cognitive neuroscience view on psychological identification', *Consciousness and Cognition* 12 (4):577-596 (2003).
19. McGilchrist, p 57
20. Allan N. Schore, 'The Right Brain Is Dominant in Psychotherapy', *Psychotherapy* (2014), Vol. 51, No.3 p. 389. All the material mentioned in this paragraph is hugely significant for our relationships and our lives generally. We will spend more time on this in the next chapter.
21. McGilchrist, p. 61.
22. McGilchrist, p. 66-67.
23. McGilchrist, p. 70.
24. McGilchrist, p. 70-77. McGilchrist devotes a whole chapter to language and music (pp. 94ff).
25. See Jill Bolte Taylor, *My Stroke of Insight* (Hodder: 2008), p. 106.
26. Here is a link with both the deeper experiences of longing that we encountered in the previous chapter, and the matters of meaning and purpose that we will explore in chapters seven and eight
27. McGilchrist, p. 78.
28. McGilchrist, pp. 78, 80, 85.
29. McGilchrist, pp. 61-62.
30. McGilchrist, p. 85.
31. Yarnell, P.H., 'The Intrinsic Goodness of Pain, Anguish, and the Loss of Pleasure', *Journal of Value Inquiry*, 35: p 454
32. McGilchrist, p. 86.
33. McGilchrist, pp. 86-87.
34. McGilchrist, p. 235.
35. Jill Bolte Taylor, 'My stroke of insight': https://www.youtube.com/watch?v=UyyjU8fzEYU
36. Jill Bolte Taylor, *My Stroke of Insight* (Hodder, London: 2008)
37. Taylor, p. 42.
38. Taylor, p. 43.
39. Taylor, pp. 49-55.
40. Taylor, p. 67-68.
41. Taylor, pp. 68-70.
42. Taylor, p. 72. These experiences and faculties of the human infant will be explored more in the next chapter of this book.
43. Taylor, pp. 67-68. Again, this mirrors the experience of the newborn in its desire for attachment. See our next chapter.
44. Taylor, pp. 74-79.
45. Taylor, pp. 121, 131.
46. Taylor, pp. 131-32.
47. Taylor, pp. 132-33.
48. Taylor, pp. 133-34.
49. Taylor, pp. 143-44.
50. Roger Sperry, quoted in Rhawn Joseph, *Neuropsychology, Neuropsychiatry, and Behavioral Neurology* (Springer Science and Business Media: 1990) p. 25.
51. McGilchrist, p. 14.

52. We'll pick up on this parable in a slightly different form (and with a crucial twist) at the end of Chapter 7.
53. There is some doubt as to whether these words actually originated with Einstein. Some consider the scholar and artist Bob Samples to have written them. Either way, the sentiment is a powerful one, and resonates with the principles outlined in this chapter.
54. McGilchrist, p. 227.
55. McGilchrist, pp. 228-29.
56. McGilchrist, pp. 242.
57. McGilchrist, pp.. 263-6, 272-9, 285-8.
58. McGilchrist, pp. 289-97.
59. Redolent of all we examined in our previous chapter on longing.
60. https://www.youtube.com/watch?v=yXjLaFbpUNo
61. McGilchrist, pp. 306-329.
62. Wikipedia, 'Rene Descartes', https://en.wikipedia.org/wiki/Ren%C3%A9_Descartes
63. McGilchrist, pp. 330-351, 382-88.
64. One of my pet hates is the automated telephone response of institutions. Although we are told 'your call is important to us', it doesn't feel that way, as we (im)patiently wait in line for a reply that we suspect will not really deliver what we want. The personal, relational basis of human transactions that we crave is almost completely absent!
65. McGilchrist, pp. 389-422.
66. McGilchrist, pp. 244, 255-6.
67. McGilchrist, pp. 438-45.
68. These findings are reported by psychology and psychiatry professor Richard J. Davidson in 'Understanding Positive and Negative Emotion': http://www.loc.gov/loc/brain/emotion/Davidson.html
69. McGilchrist, p. 3.
70. Lewis, p. 138.

Chapter 5

1. Quoted from an interview with the BBC in the programme 'The Happiness Formula'.
2. Amongst the many studies that could be mentioned, some are: Talia Kennedy, 'Can a Friend a Day Keep the Doctor Away?', 1 June, 2008: http://greatergood.berkeley.edu/article/item/can_friend_day_keep_doctor_away; Michelle Flythe, 'Survival of the Social', 1 September 2005: http://greatergood.berkeley.edu/article/item/survival_of_the_social; Stephen Aldridge and David Halpern, 'Social Capital: a Discussion Paper' (Performance and Innovation Unit: April 2002)
3. McGilchrist, p 93
4. A quote from B. F. Skinner (one of the founders of behaviourism) by Allan N. Shore in his book, *The Science of the Art of Psychotherapy* (Norton: 2012), p. 3.
5. Allan N. Schore 'The Emotional Revolution 6 of 9' (2017) https://www.youtube.com/watch?v=z1RfLyKgSPc 'Emotional Revolution – a shift in paradigms' is a helpful five-minute summary: http://whenworldwide.org/films/emotional-revolution-shift-paradigms/
6. Schore, 2012, p. 3.
7. Allan N. Schore, 'The Right Brain is Dominant in Psychotherapy', *Psychotherapy* 2014, Vol. 51, No. 3, p. 388.
8. Schore, 2012, p. 7.
9. Schore, 2012, p. 8 – he is quoting McGilchrist, *The Master and his Emissary*, p 176
10. Schore, 2012, p. 8.
11. Psalm 131:1-2.
12. Fred Ingham, 'The Four S's of Parenting: Dan Siegel's Whole-Brain Child' https://www.parentmap.com/article/the-four-ss-of-parenting-dan-siegels-whole-brain-child
13. Tim Clinton and Gary Sibcy, 'Attachments' (Thomas Nelson: 2002), pp. 21-22.
14. David Wallin, 'Attachment in Psychotherapy' (The Guilford Press, New York: 2007), pp. 17-22.
15. Clinton and Sibcy, pp. 23-24.
16. Based on Clinton and Sibcy's diagram on p. 96.
17. Questions taken from Wallin, p. 29; Siegel, p. 173.
18. Donald Winnicott was a hugely influential paediatrician and psychoanalyst who developed a prescient understanding of the parent/infant relationship in the mid-twentieth century
19. See Wallin, pp. 52-58.
20. Wallin, p. 52.
21. Peter Fonagy, quoted by Wallin, p. 53.
22. Hobson, P., 'The Cradle of Thought: Exploring the Origins of Thinking' (MacMillan: 2002), p. 2.
23. Bonnie Badenoch, 'Being a Brain-Wise Therapist: A Practical Guide to Interpersonal Neurobiology' (WW Norton and Co: 2011), p. 52.
24. Daniel Stern, quoted in Wallin, pp. 52-56.
25. Wallin, pp. 44-51.
26. Siegel, pp. 59-61. These neurophysiological processes explain the success of such exercises and therapies as mindfulness, which connect our stressed-out minds with our bodies, other people and the (real) world around us. Very much right brain territory.
27. Badenoch, pp.. 53

28. Wallin, pp. 57.
29. Schore, 2014, p. 390. He adds elsewhere, 'the specialization of the (brain) hemispheres is fundamentally involved in major psychological functions ... and it is now thought of as a marker for the dysfunctions expressed in every form of psychopathology' (Schore, 2012, p. 6).

Chapter 6

1. Rockefeller's net worth at his death was estimated to be $3.3 billion
2. In the following section I have drawn on psychotherapist Peter Steinke's helpful book, *How Your Church Family Works* (The Alban Institute: 2006). Although aimed at church congregations, the book gives many helpful insights into the dynamics of relationships in all kinds of settings.
3. As I wrote these words, an atrocity had happened just two weeks before in Manchester. A suicide bomber had killed and injured scores of (mostly) young people. The TV pictures were intensely moving, as people, young and old, from totally different backgrounds, held onto each other in their grief.
4. Steinke, p. 12.
5. Steinke, pp. 31-32.
6. Steinke, pp. 33-34.
7. Taylor, p. 42.
8. Margaret Hough's book, *Counselling Skills and Theory* (Hodder and Stoughton: London, 1998) is very helpful in describing Berne's work: pp. 144-168
9. Berne's actual definition of an ego-state is 'a consistent pattern of feeling and experience directly related to a corresponding consistent pattern of behaviour.' These feelings and experiences consistently occur together. See 'What is an ego state?', *UK Association for Transactional Analysis* http://www.uktransactionalanalysis.co.uk/news-events/articles/item/2-what-is-an-ego-state
10. If you've never read the books by A. A. Milne (or seen the films) featuring the lovable bear, Winnie-the-Pooh, you've missed a treat. One of the characters is Tigger, a very bouncy animal who is cheerful, friendly and somewhat more optimistic about his abilities than he should be! I'm not sure if I really do match up to this stereotype, but I can see some similarities!
11. Siegel, pp. 190-209.
12. Siegel, pp. 240-245.
13. Wikipedia, 'Karpman Drama Triangle': https://en.wikipedia.org/wiki/Karpman_drama_triangle
14. 'How Long Does It Actually Take to Form a New Habit?': http://www.huffingtonpost.com/james-clear/forming-new-habits_b_5104807.html
15. Siegel, p. 41. A synapse is a connection between two neurons – messages pass from cell to cell across these connections.
16. Siegel, p. 42. His whole section on neuroplasticity (pp. 38-44) is well worth reading.
17. M. Scott Peck, *The Road Less Travelled* (Rider: 2008), pp. 59-60.
18. Lyubomirsky, p. 176.
19. Everett Worthington, 'REACH Forgiveness of Others': http://www.evworthington-forgiveness.com/reach-forgiveness-of-others
20. Kim Phúc (popularly known as the Napalm girl) was the young girl running naked down the road in the famous photograph taken when US forces napalm bombed a Vietnamese village in 1972. At the time her burns were considered so severe that she was not expected to survive. She did survive however, and after 17 surgical procedures she returned home. Yet she forgave the pilot who caused her suffering and in 1996 she met him. She established the Kim Phúc Foundation in 1997 to provide support for child victims of war.
21. Harris, A.H., et al, 'Effects of group forgiveness intervention on forgiveness, perceived stress and trait anger', *Journal of Clinical Psychology*, Vol 62(6), p 715-733
22. http://theforgivenessproject.com
23. YouTube, 'Famous Movie Scene: *Good Will Hunting*, "It's Not Your Fault"': https://www.youtube.com/watch?v=UYa6gbDcx18

Chapter 7

1. I don't know who wrote this. I found it at http://www.nomad4ever.com/2007/07/18/the-meaning-of-life/
2. This is a combination of two Bible verses, Ecclesiastes 8:15, 'I commend joy, for man has no good thing under the sun but to eat and drink and be joyful', and Isaiah 22:13, 'Let us eat and drink; for tomorrow we die'.
3. The story has been told in various places and has been attributed to the writer Heinrich Boll. I discovered it on the following sites: https://bemorewithless.com/the-story-of-the-mexican-fisherman/ and https://kidzshortstories.wordpress.com/2013/08/10/the-story-of-the-mexican-fisherman-by-heinrich-boll/Nick Spencer, *Beyond the Fringe: Researching a Spiritual Age* (Cliff College Publishing: 2005), p. 15.
4. Nick Spencer, Beyond the Fringe: Researching a Spiritual Age (Cliff College Publishing: 2005), p.15.
5. 'Ask Jeeves lists 10 unanswerable questions to mark tenth anniversary', *The Metro*, 20 Sept 2010 (http://www.metro.co.uk/tech/841430-ask-jeeves-lists-10-unanswerable-questions-to-mark-10th-anniversary

6. Paul G. Hiebert, *Cultural Anthropology* (Baker Book House, Grand Rapids: 1983), p. 25.

7. This tells us immediately that we are in the territory of 'nurture' rather than 'nature'.

8. Meg Jones, 'The Development of Cultural Identity in Early Childhood Settings', MPhil thesis, De Montfort University, Leicester: May 2009, p. 34. https://www.dora.dmu.ac.uk/bitstream/handle/2086/10698/MPhil.pdf?sequence=1&isAllowed=y

9. From Gary Weaver in 'Culture, Communication and Conflict: Readings in Intercultural Relations', quoted by Howard Culbertson, Southern Nazarene University in 'Defining 'culture' and cultural anthropology', PowerPoint slideset https://home.snu.edu/~hculbert/define.pdf

10. Showing once again how humans consistently and automatically seek connection and integration.

11. Paul G. Hiebert and R. Daniel Shaw, 'The Power and the Glory', quoted in 'Relationship between World View and Religion': http://globalchristiancenter.com/bible-and-theology/systematic-theology/24569-relationship-between-world-view-and-religion

12. Hiebert, pp. 355-356. Think how this quotation resonates with all that we examined about human longing in Chapter 3. It links too with our explorations in Chapter 8.

13. Hiebert, p. 356. It's fascinating to compare these societal explanatory models with the 'internal working models' of relationships that Bowlby believed infants develop as they seek unconsciously to achieve proximity to their caregiver (see Chapter 5).

14. Lloyd Kwast, 'Understanding Culture' in *Perspectives: A Reader*, Ralph D. Winter and Steven C. Hawthorne (eds.)(William Carey Library: 1992), pp. C3-C6.

15. James W. Sire, *The Universe Next Door* (InterVarsity Press: 1988), p. 18.

16. The very words employed to describe civilisations and cultures that preceded, accompanied and even followed the modern period betray the assumptions involved. Pre-modernity is an inclusive term for *all* societies that came before the 'Enlightenment' (a loaded expression, if ever there was one!). Then came Modernity, with all the presuppositions that such a term carries. Postmodernity follows inevitably in its wake.

17. A helpful overview of the past, present and possible future of the Western Dream is given by J. Richard Middleton and Brian J. Walsh in *Truth Is Stranger Than it Used to Be* (InterVarsity Press: 1995), pp. 13-27.

18. Wikipedia, 'Idea of Progress': https://en.wikipedia.org/wiki/Idea_of_progress#cite_ref-39

19. Adapted from Sire, pp. 62-70.

20. Monod J., *Chance and Necessity: An Essay on the Natural Philosophy of Modern Biology* (Vintage: 1971), pp. 141-146.

21. Francis Crick, 'The Astonishing Hypothesis: the Scientific Search for the Soul' (Touchstone: 1994).

22. The more scientists discover about the huge dimensions of the universe and the infinitesimally small nature of subatomic particles, the less the traditional theories of physics apply. See: http://www.telegraph.co.uk/news/science/6546462/The-10-weirdest-physics-facts-from-relativity-to-quantum-physics.html; http://www.physicsoftheuniverse.com/topics_quantum.html

23. Remember Martin Seligman's comment in Chapter 2? Seligman is careful about the limitations of the answers science can give to questions like, 'What is the meaning of life?' but adds, 'science can illuminate *components* of happiness and investigate empirically *what builds those components*' [my italics].

24. See McGilchrist, p 94-96

25. Internet Encyclopedia of Philosophy, 'Martin Buber' http://www.iep.utm.edu/buber

26. Tom Wright, *Simply Christian* (SPCK: 2006), pp. 15-17.

27. McGilchrist, pp. 428-434.

28. The digital world is by definition quantified, whereas the analogue world is very different. The related word 'analogous' describes things in relation to each other – one thing is seen in terms of another, rather like a metaphor or symbol. The right brain sees the world in this way, the left brain does not.

29. I remember once seeing a photo of a crowd of spectators. Nearly everyone had their smartphones out, capturing the passing celebrity digitally (but in a mediated, indirect way). Just one old woman stood there watching, enjoying and taking in the experience directly! The image was stark and striking and has stayed with me ever since.

30. See McGilchrist, pp. 438-445.

31. Sire, pp. 82-83.

32. I want to emphasise that I am not anti-science. I was trained in science and appreciate hugely its contribution to human life. But it is not the last word in wisdom, knowledge and understanding – there are other routes to that.

33. McGilchrist, pp. 254-55.

34. This is an example of what Martin Buber meant, with his factual and objective I/It relationships versus the I/Thou relationships of subjective encounter

35. Charles Darwin, 'The Autobiography of Charles Darwin' (Harcourt, Brace & Co, New York: 1959), pp. 138-139.

36. Vladimir Lenin, quoted in *New York Times Book Review* (27 Oct 1996), review of 'Censored by his Own Regime', by Orlando Figes, p. 32.

37. http://dictionary.cambridge.org/dictionary/english/attenuate

38. Therapists seem to be ahead of the curve. Transpersonal psychology 'enhances the study of mind-body relations, spirituality, consciousness, and human transformation' (GoodTherapy.

org, 'Transpersonal psychology' http://www.goodtherapy.org/learn-about-therapy/types/transpersonal-psychotherapy); and 'Transpersonal therapists value wholeness - taking the view that the essential self is a combination of the transpersonal, self-transcendent and spiritual aspects of human experience.' (Counselling Directory, 'Transpersonal psychology': http://www.counselling-directory.org.uk/transpersonal-psychology.html)

Chapter 8

1. Dan P. McAdams, 'What do we know when we know a person?', Wiley Online Library, p. 365: http://onlinelibrary.wiley.com/doi/10.1111/j.1467-6494.1995.tb00500.x/abstract
2. McAdams, p. 385.
3. Robert A. Emmons, 'Personal goals, life meaning and virtue: Wellsprings of a positive life': http://www.psychology.hku.hk/ftbcstudies/refbase/docs/emmons/2003/53_Emmons2003.pdf   His view is reminiscent of Baumeister's conclusions about the importance of meaning for humans (Chapter 2).
4. Emmons, p. 108.
5. Jonathan Haidt gives a helpful summary of this in his book, *The Happiness Hypothesis* (Arrow Books: 2006), pp. 141-144.
6. Lissa Rankin, 'The Healing Power of Telling Your Story': https://www.psychologytoday.com/blog/owning-pink/201211/the-healing-power-telling-your-story
7. Siegel, p. 74.
8. Tom Sine, *Living on Purpose* (Monarch, London: 2002), pp. 20-21
9. https://en.oxforddictionaries.com/definition/metanarrative
10. McGilchrist, pp. 254-55.
11. Jean-Francois Lyotard, 'The Postmodern Condition: A Report on Knowledge' Translation from the French by Geoff Bennington and Brian Massumi. Minneapolis: University of Minnesota Press, 1993 http://faculty.georgetown.edu/irvinem/theory/Lyotard-PostModernCondition1-5.html
12. Iain McGilchrist repeatedly refers to the right brain's orientation towards the 'Other'. Remember the quote from his book in Chapter 5: 'The right hemisphere pays attention to the Other, whatever it is that exists apart from ourselves, with which it sees itself in profound relation. It is deeply attracted to, and given life by, the relationship, the betweenness, that exists with this Other.' It is this connection with the Other that lies behind so many of our longings in life, as we saw in Chapter 3. The description of intersubjectivity in Chapter 5 expands on this betweenness and points to something very profound in the human psyche and communities.
13. The foundational nature of personhood and purpose provide further evidence (if we needed it) for the central significance of our two key words for lasting happiness, relationships and meaning.
14. C. S. Lewis puts another slant on this in his book, *The Problem of Pain*: 'Pain insists upon being attended to. God whispers to us in our pleasures, speaks in our conscience, but shouts in our pain: it is His megaphone to rouse a deaf world.'
15. I have no idea whether Wright knows about the fable that McGilchrist refers to for the title of his book, *The Master and his Emissary*, but the two stories are remarkably similar – except that the true master for McGilchrist does not dominate and control (quite the opposite) whereas Wright's story's dictator bears a striking likeness to McGilchrist's Emissary!
16. Tom de Castella, *BBC News Magazine*, 'Spiritual, but not religious': http://www.bbc.co.uk/news/magazine-20888141
17. Wright, p. 16.
18. Philip Yancey, *Rumours of Another World* (Zondervan: 2003), p. 9.
19. As I write these words, I feel some defensiveness inside. I'm anticipating a rush to the door, with cries of 'No - not religion!' Why is it that when anything smacking of 'religion' emerges, there is for some people a sharp intake of breath and a desire to move on from it all? It's interesting that in all the articles and books I have read on happiness, wellbeing and related subjects, I can remember encountering Aristotle, the Buddha and various philosophers, but nothing from the Bible.
20. This latter phrase distinguishes theism from deism, which proposes that the creator God was subsequently not directly involved in his creation. Deism rejects any kind of revelation from God, insisting that human reason is sufficient to support belief in God.
21. I'm told that most psychotherapies agree that the relationship itself is what heals psychological pain.
22. This is not as strange as you might think - or at least, the strange phenomenon of the Law of Entanglement has been described in quantum physics for many years. As cognitive neuroscientist Caroline Leaf observes, 'The law of entanglement ... states that relationship is the defining characteristic of everything in space and time. Because of the pervasive nature of the entanglement of atomic particles, the relationship is independent of distance and requires no physical link. Everything and everyone is linked, and we all affect each other' (Caroline Leaf, 'Switch on your brain' (Baker Books, Grand Rapids: 2013) p 110. The term 'entanglement' was coined by physicist and Nobel Laureate Erwin Schrodinger. He wrote that when two systems interact temporarily and then separate, 'they can no longer be described in the same way as before. I would not call that one but rather the characteristic trait of quantum mechanics, the one that enforces its entire departure from classical lines of thought. By the interaction the two systems have become entangled' (Gerardo Adesso, 'The social aspects of quantum entanglement': https://arxiv.org/pdf/0706.0286.pdf)

23. There is a lot more to this statement of course, but this is not the place to expand on it. My aim in writing out this list is to promote an alternative worldview or storyline, not to develop the plot. That would require another book.

24. This reflects the very different ways in which our right and left brains perceive and conceive the world around us. The left seeks proof and completion, whereas the right is comfortable with mystery, ambiguity and narrative, engaging with and reaching out towards the Other that lies beyond.

25. N. T. Wright, 'Righteousness' in *New Dictionary of Theology*, David F. Wright, Sinclair B. Ferguson, J.I. Packer (eds.) (IVP: 1988), pp. 590-592; *Present Truth Magazine*, 'Righteousness by Faith (Part 2)': http://www.presenttruthmag.com/archive/XXXIII/33-2.htm

26. In our age of word processing, we encounter the word 'justify' or 'justification' every time we want to straighten the edge of our text document. This is a simple but striking illustration of how justice and justification is based on straightness.

27. The Refiner's Fire, 'Meaning of the word 'Shalom': http://www.therefinersfire.org/meaning_of_shalom.htm

28. Perry B. Yoder, *Shalom: The Bible's Word for Salvation, Justice, and Peace* (Evangel: 1987), pp. 10-18.

29. Psalm 85:10.

30. Martin E.P. Seligman, Acacia C. Parks and Tracy Steen, *Phil. Trans. R. Soc. Lond.* B (2004), Vol. 359, p. 1380.

31. At the risk of pushing the illustration too far, you could equate *tsedek* with the secure base and safe haven of attachment and *shalom* with the interpersonal connection of intersubjectivity. Both elements need to be in place: first, a strong and secure framework, which then enables healthy personal, connected and harmonious living. This is the basis of true health and safety.

32. Nevertheless, understanding what my presuppositions and underlying worldview are may help you to appreciate why I propose my particular route to 'lasting happiness'.

33. 'A tree from good stock doesn't produce scrub fruit nor do trees from poor stock produce choice fruit. A tree is identified by the kind of fruit it produces ... A good person produces good deeds from a good heart. And an evil person produces evil deeds from his hidden wickedness. *Whatever is in the heart overflows into speech*.' (Luke 6:43-45, my italics)

34. Wikipedia, 'Locard's exchange principle' https://en.wikipedia.org/wiki/Locard%27s_exchange_principle; Paul L. Kirk, *Crime Investigation: Physical Evidence and the Police Laboratory* (published in 1953).

35. Genesis 2:9. Interestingly the Tree of Life crops up throughout the Bible, right through to the very last chapter, Revelation 22:2.

36. Wikipedia, 'Resource': https://en.wiktionary.org/wiki/resource.

37. Tom Wright, *Simply Christian* (SPCK: 2006), pp. ix-x.

38. Reminiscent once more of C. S. Lewis' words from Chapter 3: 'the beauty, the memory of our own past are ... the echo of a tune we have not heard'.

39. In our age of word processing, we are familiar with this word's variant, since we 'justify' the margins of our text every day. It simply means to straighten the edge of the text.

40. Paul Simon, 'America'. Find the lyrics of the song on http://www.azlyrics.com/lyrics/simongarfunkel/america.html

41. Read the whole text on: https://www.archives.gov/files/press/exhibits/dream-speech.pdf

42. Jean Bethke Elshtain, 'Everything for Sale', *Books and Culture*, May/June 1998, p. 9.

43. C. S. Lewis (1941).

44. Seligman (2002), p. 14.

45. Rob Bell, 'Everything is Spiritual': https://www.youtube.com/watch?v=i2rklwkm_dQ

46. Once again, suggestive of right and left perspectives (respectively).

47. Quoted by Matthew Linn, Sheila Fabricant and Dennis Linn, *Healing the Eight Stages of Life* (Paulist Press: 1988), p. 3.

Appendix 1

1. A sabbatical is a period of paid leave granted to allow reflection, study or travel. It is of course derived from the principle of 'sabbath' in the Bible, giving rest and recuperation in the ratio of one day of rest to every six days of work.

Appendix 2

1. Michael Rosen, *We're Going on a Bear Hunt*: See http://www.funnysongsforkids.com/childrens-classics/were-going-on-a-bear-hunt

2. Genesis 2:18

3. Matthew O'Reilly: 'Am I dying?' https://www.youtube.com/watch?v=IaMnRrrQx48

4. Tom Sine, 'Living on Purpose' (Monarch, London: 2002), p 20-21